HOW TO DRAW HISTORIC HORSES
HORSEPOWER FROM 2000 BCE TO 1400 CE

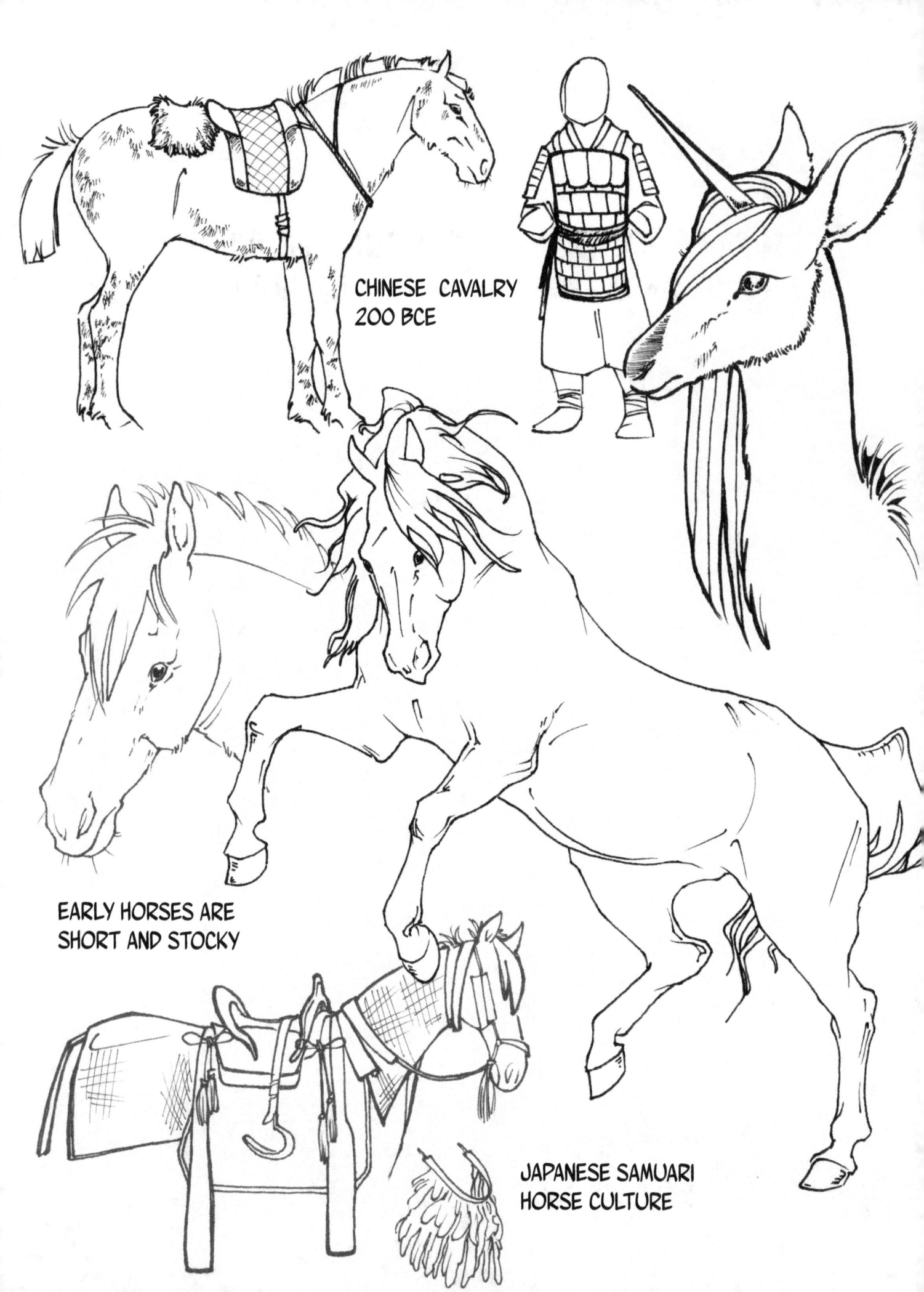

CHINESE CAVALRY
200 BCE

EARLY HORSES ARE
SHORT AND STOCKY

JAPANESE SAMUARI
HORSE CULTURE

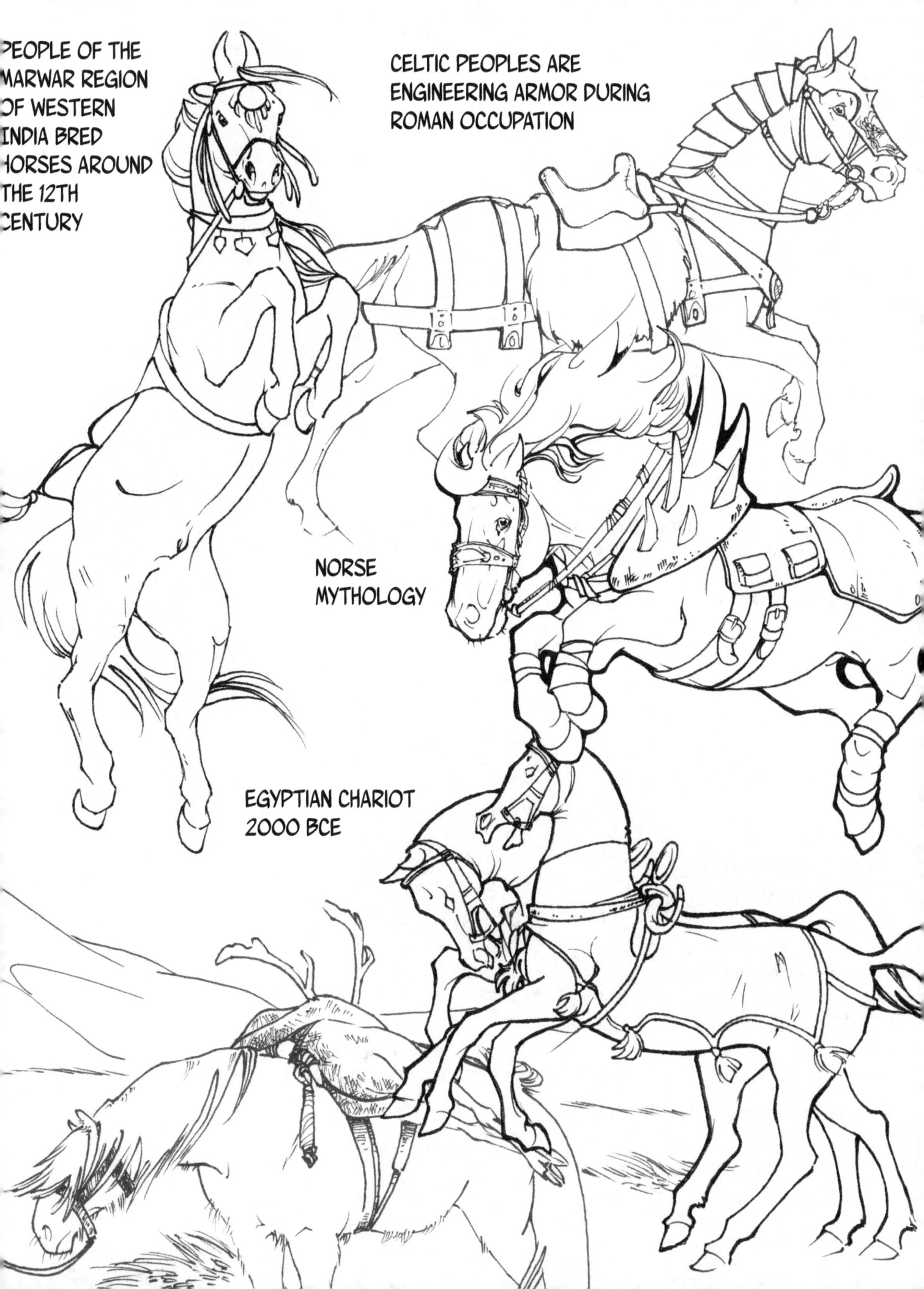

PEOPLE OF THE MARWAR REGION OF WESTERN INDIA BRED HORSES AROUND THE 12TH CENTURY

CELTIC PEOPLES ARE ENGINEERING ARMOR DURING ROMAN OCCUPATION

NORSE MYTHOLOGY

EGYPTIAN CHARIOT 2000 BCE

To everyone who kept this project alive,
even when they should have had enough sense to turn back.

Heels down. Head up. Ride on.

ISBN-13: 978-1508595472
ISBN-10: 150859547X

Printed in the United States of America

TABLE OF CONTENTS

THE "NERDY" BIT:

G'day me arty-hearties! Grab your art tools because we have a lot of ground to cover. It was around 4 million years ago that the genus of all modern horses arose. Thanks to the Canadians, we also have the last 700,000 years of the horse's complete genetic profile.

The entire genome shows that Prezewalski's diverged about 50,000 years ago, and hasn't looked back. Environment is also key when considering your historic horses - horse populations plumit when its warm, but do well when its cold.

Now, the end of the last glacial period hit North America pretty hard. A lot of mammals didn't make it. By about 8,000 BCE, horses and wild ass are gone from the place where they evolved.

SPOILER ALERT: They'll be back.

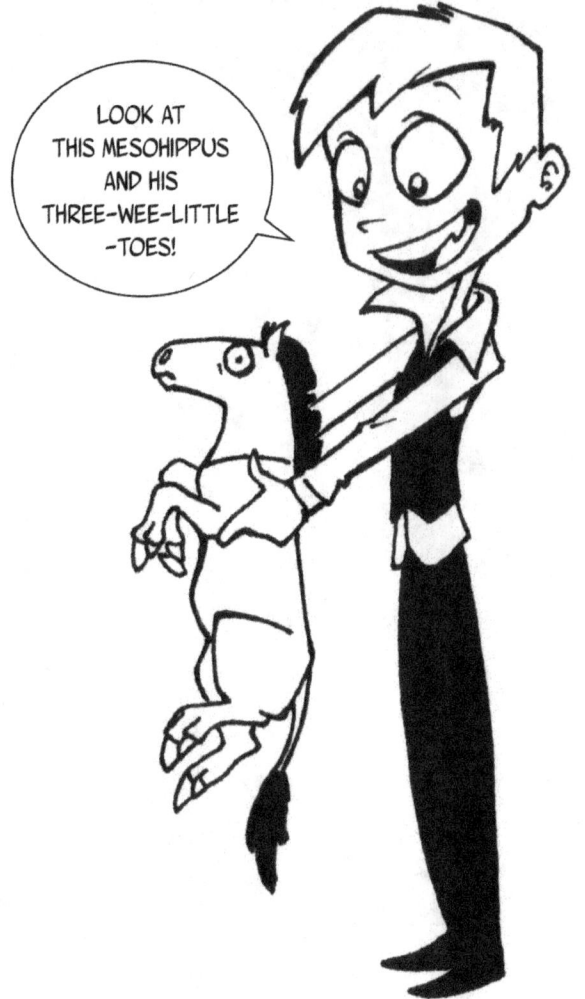

THE "I KNOW I'LL GET EMAILS" BIT:

Here's the messy part. It's a fact that historians love to argue.

And the prize for "earliest domestication" of the horse depends a great deal on how you define "domestication." There is some indication for human/horse coexistence for around 4000 BCE, but the evidence for humankind's love affair with horses is undeniable from about 2,000 BCE onwards.

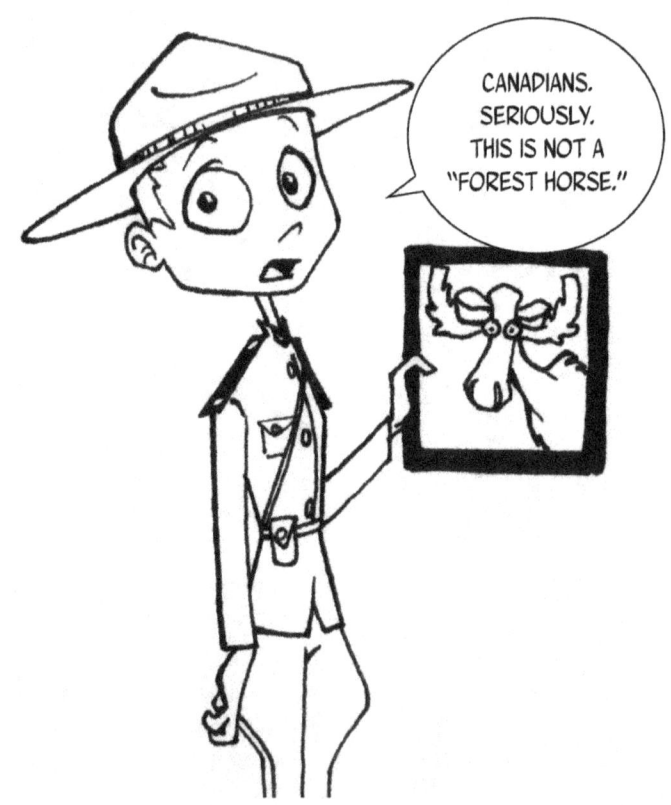

THE "I CAN'T BELIEVE I HAVE TO EXPLAIN THIS" BIT:

This book is a resource of the equine world from 2000 BCE to about 1400 CE. There are lot of facts in here. Except for the bits I just made up. Come to think of it, if you're getting your history from a how-to-draw book, you probably deserve it.

Here's how to get the best of the real deal:

STEP 1) Go to a museum
STEP 2) Ask and the archives shall open
STEP 3) See all the sweet treasures that never get daylight.

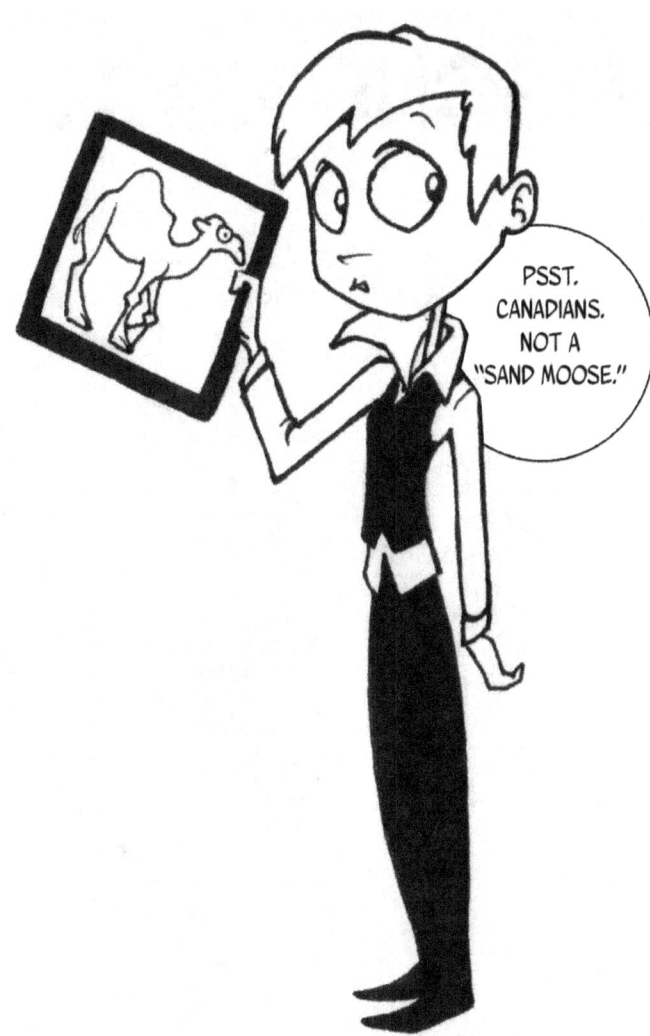

PSST. CANADIANS. NOT A "SAND MOOSE."

THE "YOU'VE BEEN WARNED" BIT:

Beware what you may find in the museum collections, however. The history of the horse is often not a pretty one. But for all the period films you've ever seen with the actors clad in plastic and which give the Greek and Roman cavalry stirrups and medieval knights with shires, be glad that they don't give them spiked bits, or have them running over caltrops, or serve them as the main course.

But you already knew history was full of violence, sex, and gore. And we bring the horses and the humor. You're welcome.

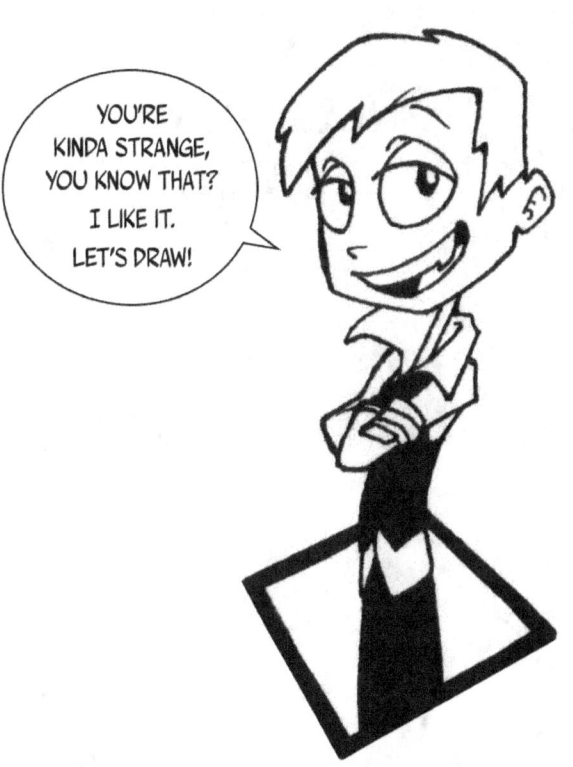

YOU'RE KINDA STRANGE, YOU KNOW THAT? I LIKE IT. LET'S DRAW!

AWESOME ANATOMY

Before you get to drawing dynamic equines, you really should get acquainted with a few features. Let's start with the head.

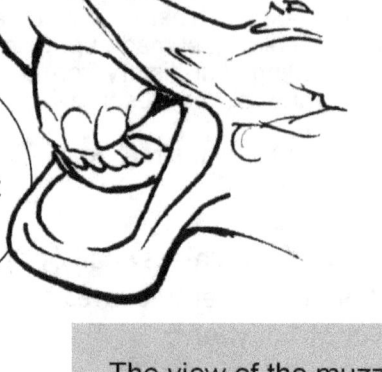

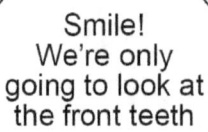

Smile! We're only going to look at the front teeth

THIS IS THE HORSE'S MUZZLE, AND IT INCLUDES THE NOSTRILS, MOUTH, LIPS, CHIN, AND SO ON. IF SHAVED, IT'LL LOOK SMOOTH AND PRETTY, BUT LEFT NATURAL, IT'LL BE COVERED IN WHISKERS.

The view of the muzzle from the front, with "relaxed banana" nostrils and flared.

"Relaxed banana" is a highly technical, anatomical term.

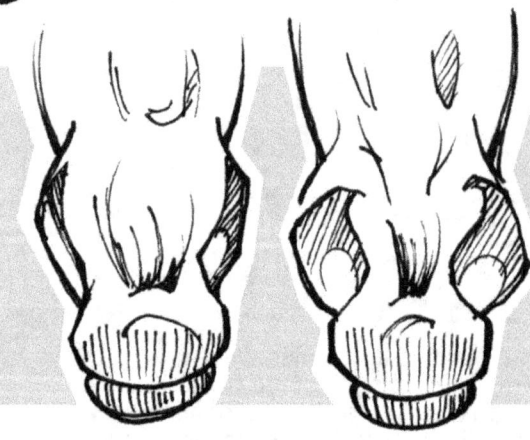

THE SIMPLE NOSE JOB

The equine nose has driven many an accomplished artist to drink. For starters, let's take a look at the three, basic positions of the horse's nostrils.

The first is relaxed, and looks like a number 6.

Second is excited. The nose is really pumping, so the nostrils extend to an 0.

Third is inquisitive. This squishes and stretches our nostril shape.

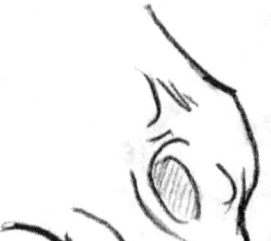

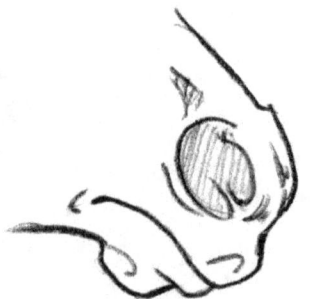

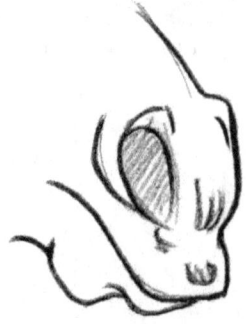

ALL IN THE NOSE

The nose is a very tactile and sensitive area of the horse, and it stretches to accommodate all sorts of expressions.

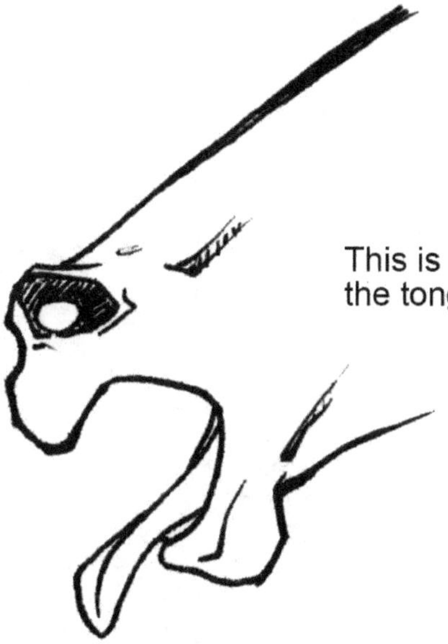

This is how it looks with the tongue out.

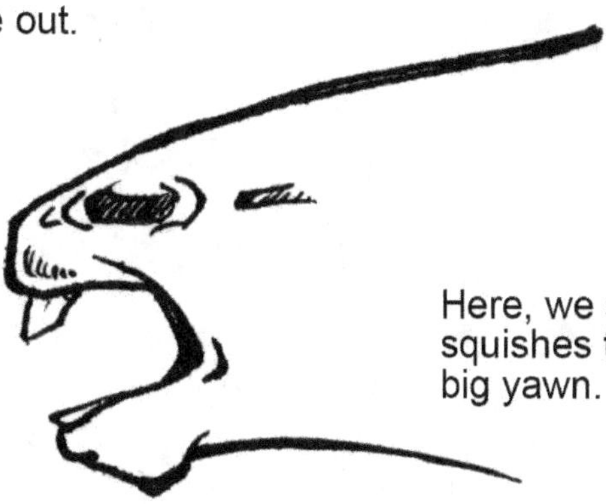

Here, we see the nose squishes to take a big yawn.

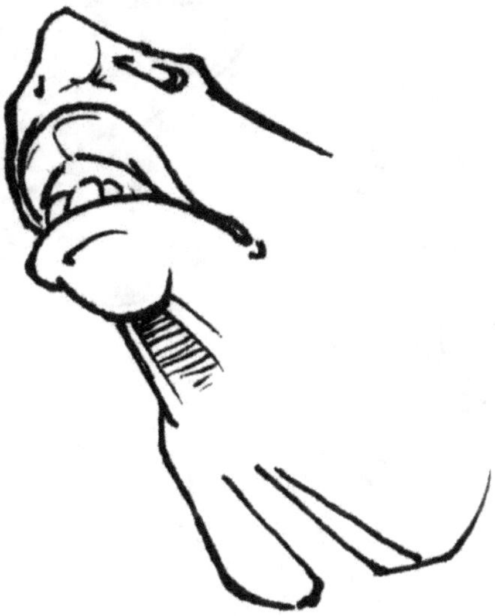

This is the same elevated lip pose from a side view– low angle.

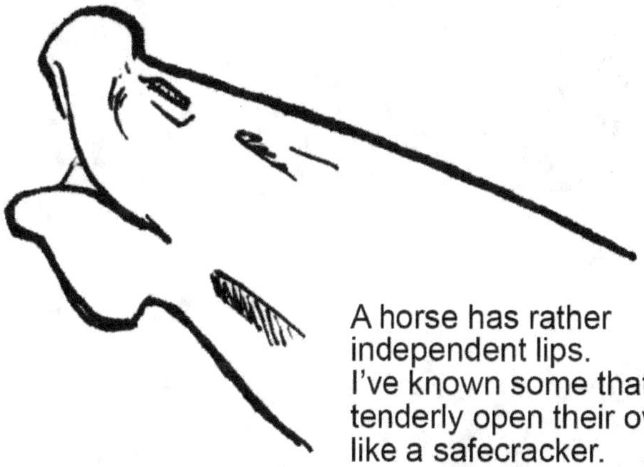

A horse has rather independent lips. I've known some that could tenderly open their own gates like a safecracker.

This nose/lip pose is due to whatever smell has caught the horse's attention.

BASIC NOSE-JOBS

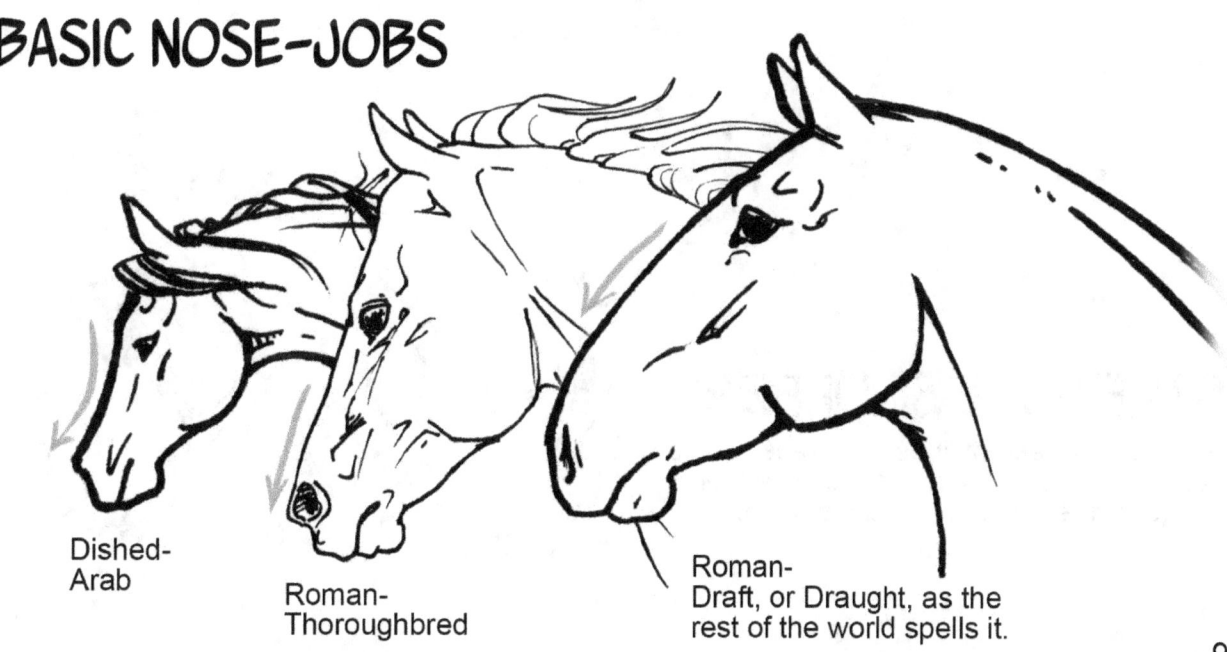

Dished-Arab

Roman-Thoroughbred

Roman-Draft, or Draught, as the rest of the world spells it.

NOSE FEATURES

There are an endless number of angles and positions from which to draw a horse. Here are just a few, facial examples.

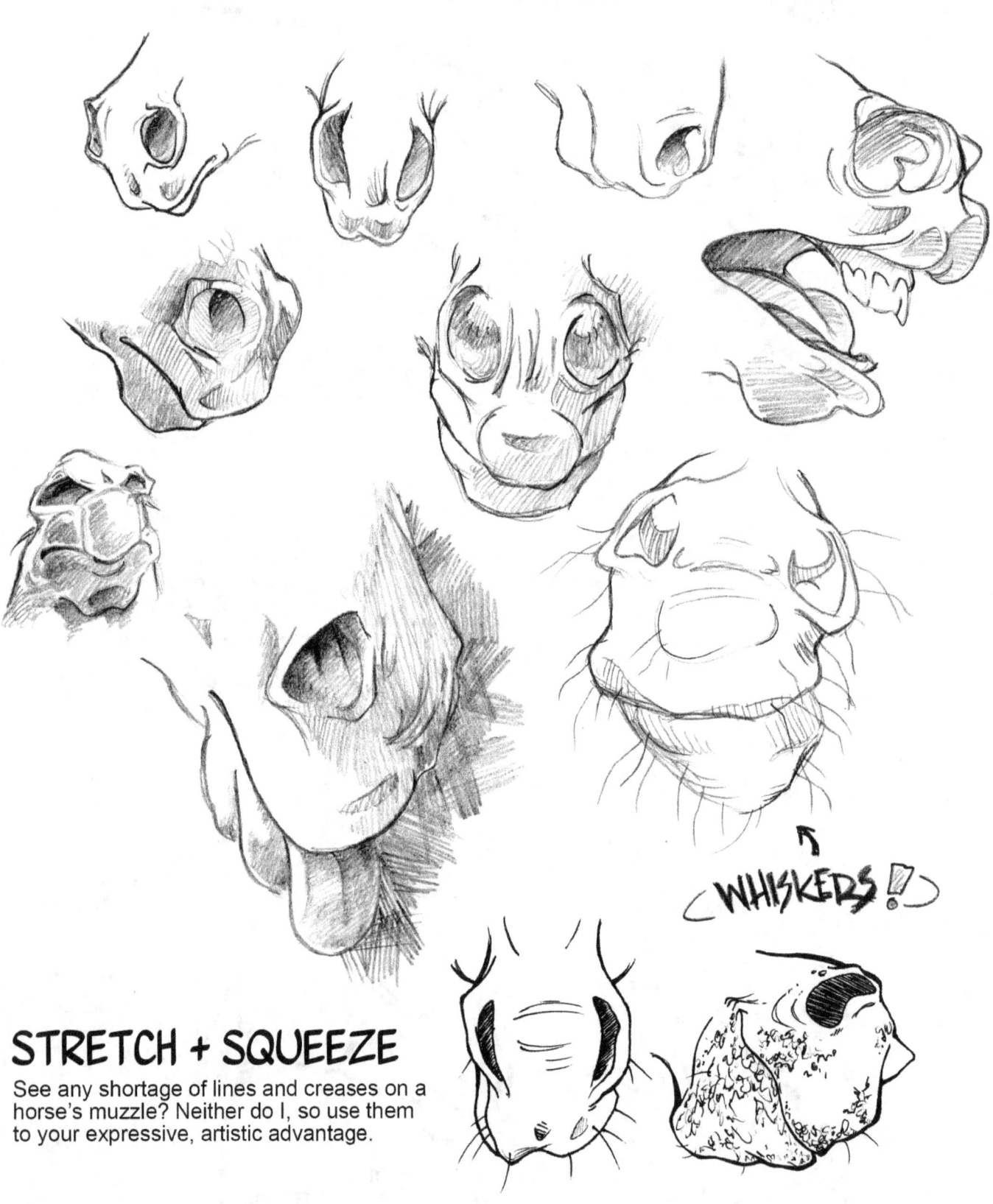

WHISKERS !

STRETCH + SQUEEZE

See any shortage of lines and creases on a horse's muzzle? Neither do I, so use them to your expressive, artistic advantage.

MOUTH FEATURES

A wide-mouthed grin is probably the most flattering expression, but when your horse is having a "less-than-carefree-moment," arm it with an attitude to match.

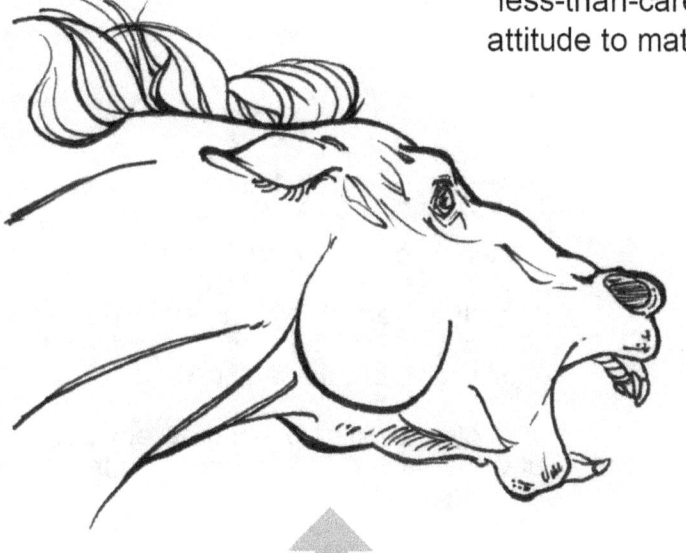

There are different levels of button-pushing in the world. The above horse is certainly angry, but the horse below, well, *irrate* doesn't even begin to cover it.

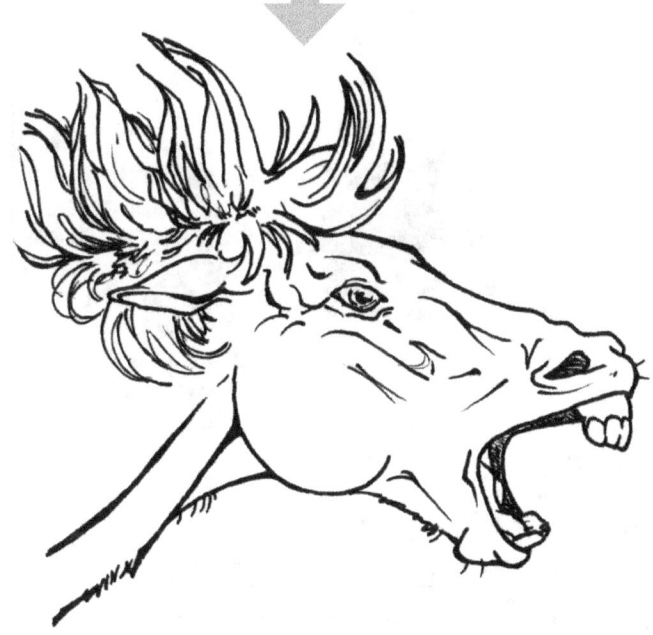

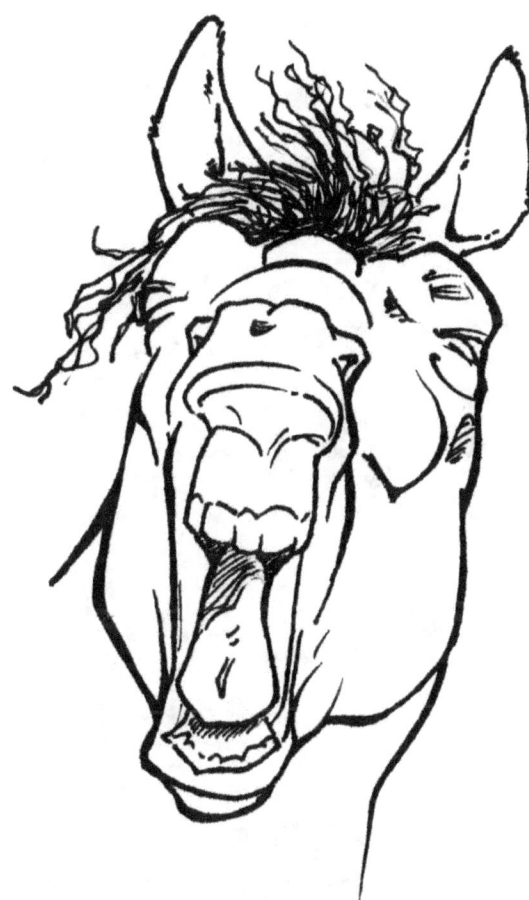

BIG YAWN

I doubt that you, dear reader, will ever be professionally commissioned to illustrate this pose, but it's great fun, and an excellent stretch + squeeze exercise.

WINDOWS TO THE SOUL

H orses aren't color blind, although, they do have dichromatic vision, which is a spiffy term that means they see two, of the three, basic wavelengths of color. Your horse does OK with blue and green, but cannot tell the apple you just fed it was red.

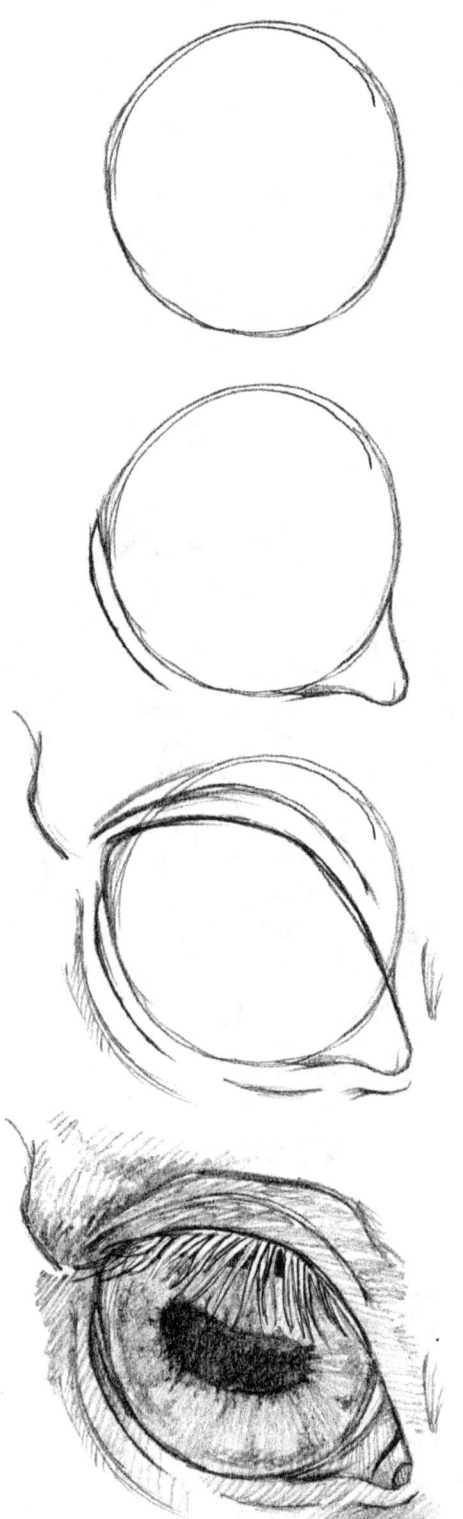

EYEING IT UP

Horses have the largest eyes of any land mammal, and their eye balls are not perfectly spherical. Your horse also sees better in the dark than you do, and it has roughly, give or take, a 350^0 range of vision.

None of that will help you draw any better, but what did you expect from me other than useless information?

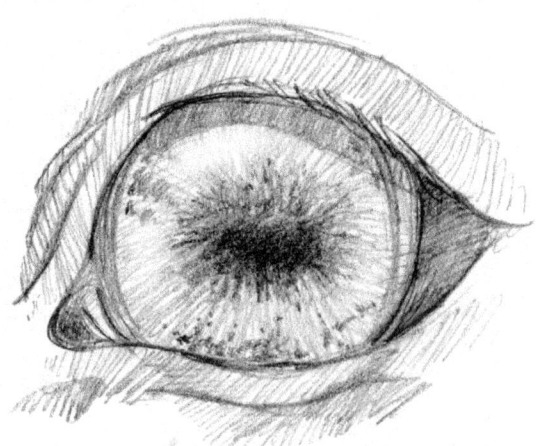

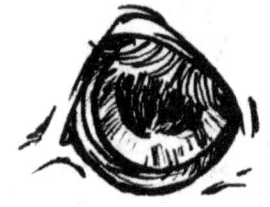

The color of the horse's eye bursts out from the center. Keeping that in mind will save you grief when you're drawing them.

NOTE

Horses don't have a spherical iris, but a rounded, rectangular one. Since most horse eyes are dark brown, an artist rarely has to pay attention to this fact, but in the case of a blue eyed horse, example left, it is obvious.

EYE POPPING

Using your knowledge of the eye, keep in mind your light source. Highlights don't just happen.

Eyes wide shut.

Eyes are quite asymmetrical and must flow with the tilt of the head.

Eyes wide open.

Lots of white suggests fear or fury.

This gentle expression is alert and kind.

WRONG!

It might be tempting to put the eyes on the front, especially if you're used to drawing dogs and cats, but don't. Eyes go on the sides of the face, not the front.

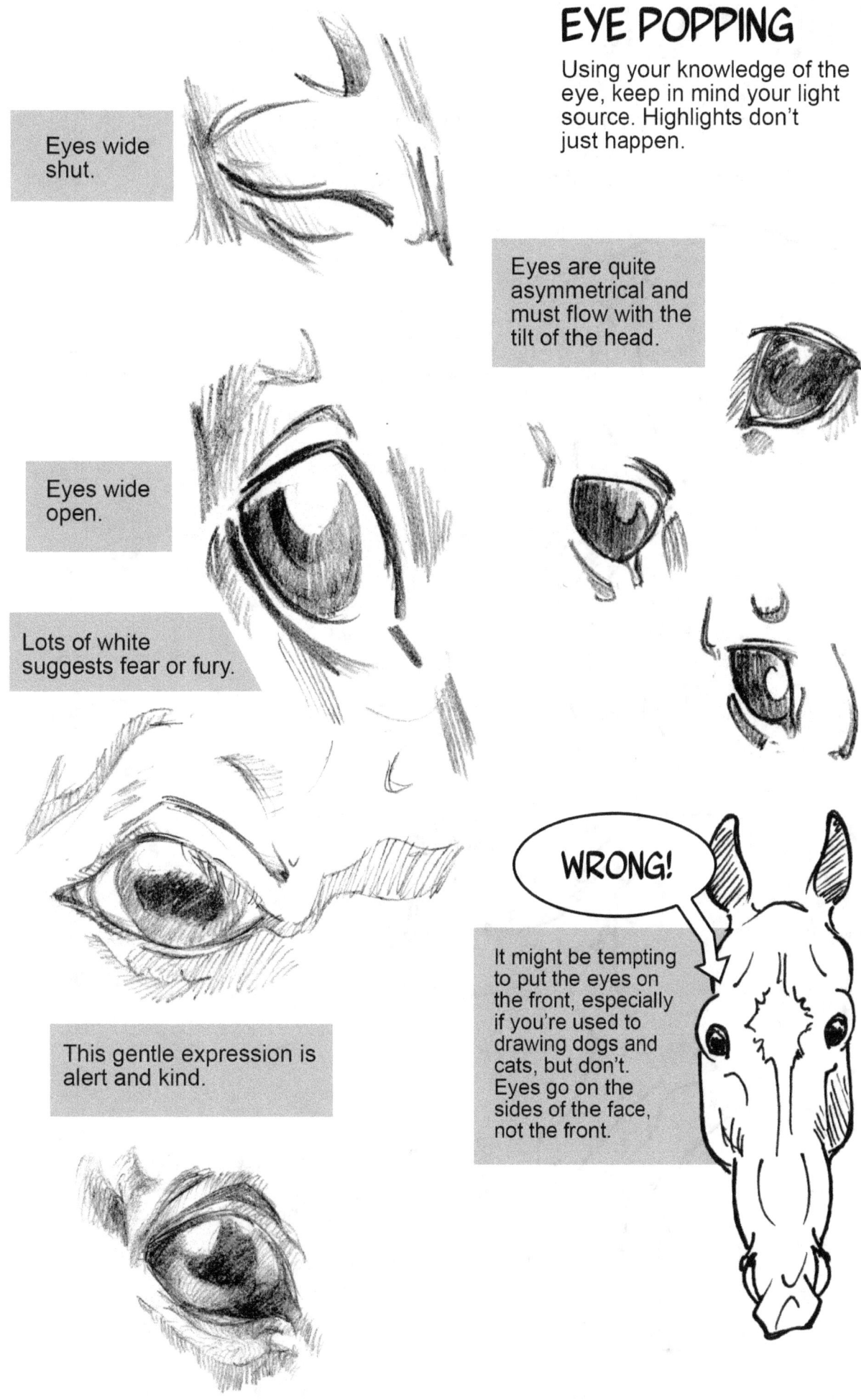

TAIL TALK

Horses are mostly body language communicators, and while plenty of attention is given to the head, let's not ignore the other end. Here's a cheat-sheet about what the tail might be telling you.

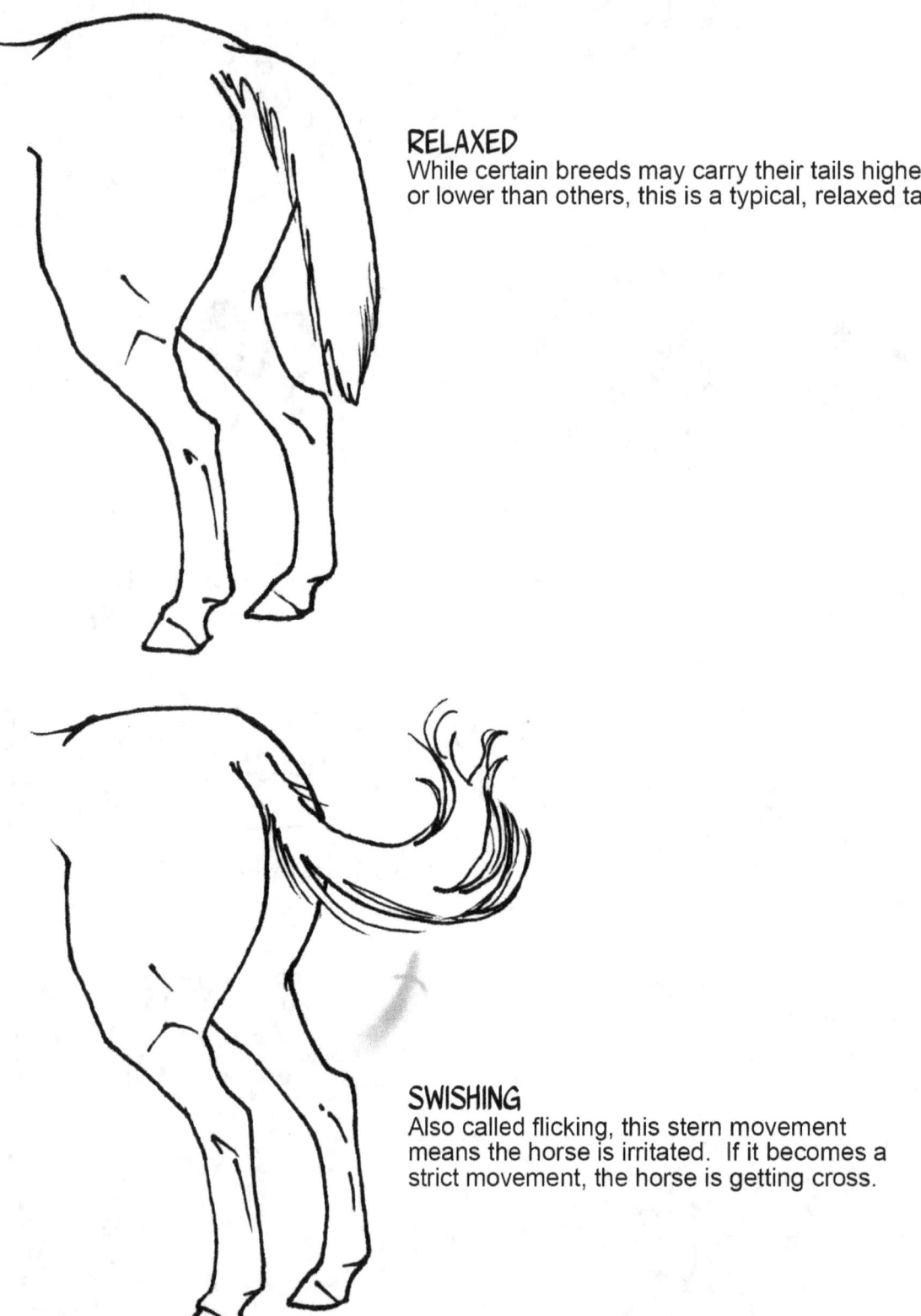

RELAXED
While certain breeds may carry their tails higher or lower than others, this is a typical, relaxed tail.

SWISHING
Also called flicking, this stern movement means the horse is irritated. If it becomes a strict movement, the horse is getting cross.

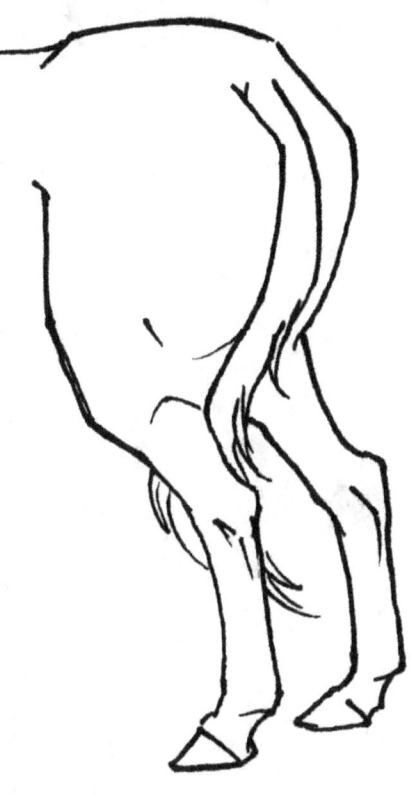

CLAMPED
Watch out for this one. A clamped
tail means the horse is tense.
This is saying, "I'm about to kick
or bolt. Possibly both."

RAISED
This can mean many things.
Alertness. Feeling spirited. All of
these are symptoms of a raised tail.
But mostly, it just means your horse
hears the "call of nature."

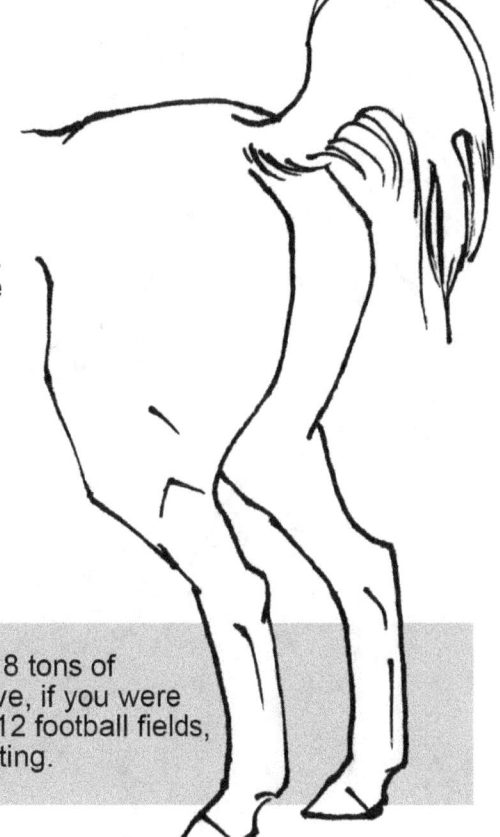

A 1400 pound horse will create around 8 tons of
manure a year. To put that in perspective, if you were
to lay that out over an area the size of 12 football fields,
your hands would be absolutely disgusting.

HOOVES AND LEGS

H ooves and legs come as a package deal.
You should learn to draw them.

Or grass.

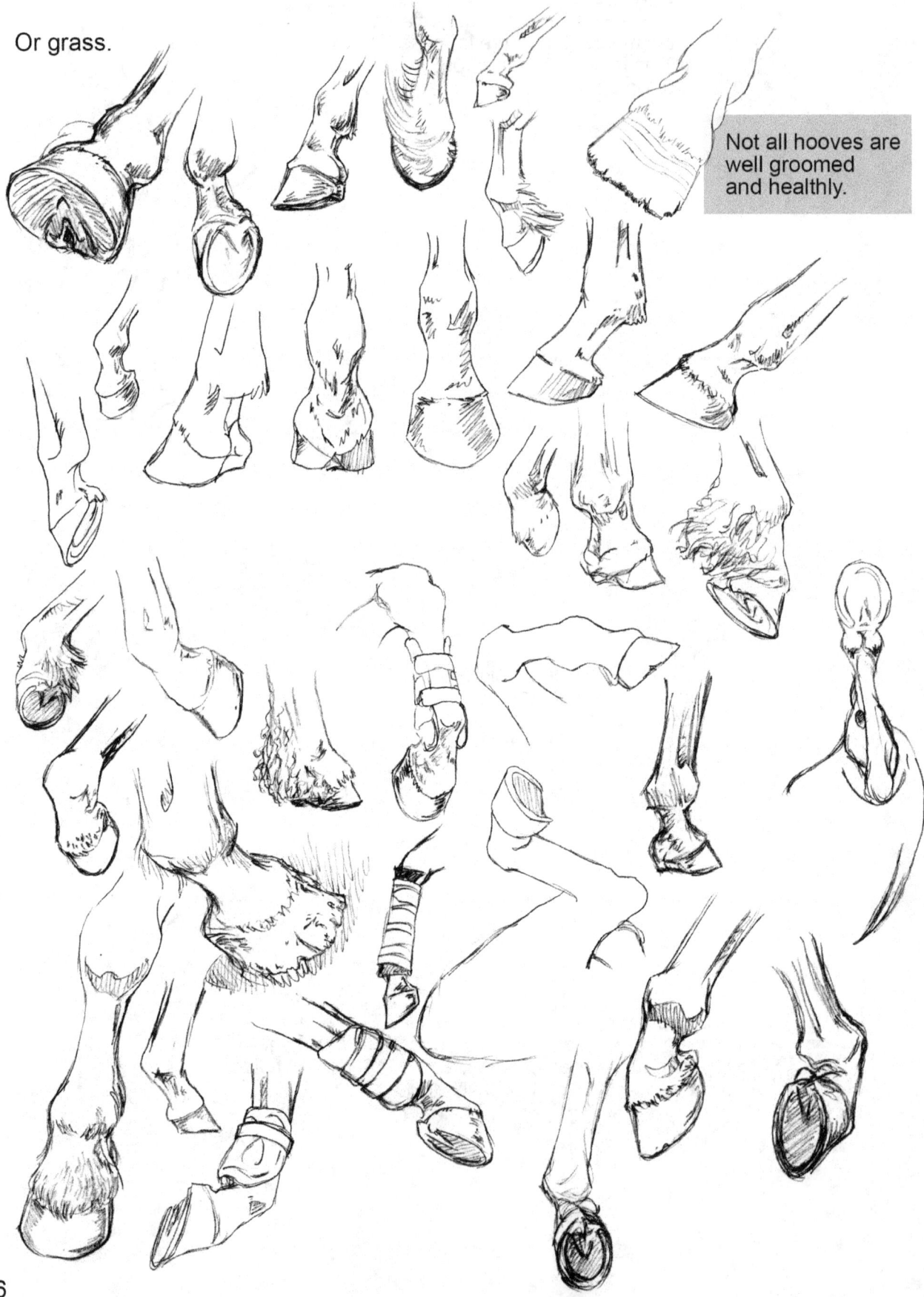

Not all hooves are
well groomed
and healthly.

ALL TOGETHER NOW...

W hile I'm a fan of not making people memorize things, learning the parts of the horse will help you follow along with the text of this book. Also, they made me add it.

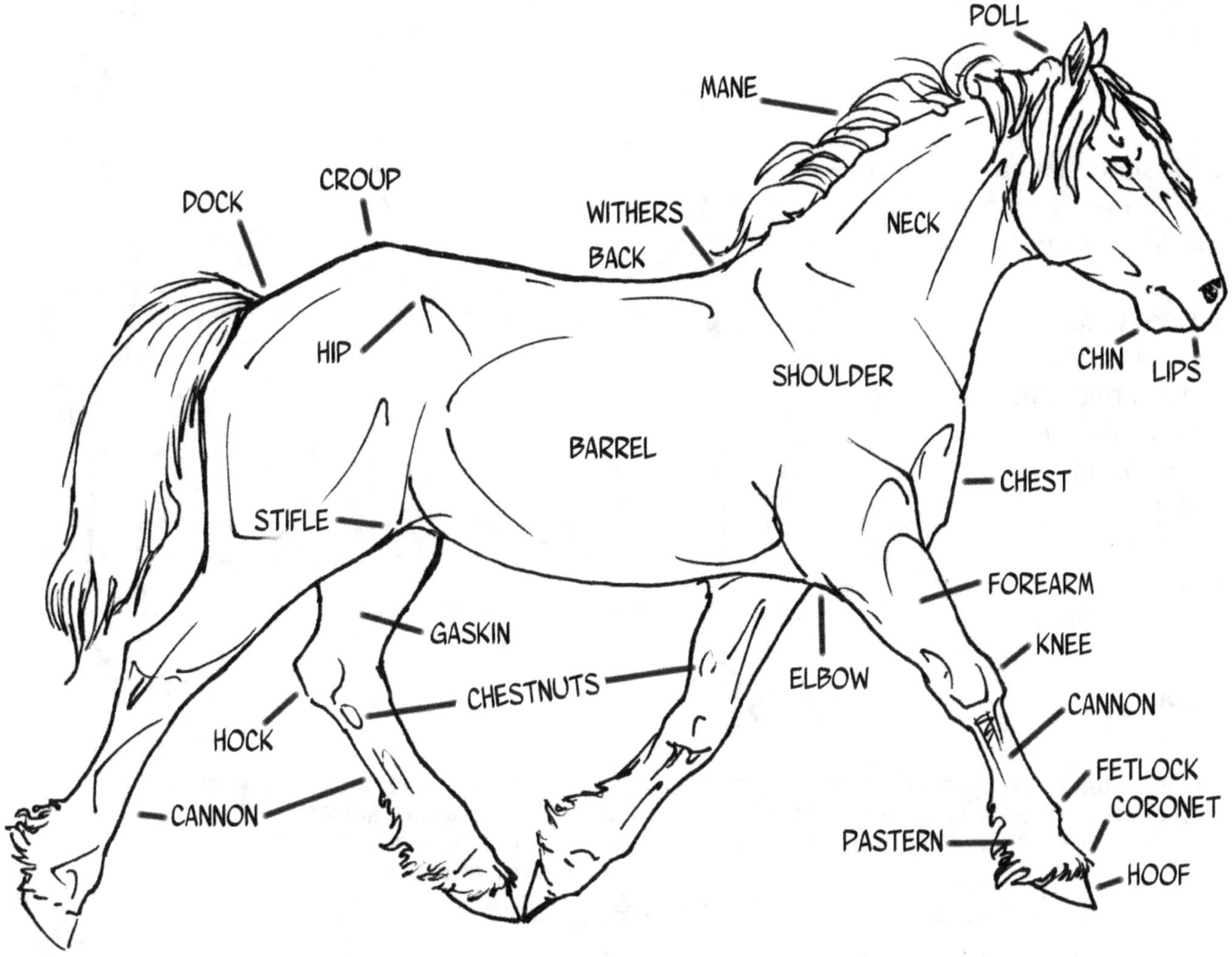

POLL

MANE

DOCK   CROUP   WITHERS   NECK
        BACK

HIP   SHOULDER   CHIN   LIPS

BARREL   CHEST

STIFLE   FOREARM

GASKIN   KNEE

CHESTNUTS   CANNON

HOCK   ELBOW   FETLOCK
                 CORONET

CANNON   PASTERN   HOOF

DRAWING TIPS

Since having a reference available for every drawing occasion is rarely an option in the real world, here are some easy self-checks.

- Knees are lower than the hocks.

- Elbows should be above the belly line; stifles below.

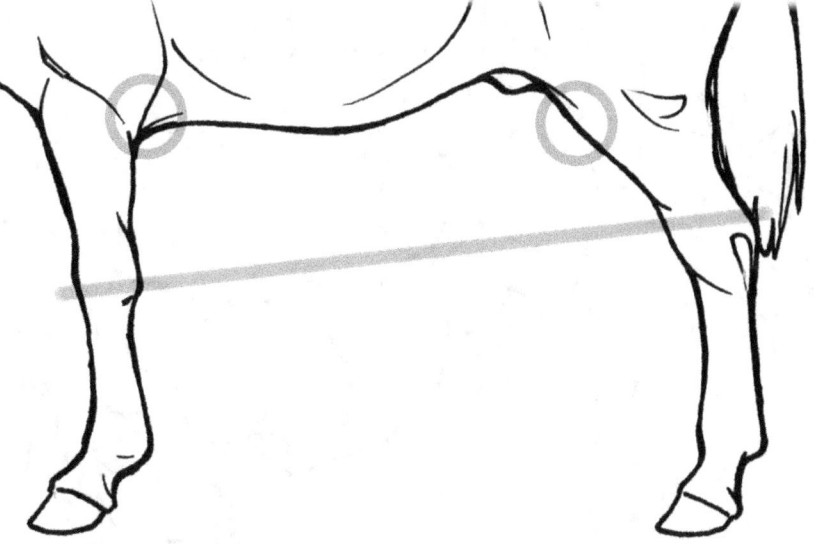

17

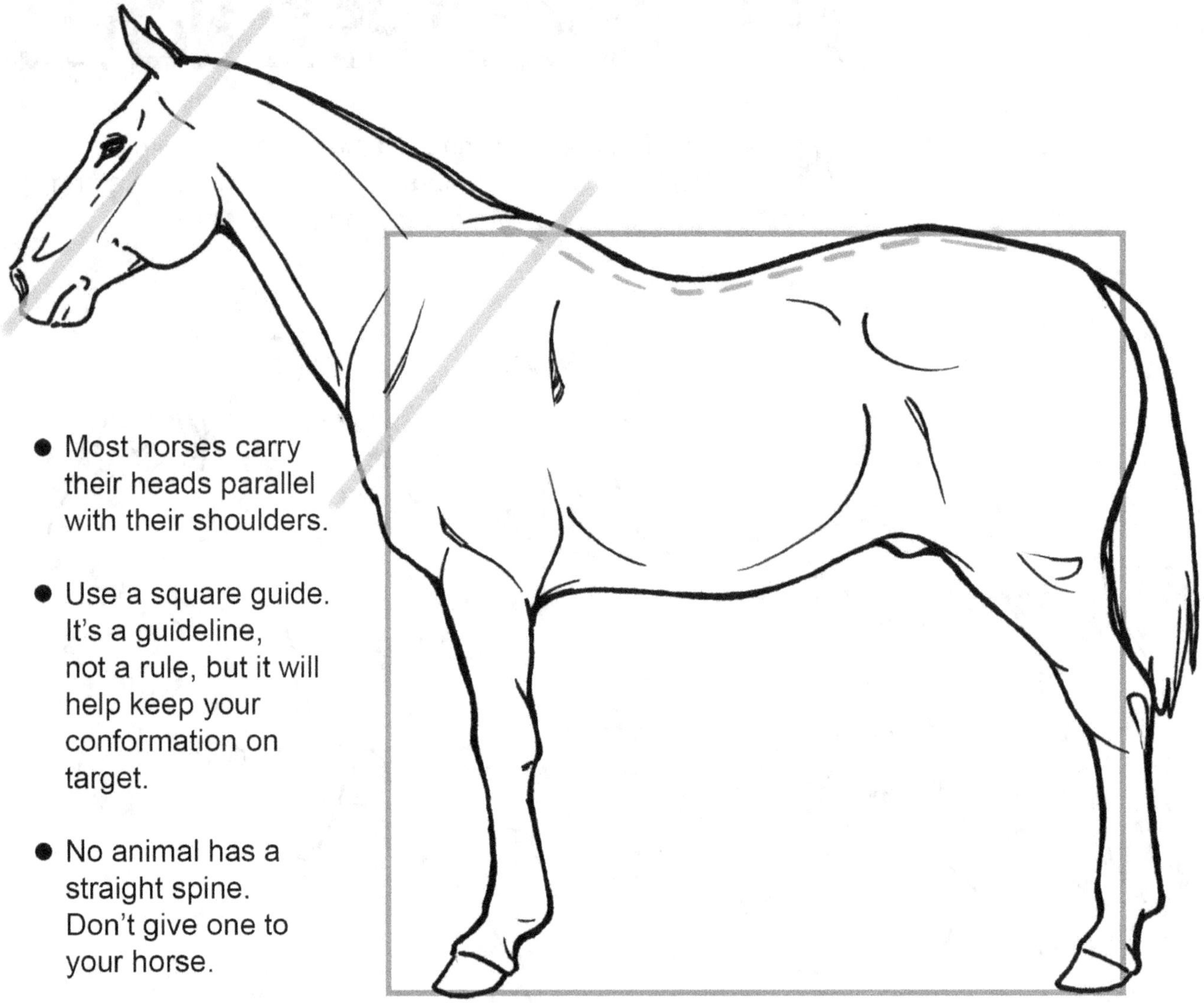

- Most horses carry their heads parallel with their shoulders.

- Use a square guide. It's a guideline, not a rule, but it will help keep your conformation on target.

- No animal has a straight spine. Don't give one to your horse.

Nature tends to prefer wild horses that are smaller, tougher, and can get fat on what little there is available in their native habitats.

Mongolian, Mountainous, and Arab breeds are good examples of the tiny, but feisty, bodies natural selection tends to elect.

14.25 Hands High

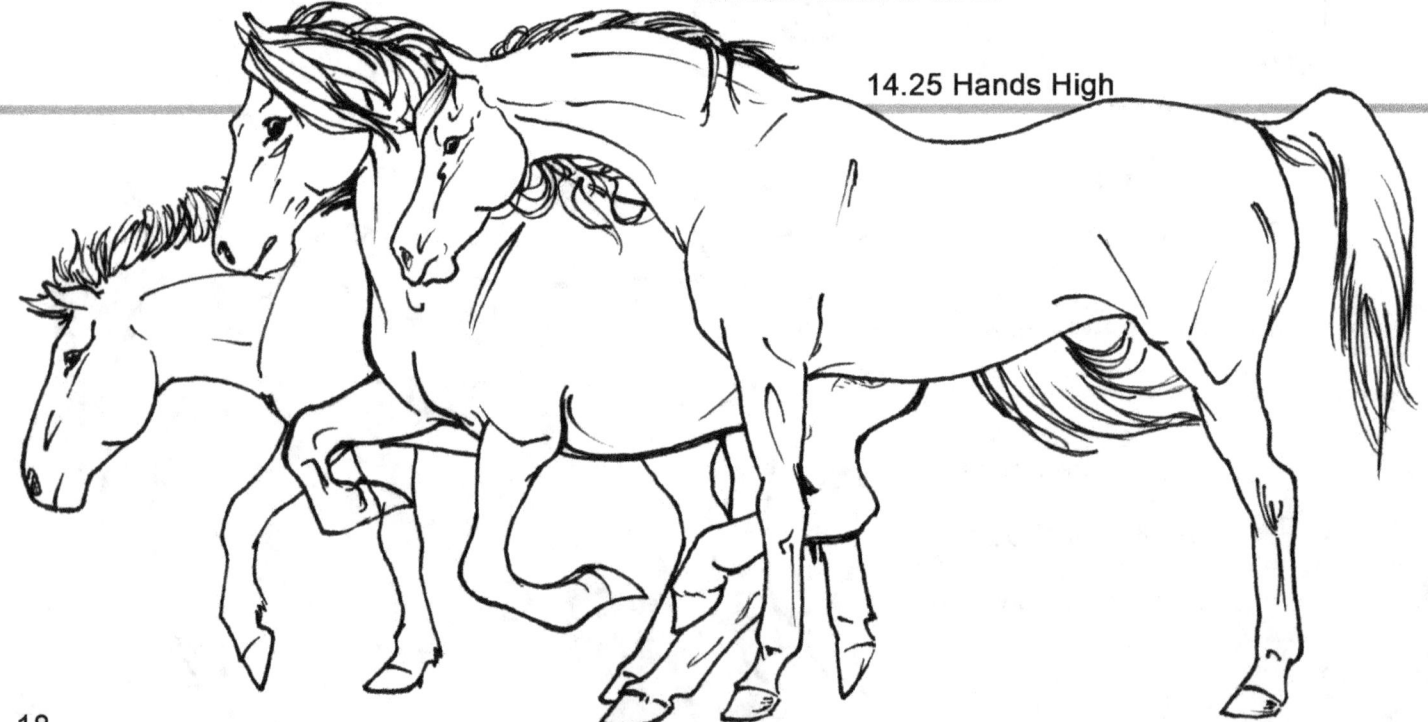

18

OVERLAY METHOD

As you already know, shapes and layers are your friends. And while there are many ways to sketch, my favorite is the "I'm too lazy to erase my lines, so I'll just draw a new one right over it" method.

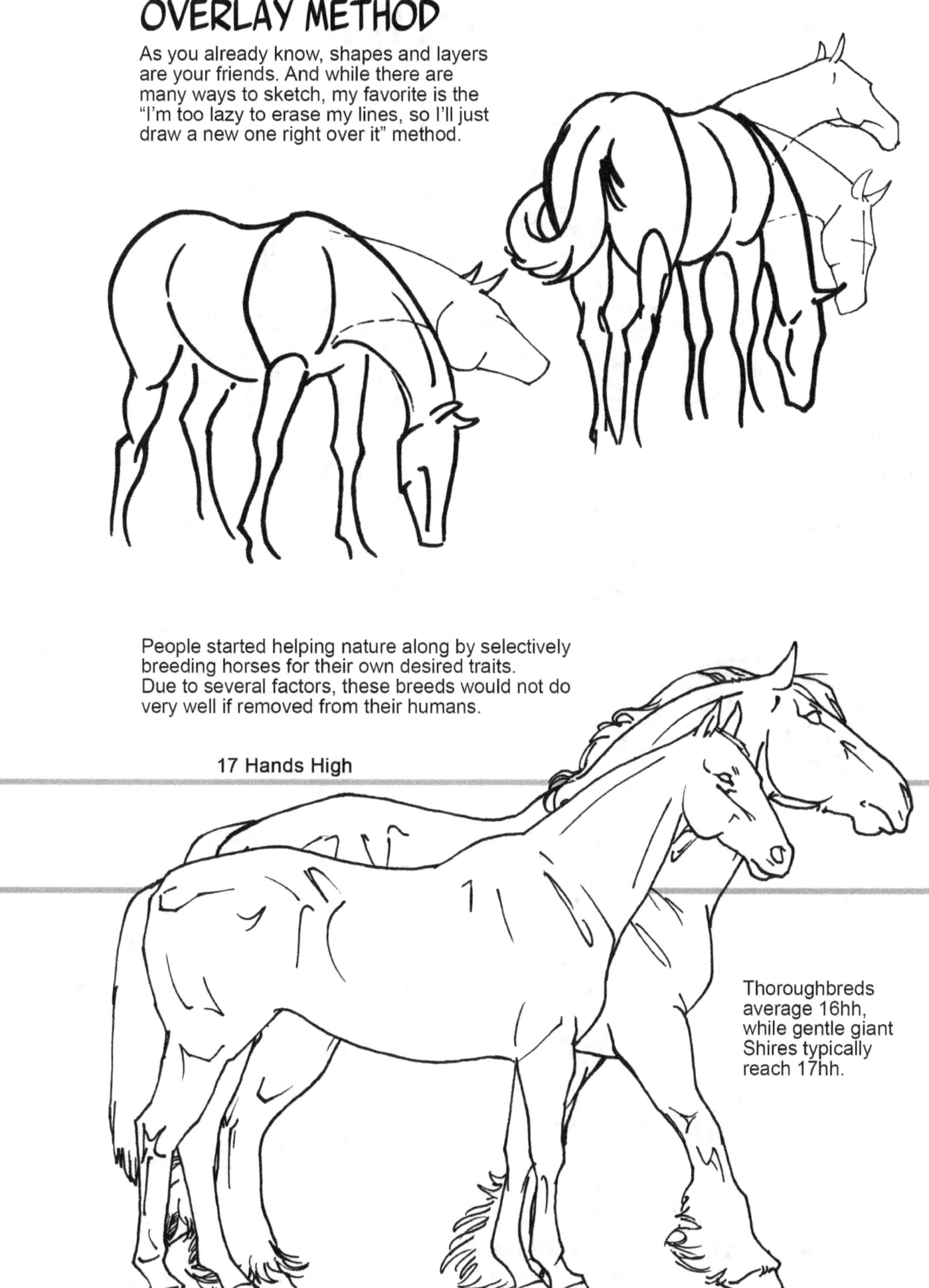

People started helping nature along by selectively breeding horses for their own desired traits. Due to several factors, these breeds would not do very well if removed from their humans.

17 Hands High

Thoroughbreds average 16hh, while gentle giant Shires typically reach 17hh.

19

MAJESTIC MOVEMENT

Stiff is boring. We're here to draw horses, not bowls of fruit on a table, and horses are full of potential energy. Let's go!

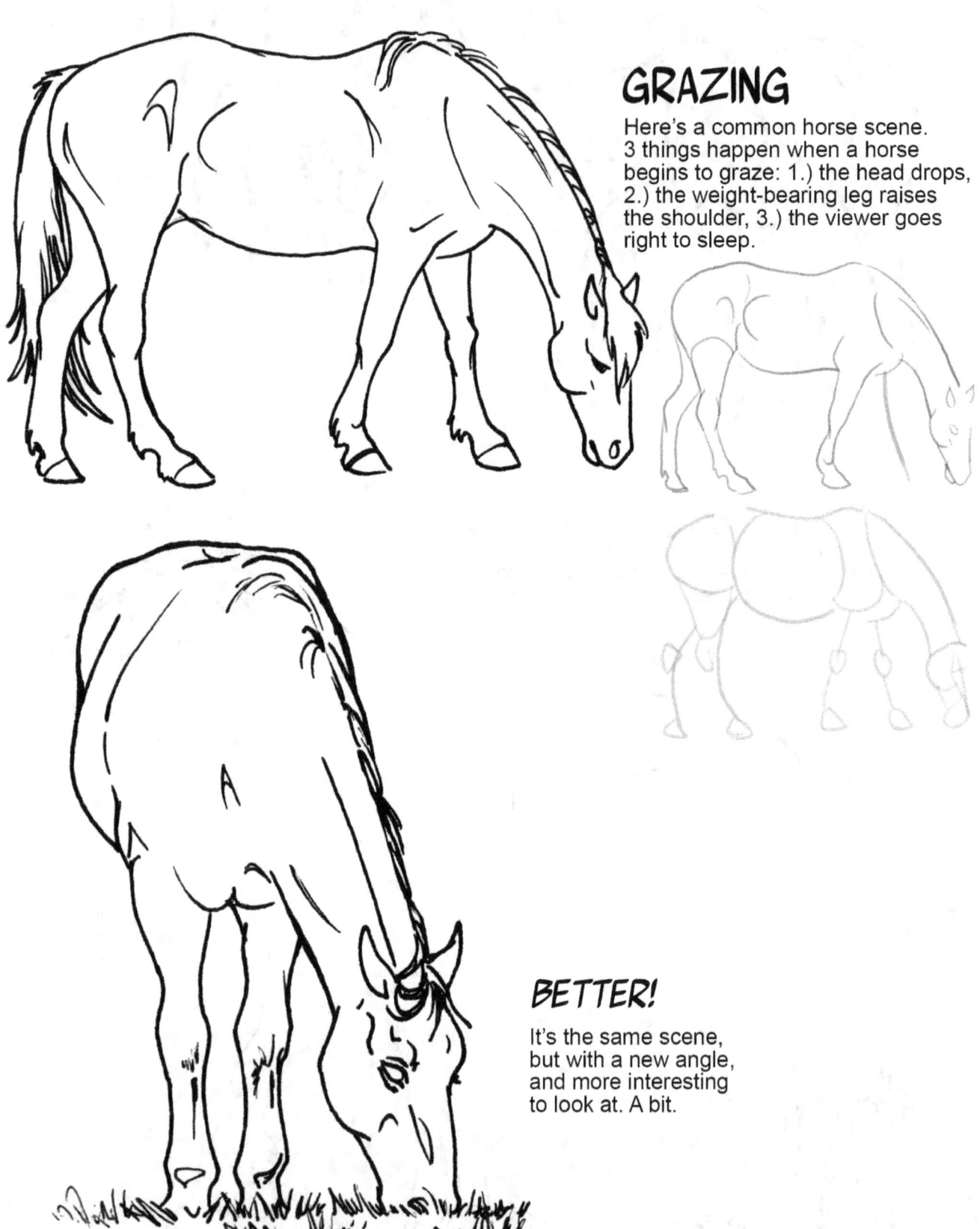

GRAZING

Here's a common horse scene. 3 things happen when a horse begins to graze: 1.) the head drops, 2.) the weight-bearing leg raises the shoulder, 3.) the viewer goes right to sleep.

BETTER!

It's the same scene, but with a new angle, and more interesting to look at. A bit.

GENTLE CURVES

Grazing horses are not on high-alert, and a basic sketch will keep those necklines, longer above, shorter below, at a jaunty angle.

The only time a horse isn't perfectly proportioned for feeding is when it's very young. A youngster's comical proportions make for difficult grazing. When your colt is absurdly bum-up and knees-wonky, you're drawing 'em right.

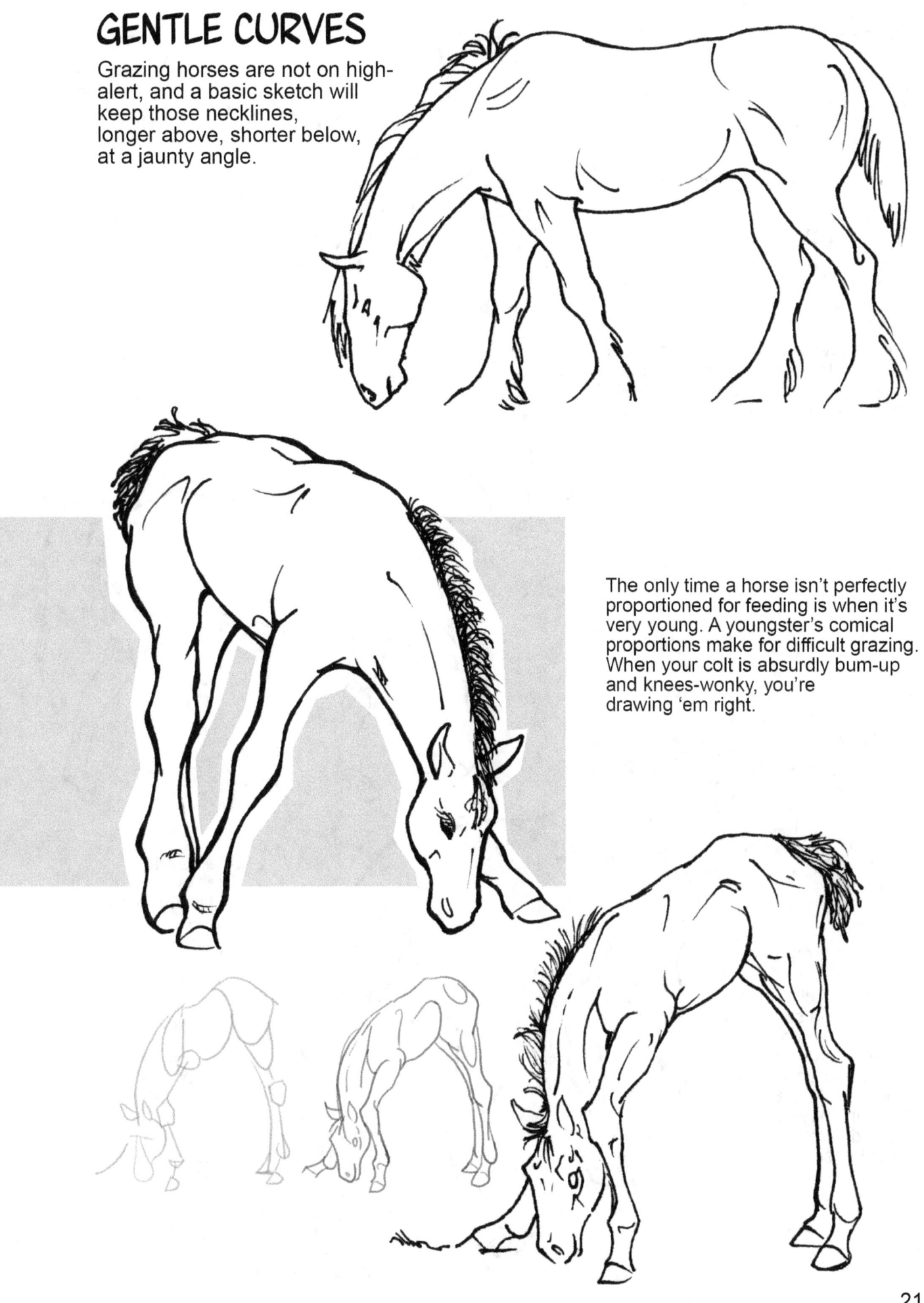

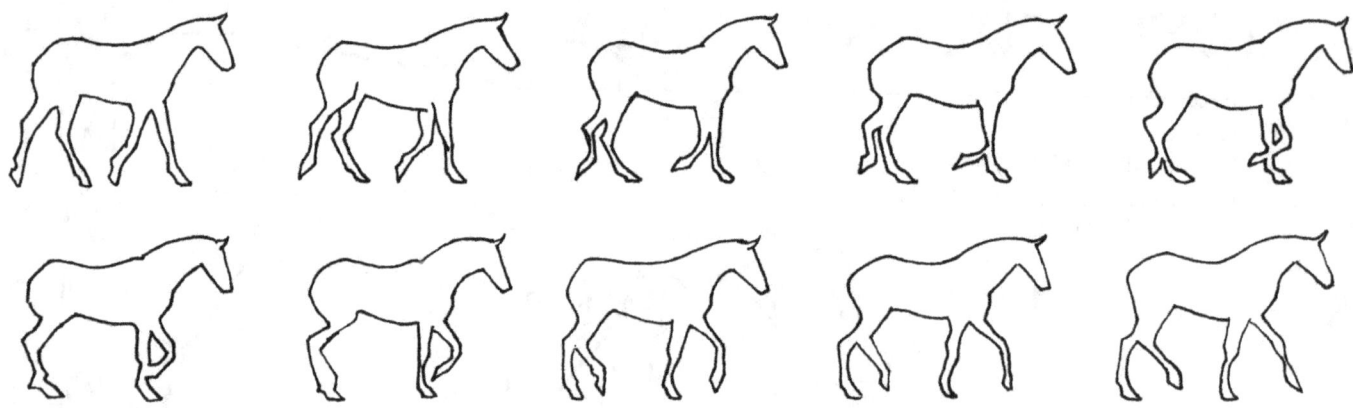

WALK

In this Muybridge-moment, we see the walking cycle. As long as you notice that at the walk, a horse never has more than 2 feet off the ground, your time has been well spent.

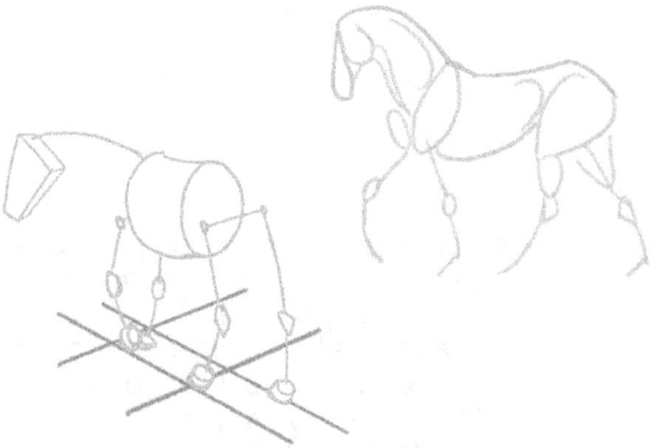

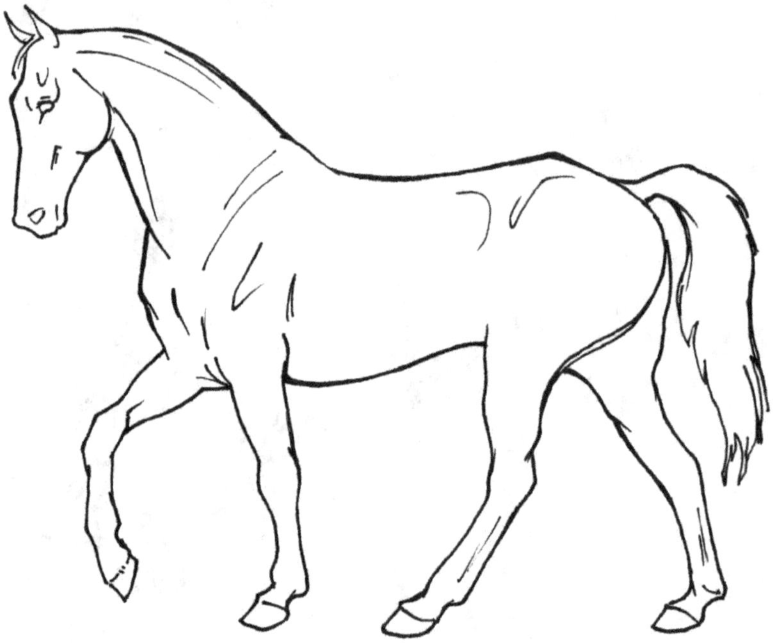

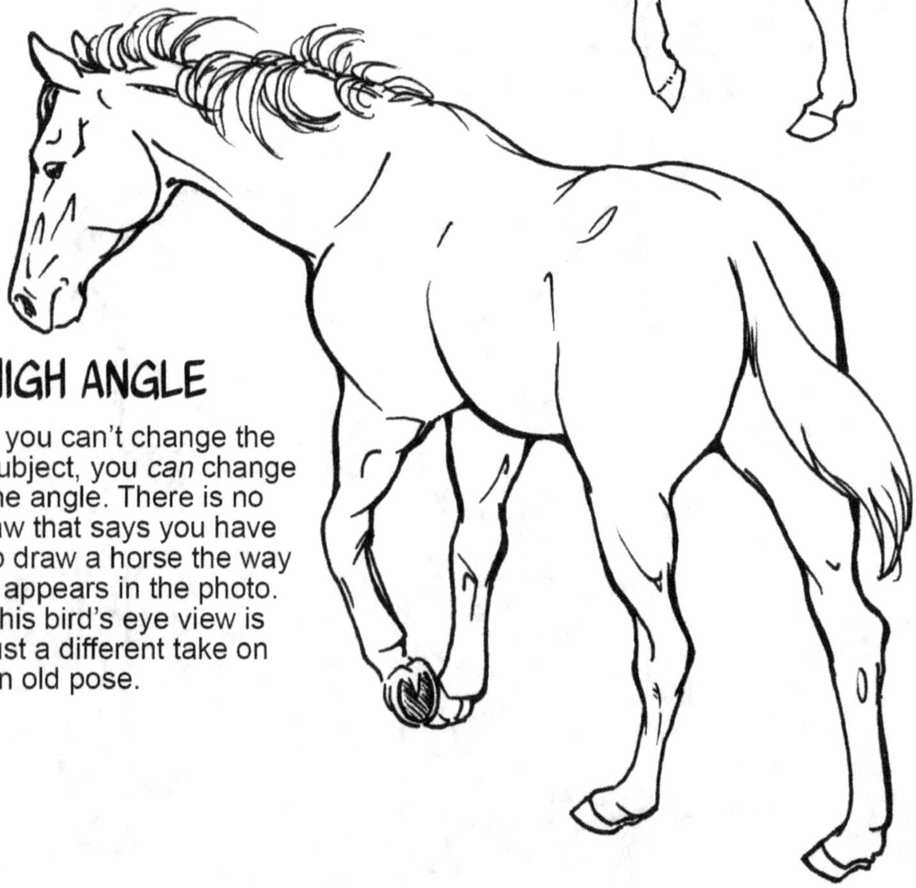

HIGH ANGLE

If you can't change the subject, you *can* change the angle. There is no law that says you have to draw a horse the way it appears in the photo. This bird's eye view is just a different take on an old pose.

UP & DOWN
When one end goes up, the other goes down.

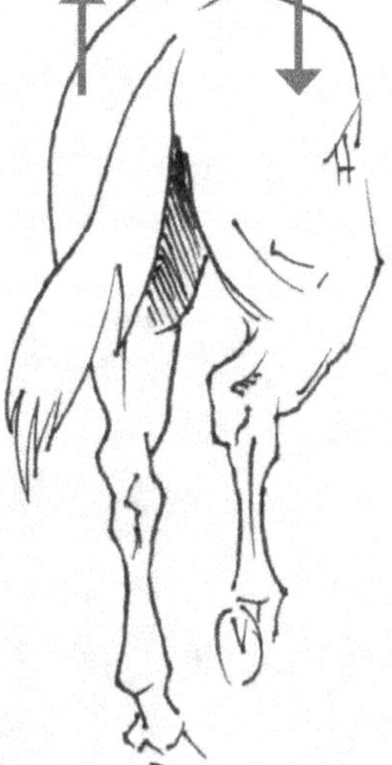

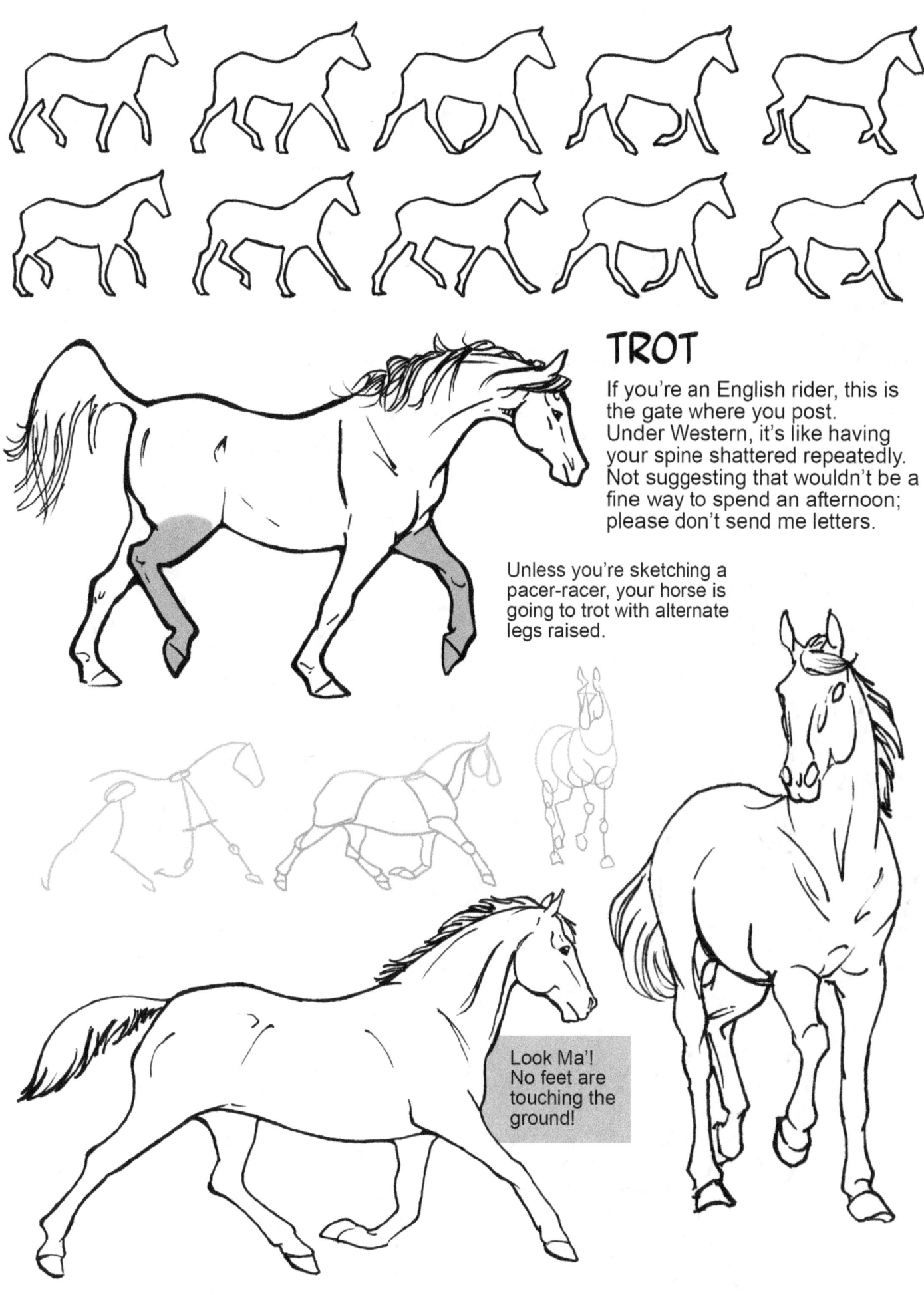

TROT

If you're an English rider, this is the gate where you post. Under Western, it's like having your spine shattered repeatedly. Not suggesting that wouldn't be a fine way to spend an afternoon; please don't send me letters.

Unless you're sketching a pacer-racer, your horse is going to trot with alternate legs raised.

Look Ma'! No feet are touching the ground!

23

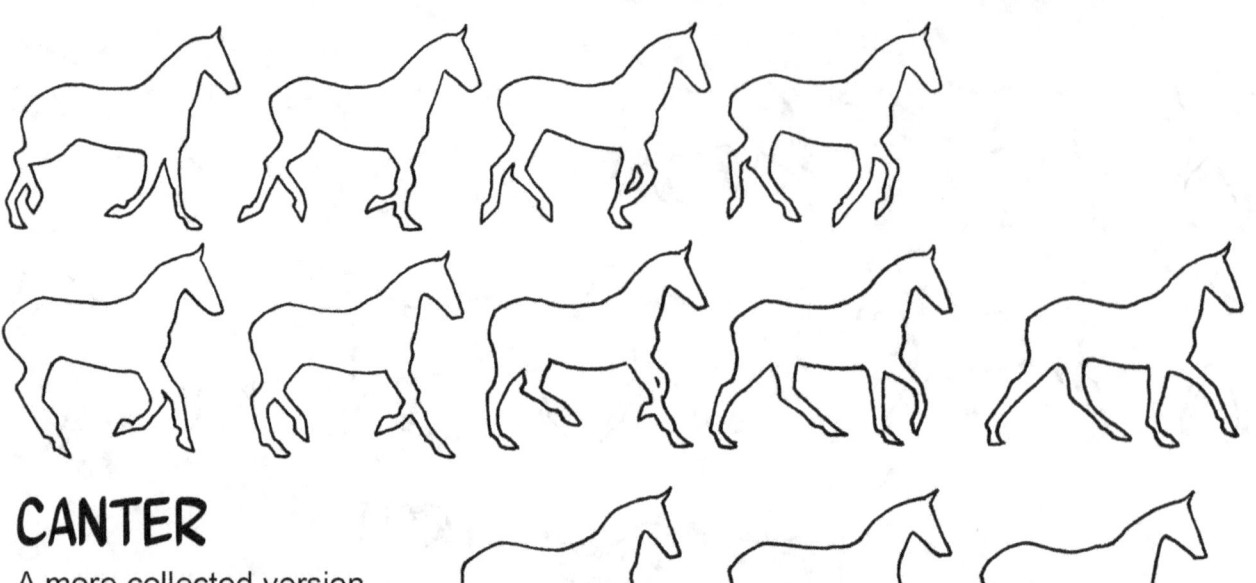

CANTER

A more collected version of travel than the gallop, to move at the canter is akin to riding at a 3-beat hop.

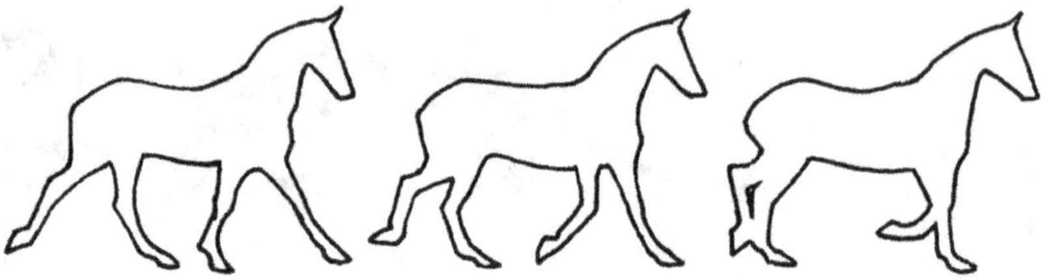

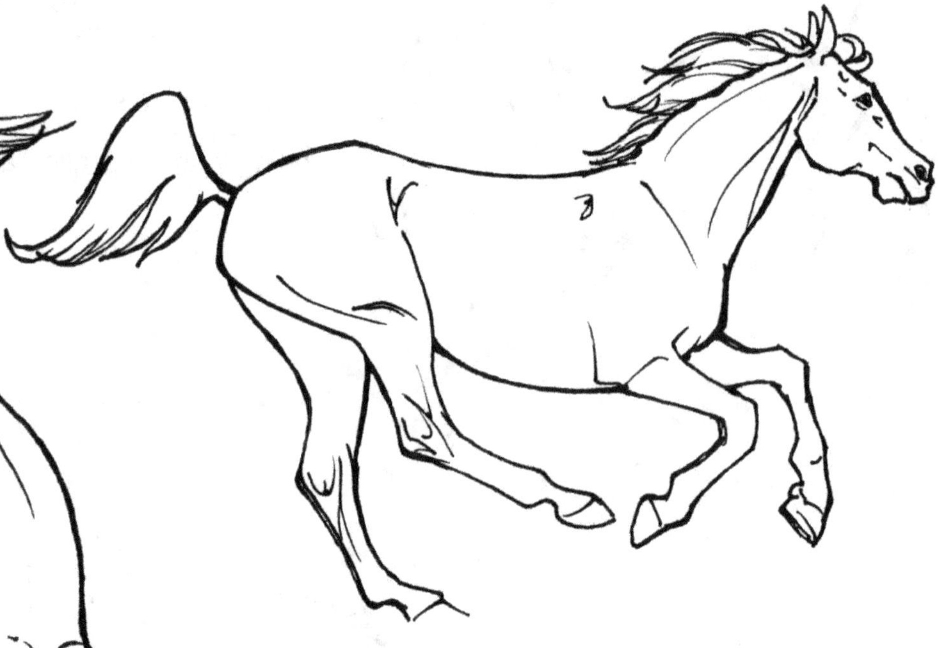

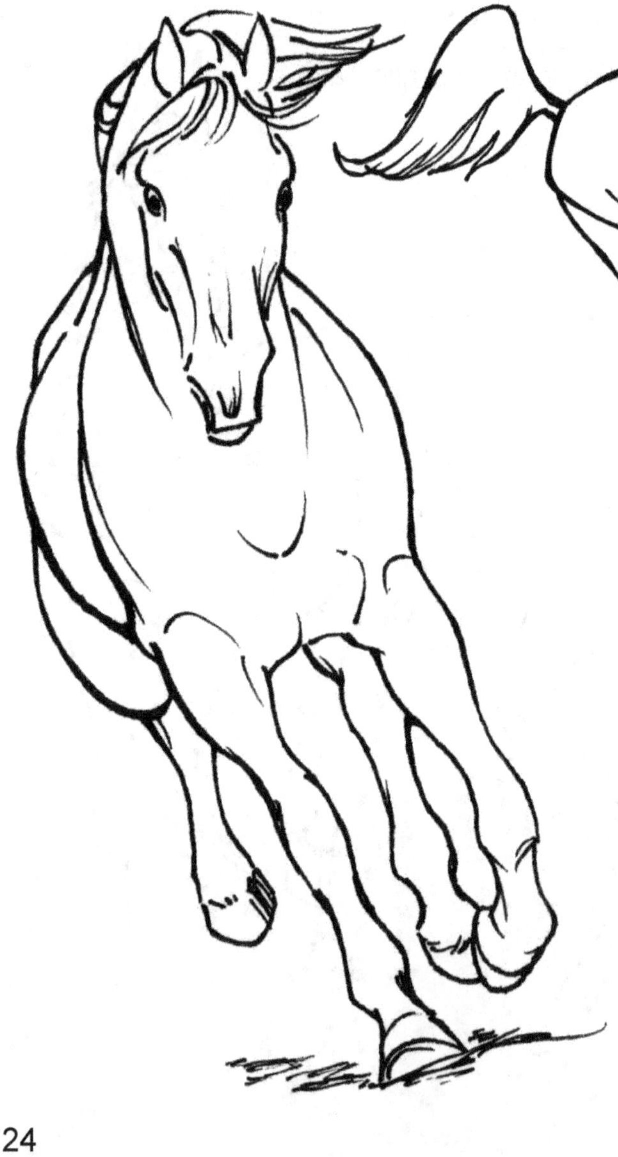

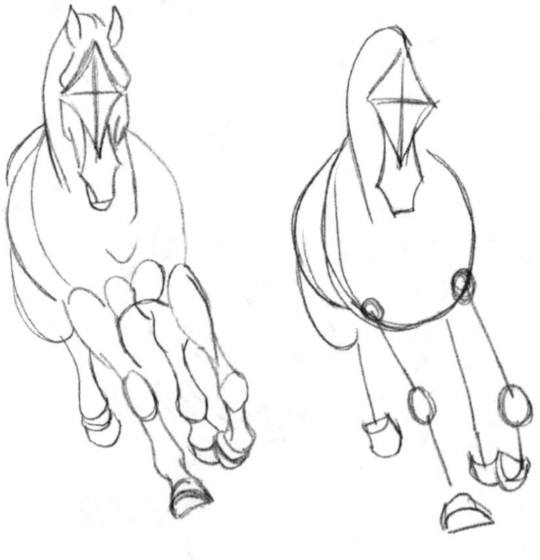

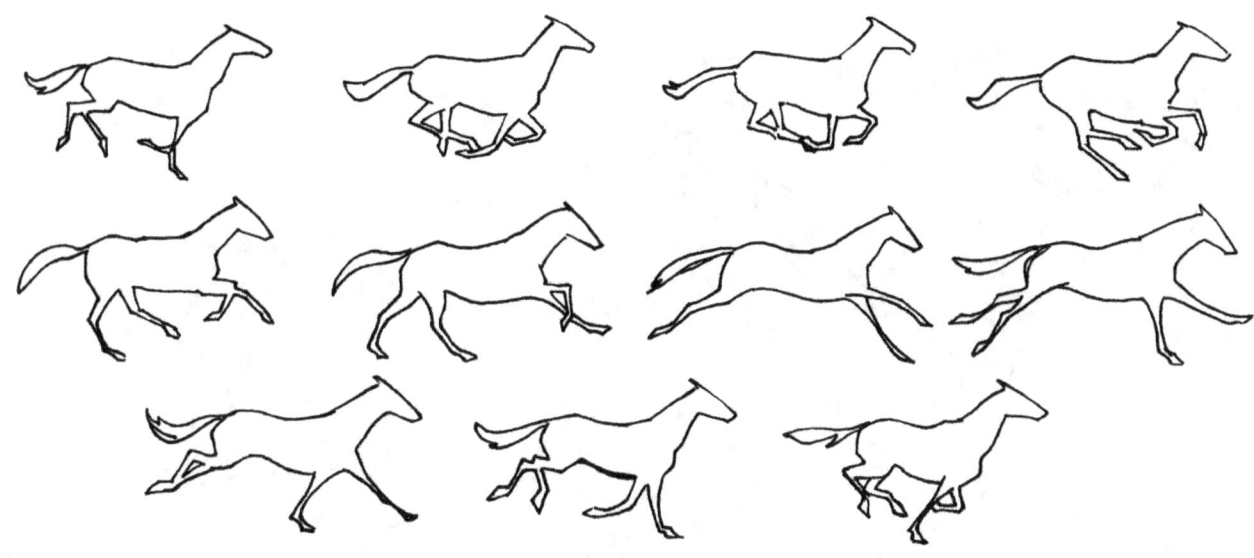

GALLOP

An all-out running gate, the gallop is top speed, and most horses can't hold it for too long.

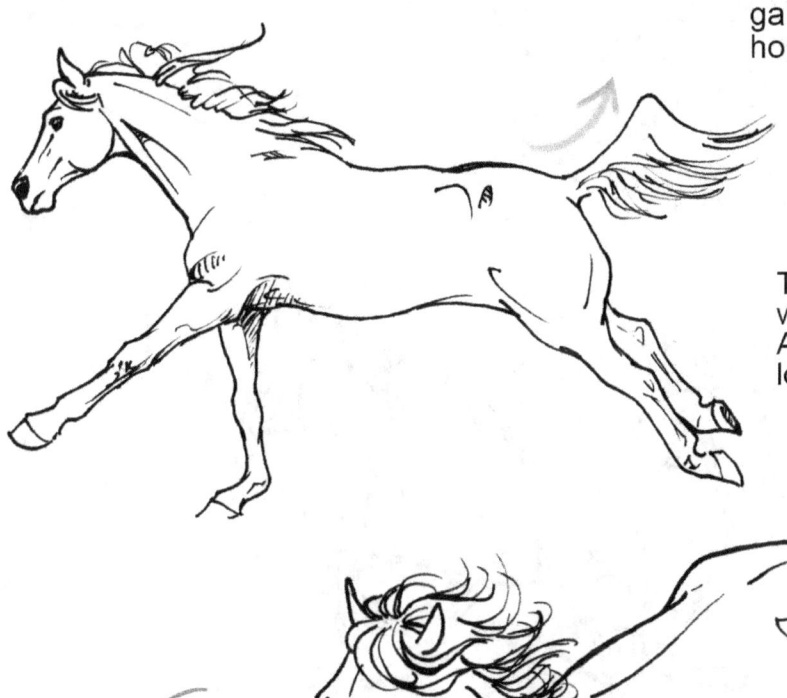

The Arab typically takes flight with the tail in the air.
Arabians are well known for their long-range capabilities.

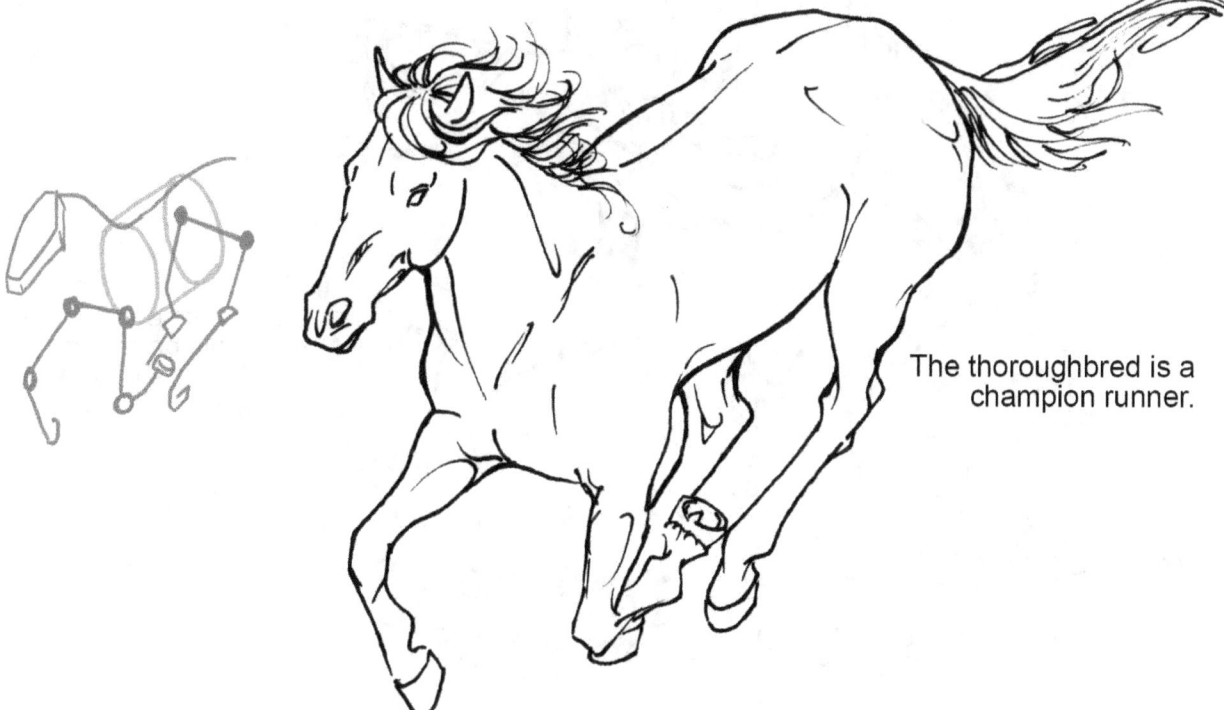

The thoroughbred is a champion runner.

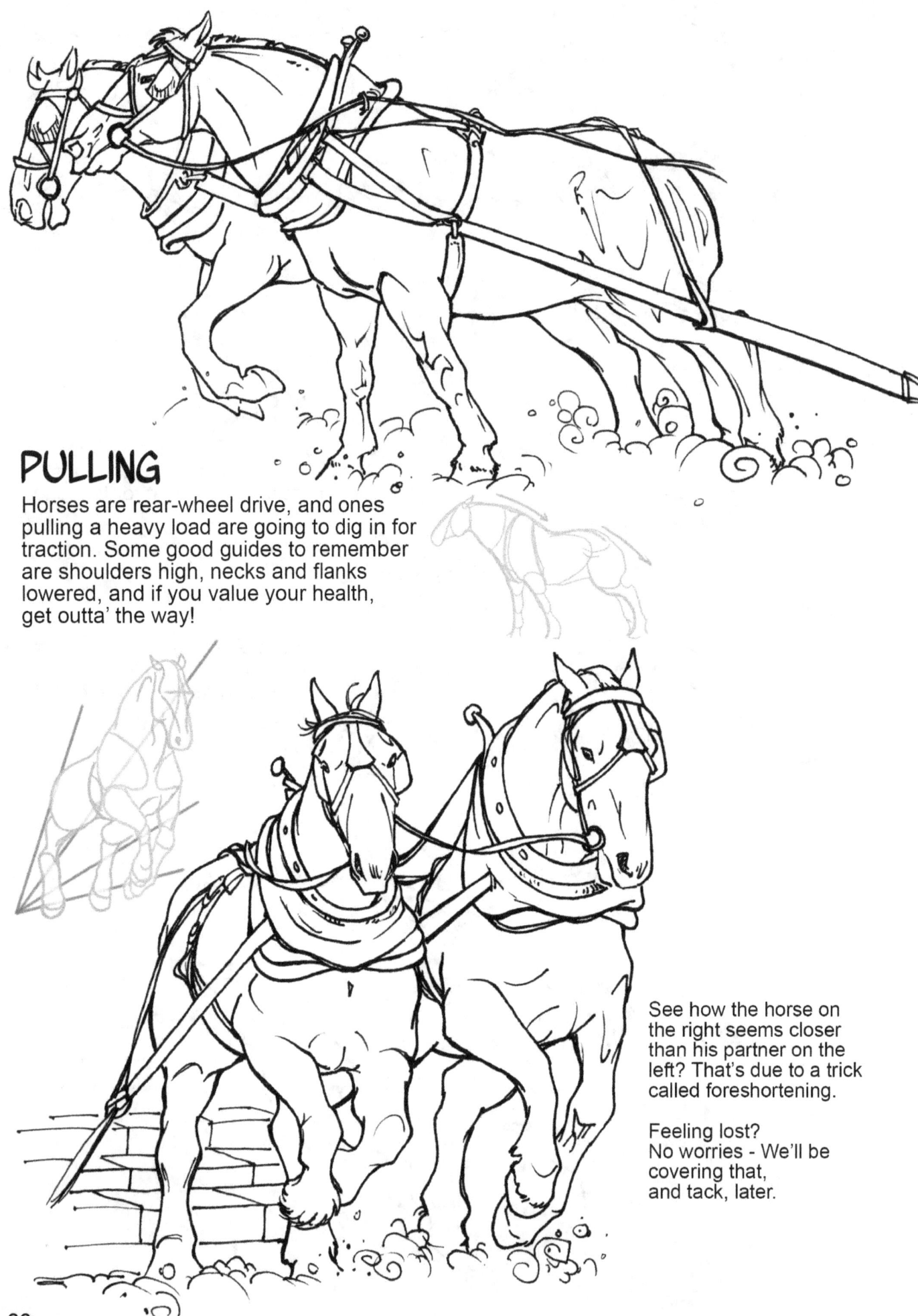

PULLING

Horses are rear-wheel drive, and ones pulling a heavy load are going to dig in for traction. Some good guides to remember are shoulders high, necks and flanks lowered, and if you value your health, get outta' the way!

See how the horse on the right seems closer than his partner on the left? That's due to a trick called foreshortening.

Feeling lost?
No worries - We'll be covering that, and tack, later.

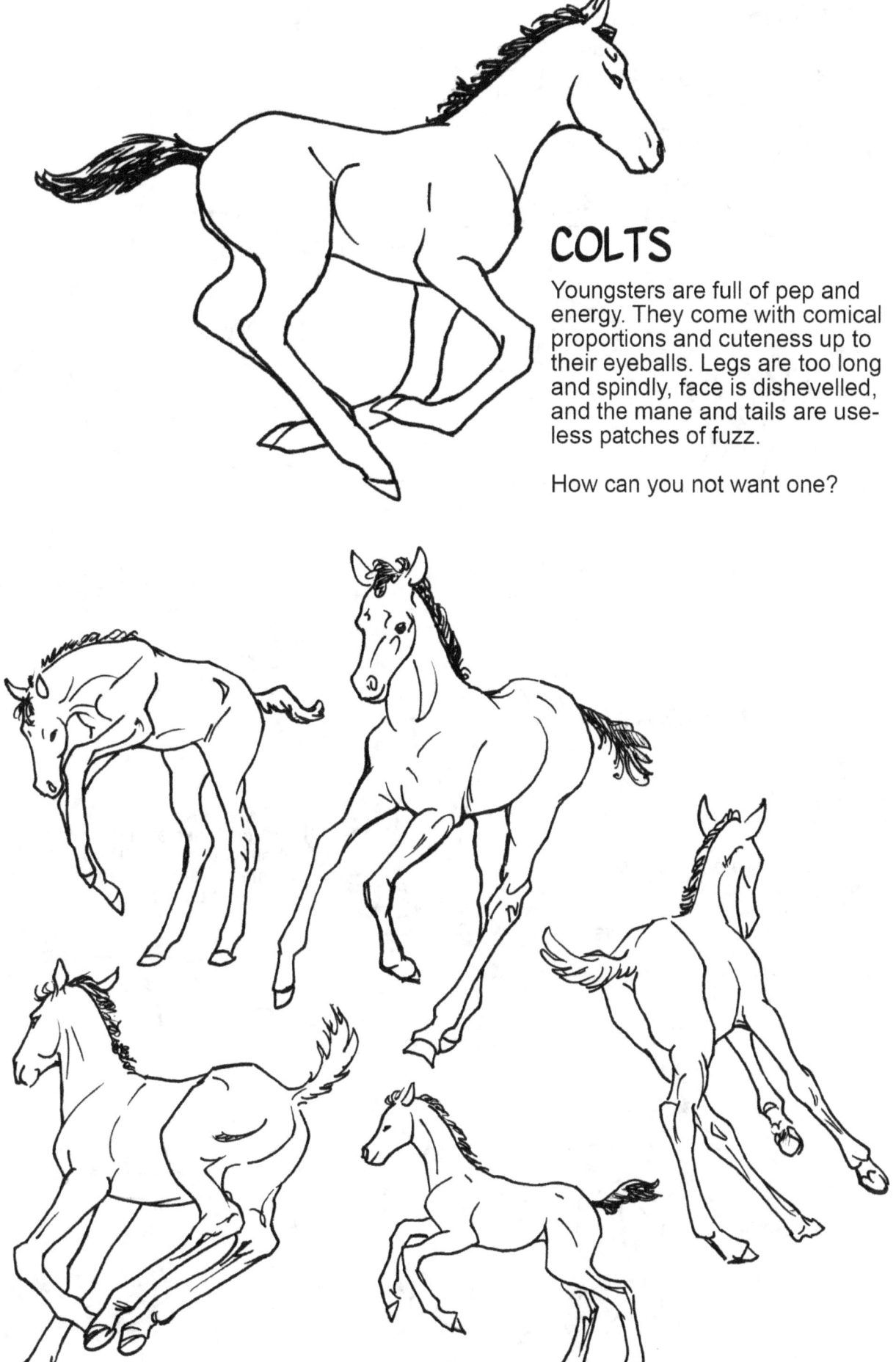

COLTS

Youngsters are full of pep and energy. They come with comical proportions and cuteness up to their eyeballs. Legs are too long and spindly, face is dishevelled, and the mane and tails are useless patches of fuzz.

How can you not want one?

SPOOK

When a horse's flight response kicks into gear, it's called spooking or shying. In the wild, this first-response meant the horse could "run away another day." In modern times, it will likely earn you an "unscheduled dismount."

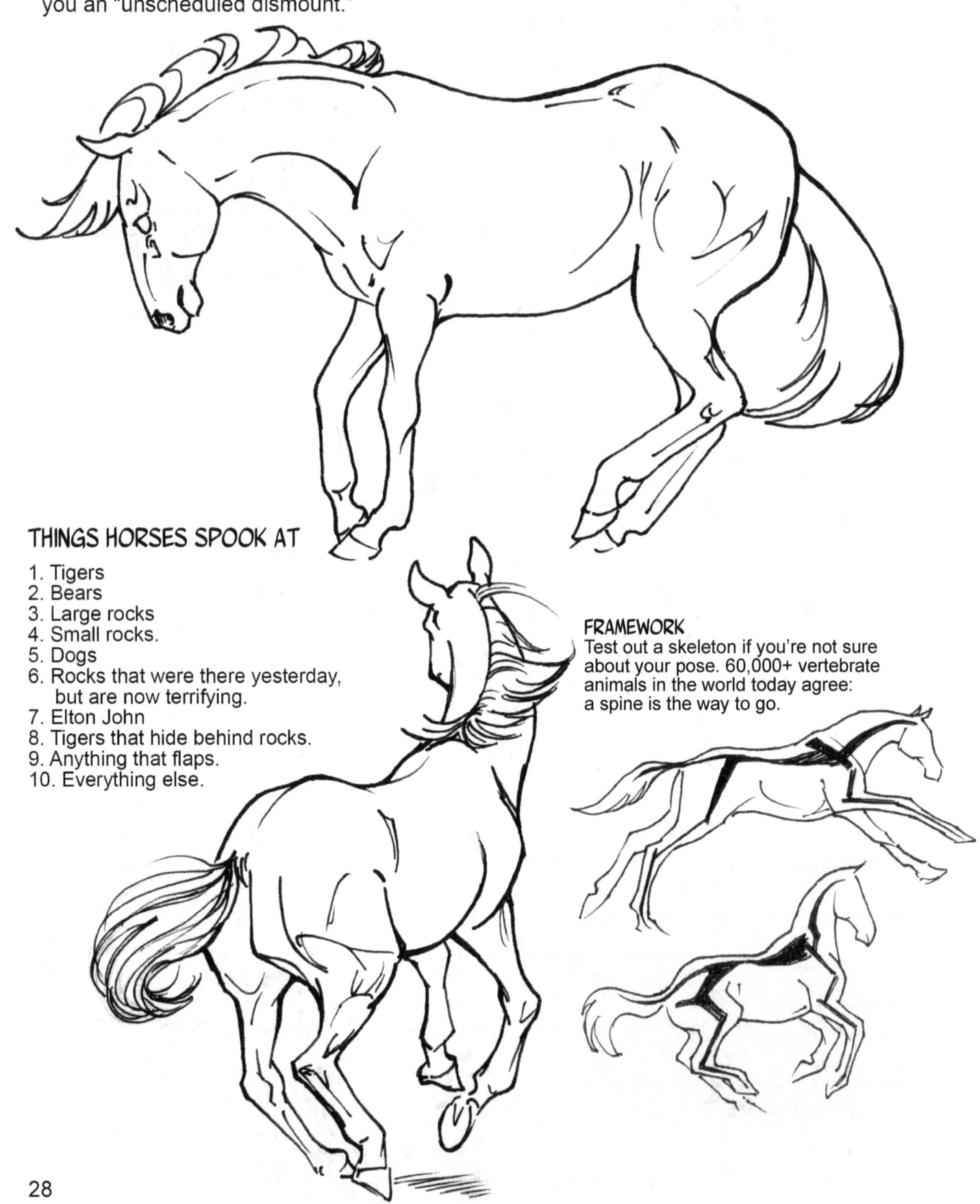

THINGS HORSES SPOOK AT

1. Tigers
2. Bears
3. Large rocks
4. Small rocks.
5. Dogs
6. Rocks that were there yesterday, but are now terrifying.
7. Elton John
8. Tigers that hide behind rocks.
9. Anything that flaps.
10. Everything else.

FRAMEWORK

Test out a skeleton if you're not sure about your pose. 60,000+ vertebrate animals in the world today agree: a spine is the way to go.

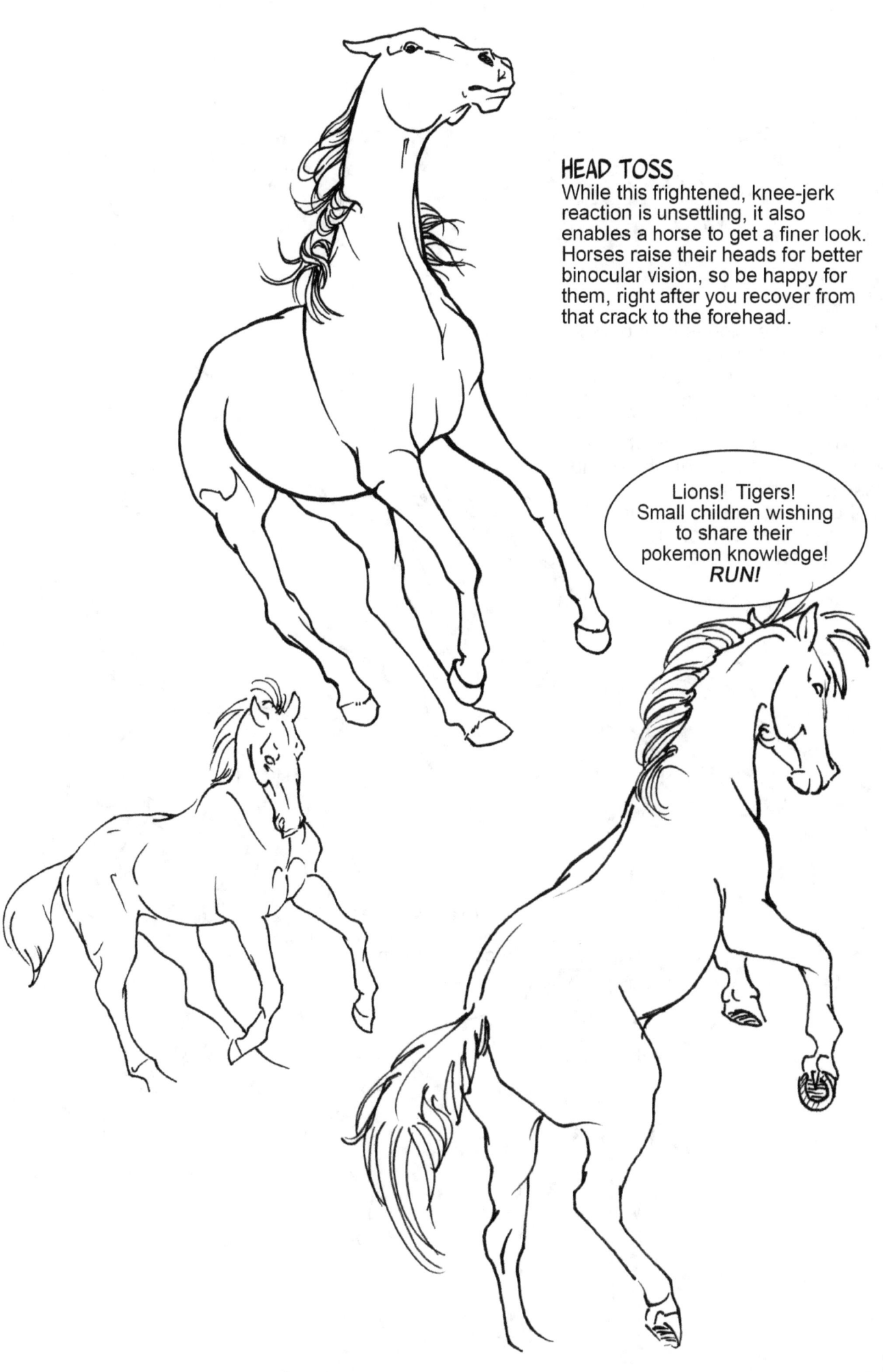

HEAD TOSS

While this frightened, knee-jerk reaction is unsettling, it also enables a horse to get a finer look. Horses raise their heads for better binocular vision, so be happy for them, right after you recover from that crack to the forehead.

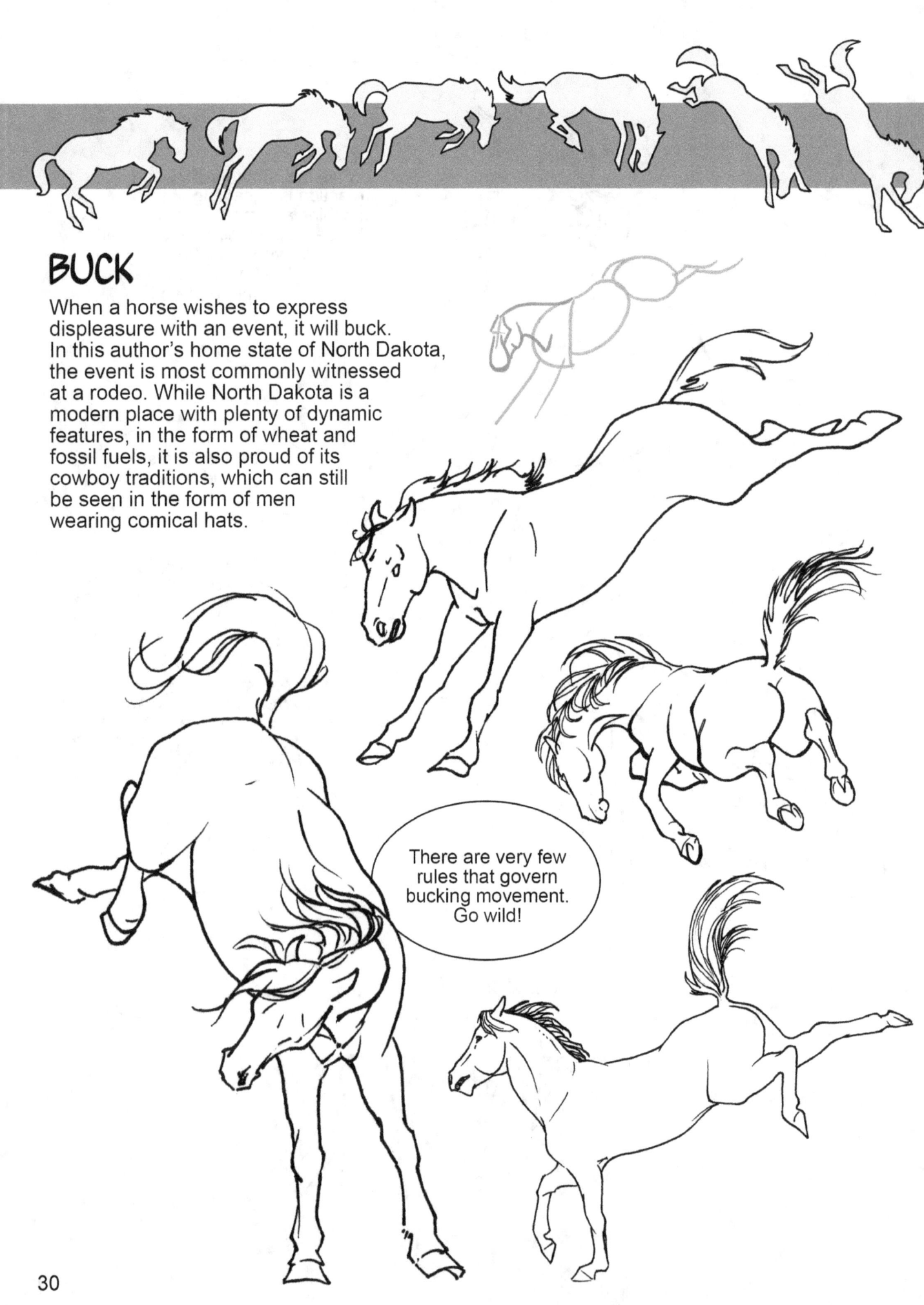

BUCK

When a horse wishes to express displeasure with an event, it will buck. In this author's home state of North Dakota, the event is most commonly witnessed at a rodeo. While North Dakota is a modern place with plenty of dynamic features, in the form of wheat and fossil fuels, it is also proud of its cowboy traditions, which can still be seen in the form of men wearing comical hats.

There are very few rules that govern bucking movement. Go wild!

Serious bucking is full of twists and turns. And stomps. And kicks.

But there is very little screaming in cereal aisles, so while a similar experience, it's still preferable to hanging with your cousin's two year old.

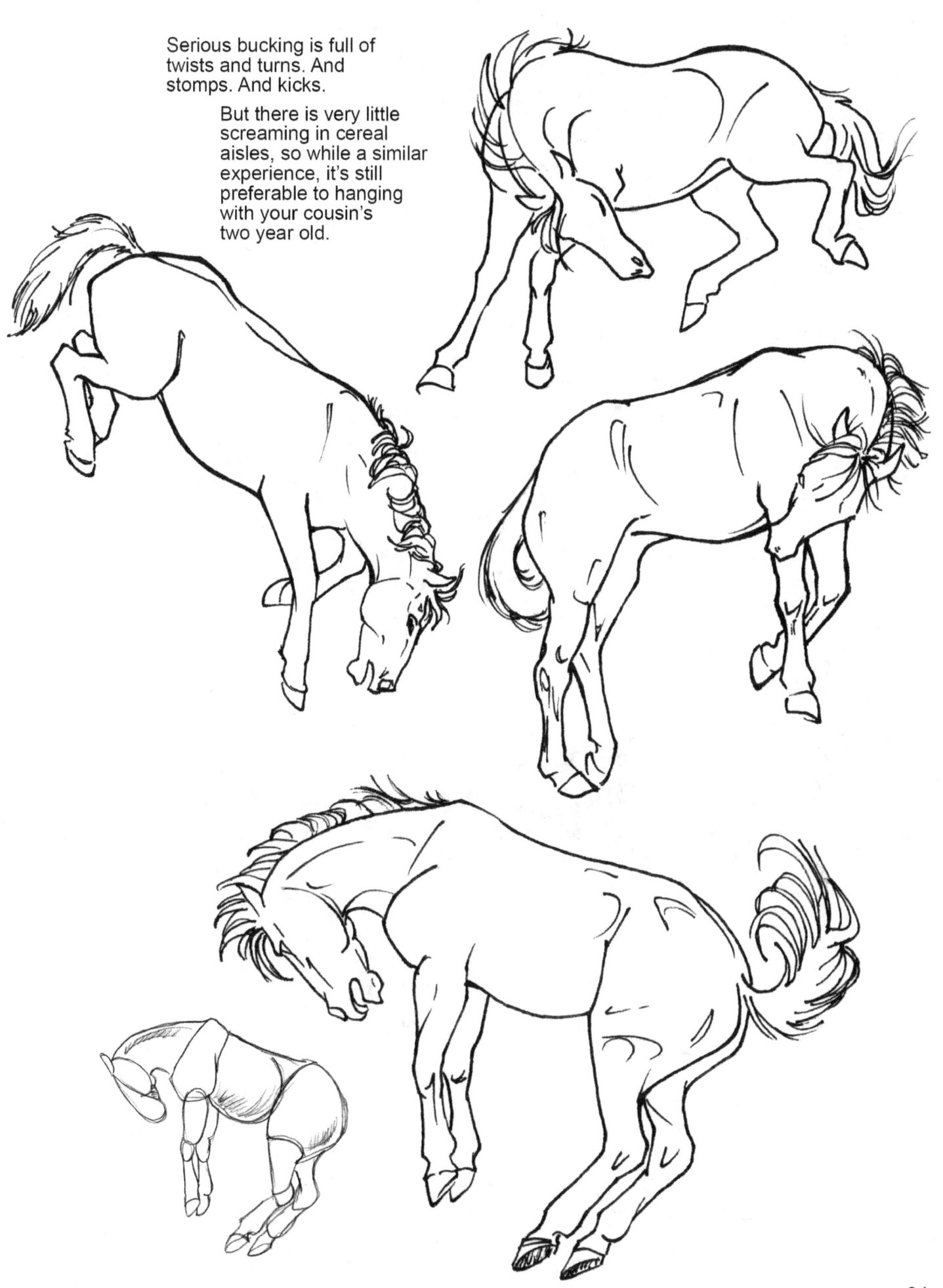

ROLLING

Horses love a good scratch, and roll, and rubbing, and if you have been recently, laboriously grooming him, the nearest patch of mud will prove irresistible. Especially if you really needed him clean and presentable that day.

LYING DOWN

Drawing a horse rolling is largely just an exercise in the stages of how a horse lies down.

1) Leans down the front first
2) Kneels
3) Lowers his bum

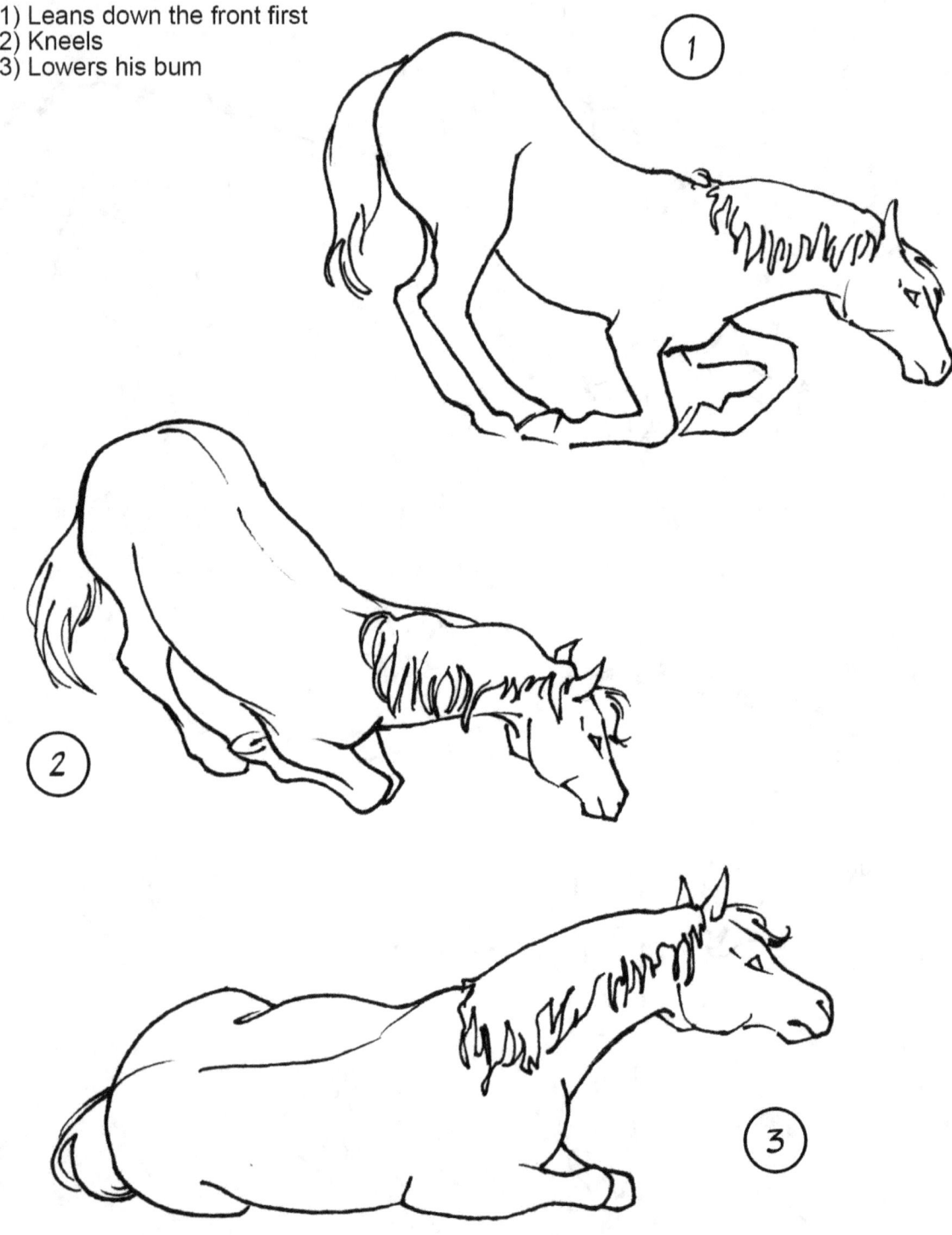

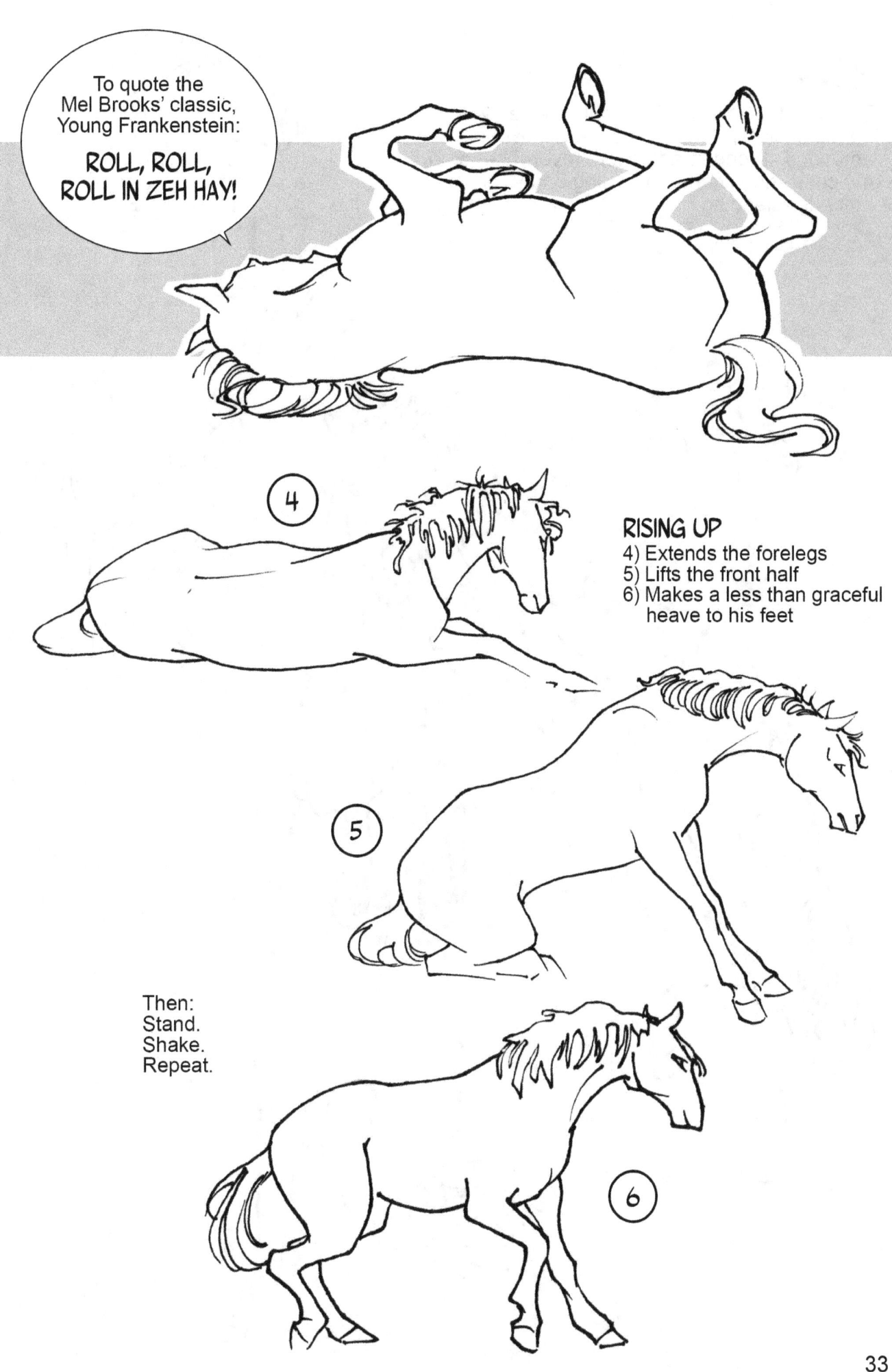

To quote the Mel Brooks' classic, Young Frankenstein:

ROLL, ROLL, ROLL IN ZEH HAY!

④

RISING UP
4) Extends the forelegs
5) Lifts the front half
6) Makes a less than graceful heave to his feet

⑤

Then:
Stand.
Shake.
Repeat.

⑥

REAR

The only time this isn't brilliant, is when you're on his back. The rearing horse can evoke many emotions - wonder, adoration, reverence, or in my case, significant arm flailing and a hefty dry-cleaning bill.

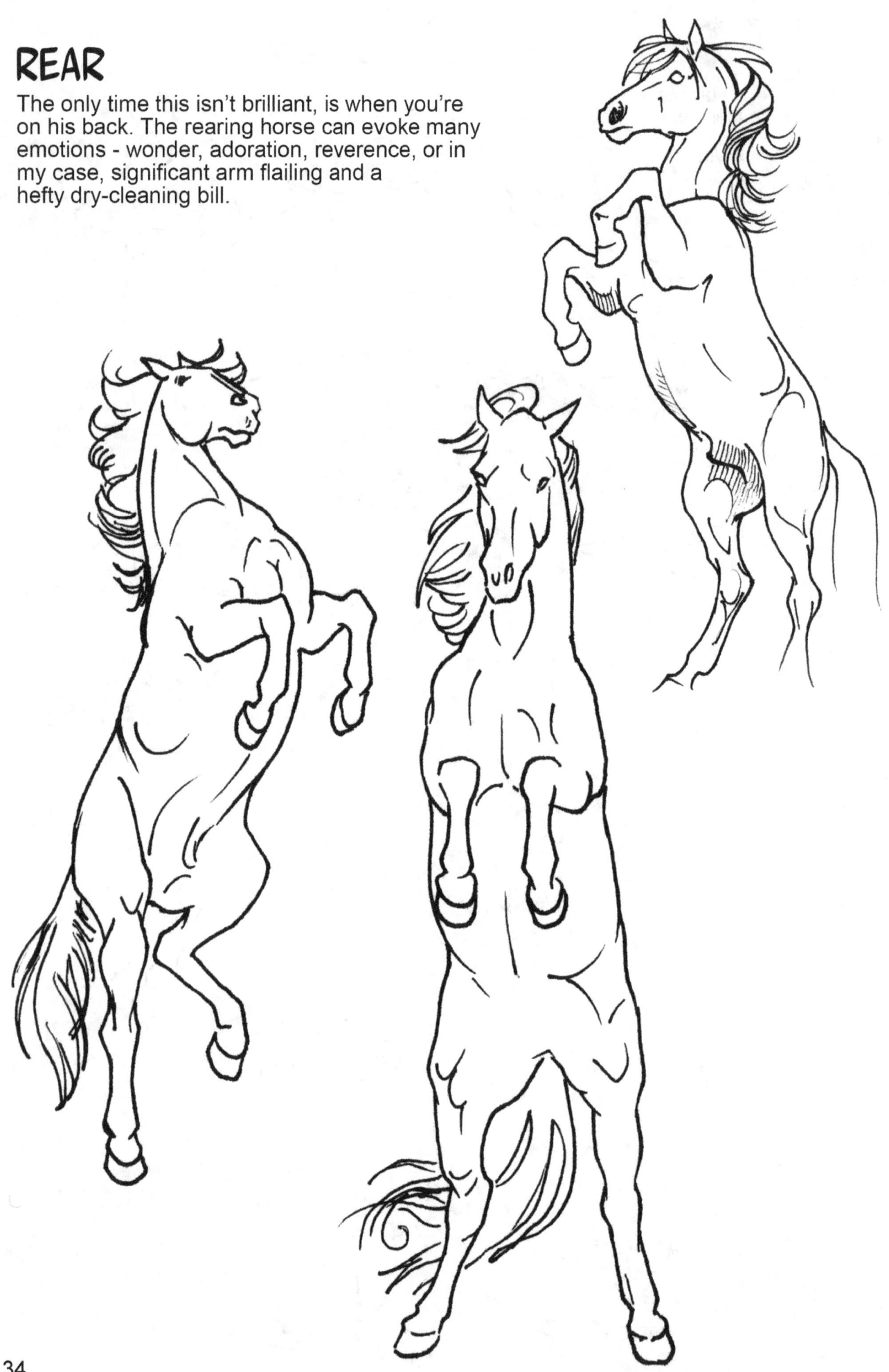

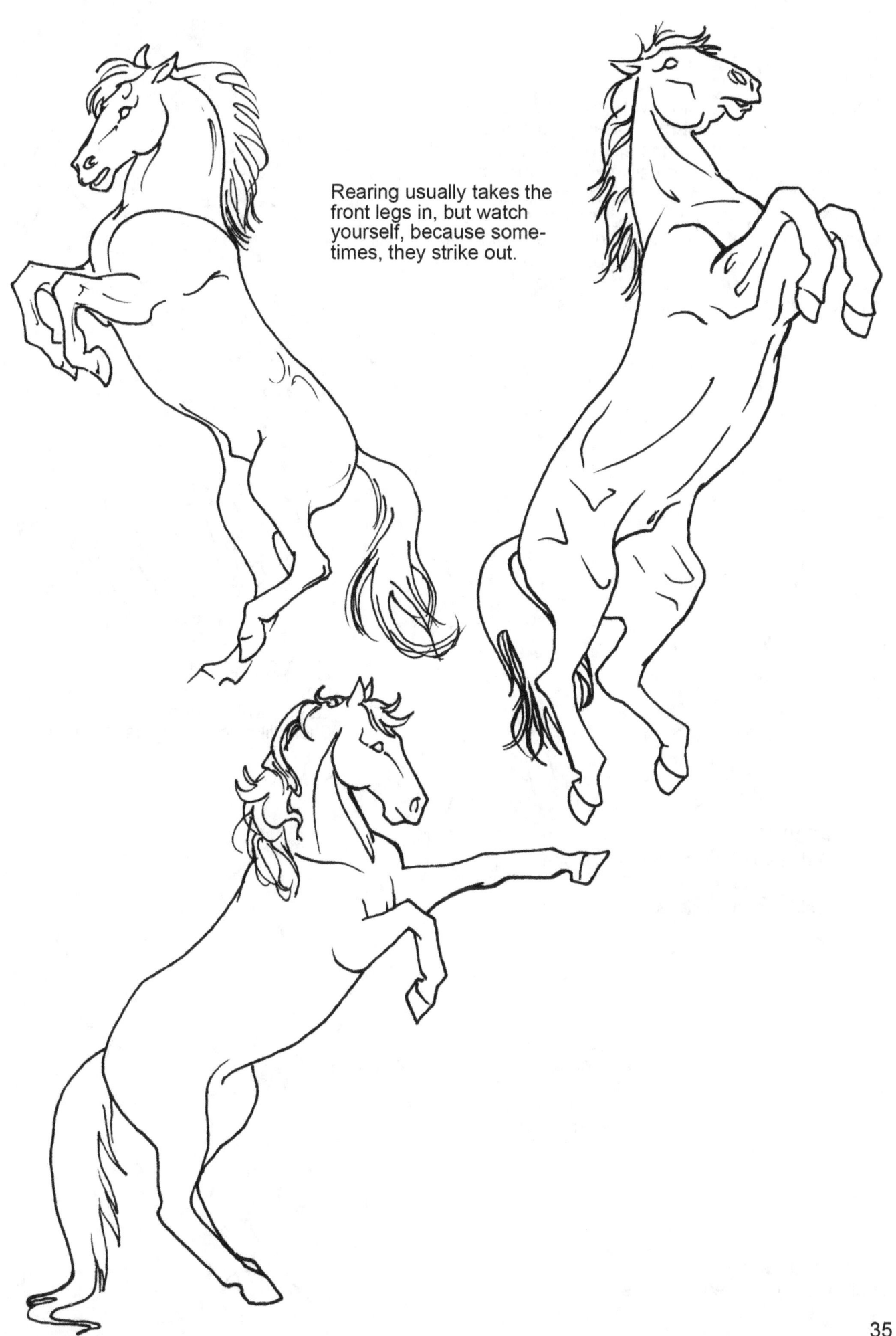

Rearing usually takes the front legs in, but watch yourself, because sometimes, they strike out.

DRESSAGE

"Dressage" is a ye olde word that means "Horse dancing that will cost more than your house." While any horse can master the art, at one level or another, the sport is usually performed by warmbloods who are the equine equivalents of suburban SUVs*: Big, bold gas guzzlers, with the turning radius of a small moon. Essential if you must be seen with the "*right*" badge, or you might cover a path that sometimes has hazardous, tricky terrain, i.e., occasionally has leaves on it.

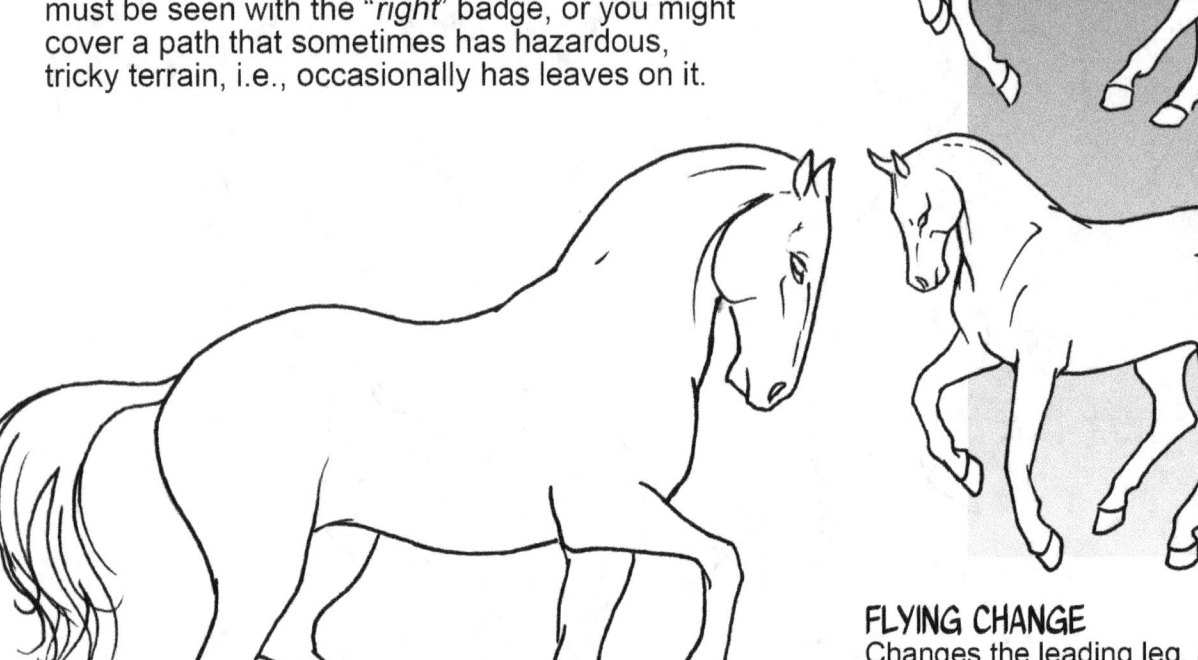

FLYING CHANGE
Changes the leading leg, at the canter, while in the air.
Looks like your horse is skipping.

PIAFFE
A rhythmic trot, performed on one spot.
Looks like prancing in place.
Called **PASSAGE** when you're moving.

PIROUETTE
The horse turns without moving backwards or sideways, while the hind legs stay on target.
Performed at either a walk or a canter.

*For readers across the pond, substitute Chelsea Tractors.

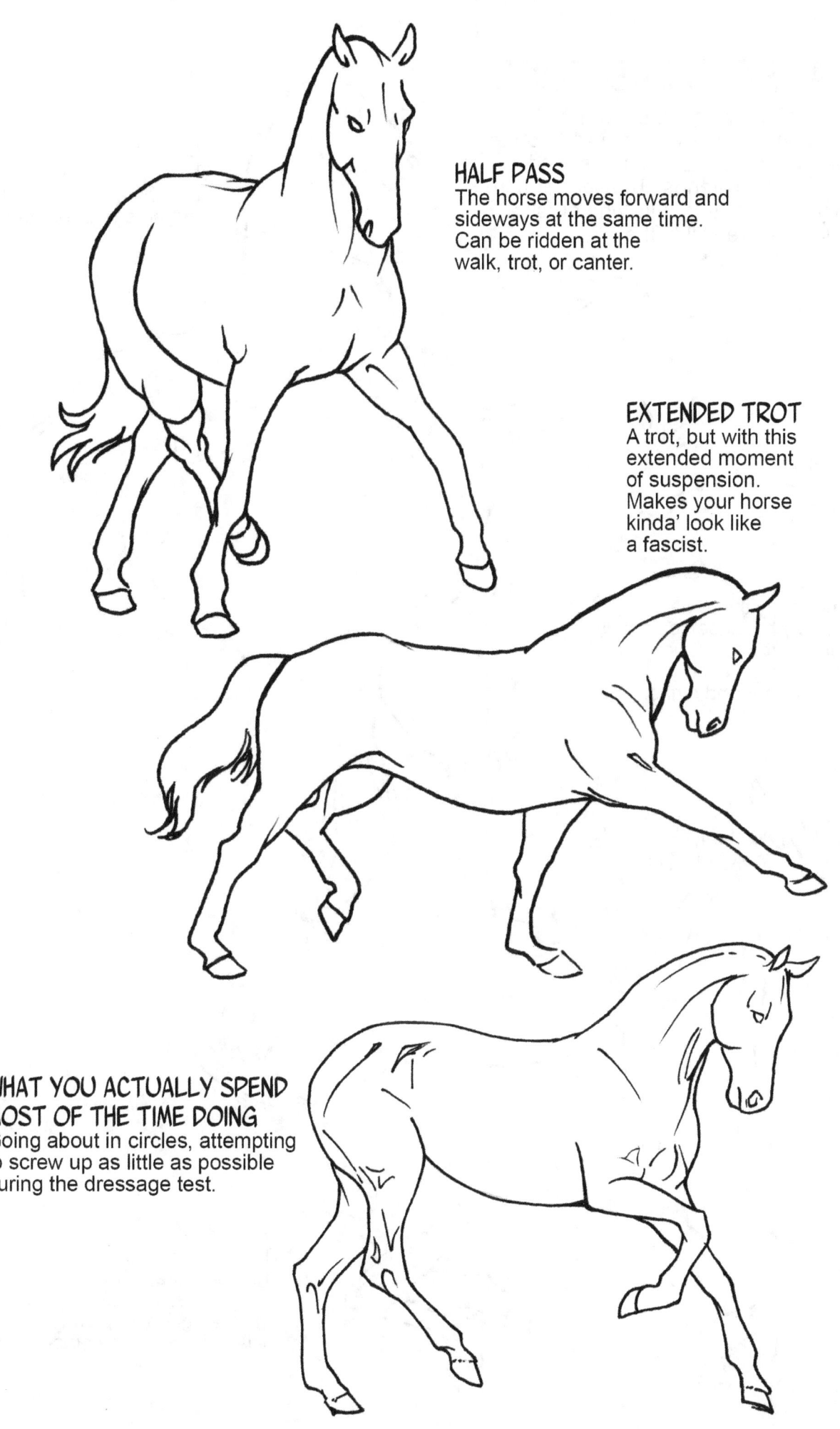

HALF PASS
The horse moves forward and sideways at the same time. Can be ridden at the walk, trot, or canter.

EXTENDED TROT
A trot, but with this extended moment of suspension. Makes your horse kinda' look like a fascist.

WHAT YOU ACTUALLY SPEND MOST OF THE TIME DOING
Going about in circles, attempting to screw up as little as possible during the dressage test.

CLASSICAL DRESSAGE

Classical dressage is performed by what are commonly known as the "Baroque Breeds", namely, Lipizzaners, Andalusians, and Lusitanos. They perform in fancy dress, with adults who dress as though we are still in the Napoleonic Wars.

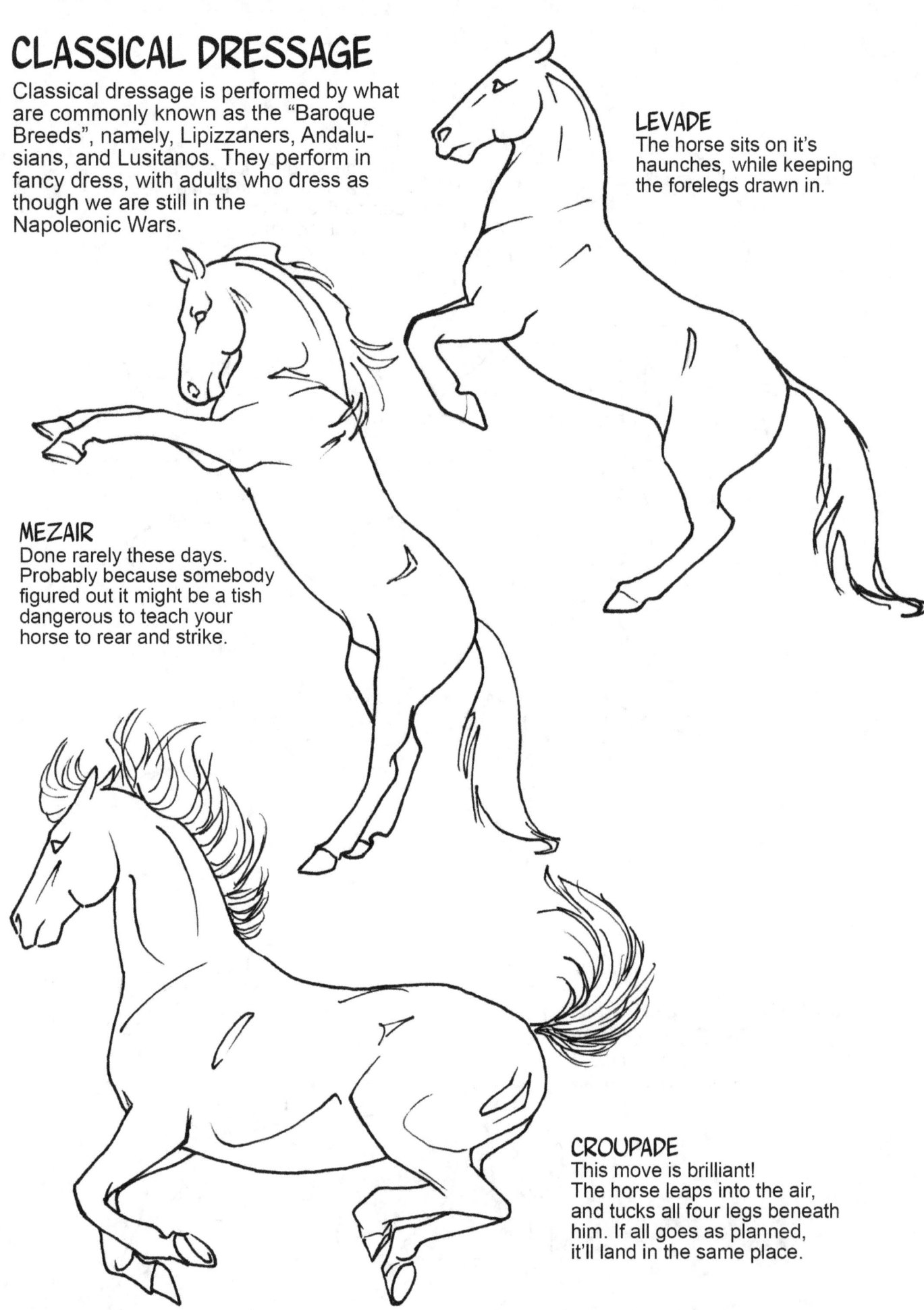

LEVADE
The horse sits on it's haunches, while keeping the forelegs drawn in.

MEZAIR
Done rarely these days. Probably because somebody figured out it might be a tish dangerous to teach your horse to rear and strike.

CROUPADE
This move is brilliant! The horse leaps into the air, and tucks all four legs beneath him. If all goes as planned, it'll land in the same place.

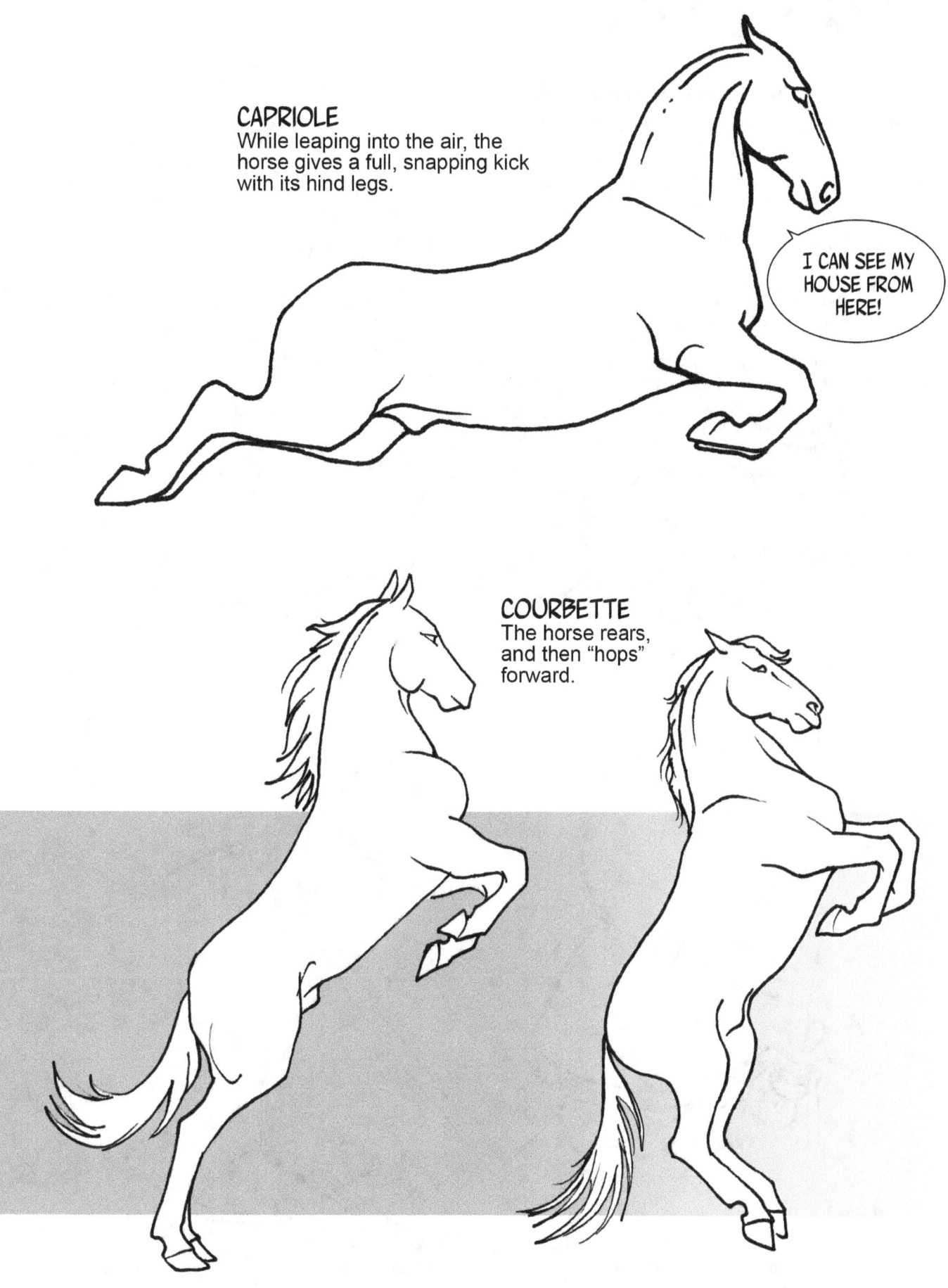

CAPRIOLE
While leaping into the air, the horse gives a full, snapping kick with its hind legs.

COURBETTE
The horse rears, and then "hops" forward.

GREAT GEAR

Tack will be our topic, and we'll stick to the modern stuff. No matter what suits your function or fashionable fancy, it all looks brilliant oiled and polished. If you walk into the tack room and take a deep breath, it's the smell of peeled cows you're in love with.

BITLESS BRIDLES
Not all bridles have bits. These are more common in western styles, or when a horse had a dental or mouth issue. I can see the certain advantage of not having a cold piece of steel inserted into your mouth on any given frosty morning.

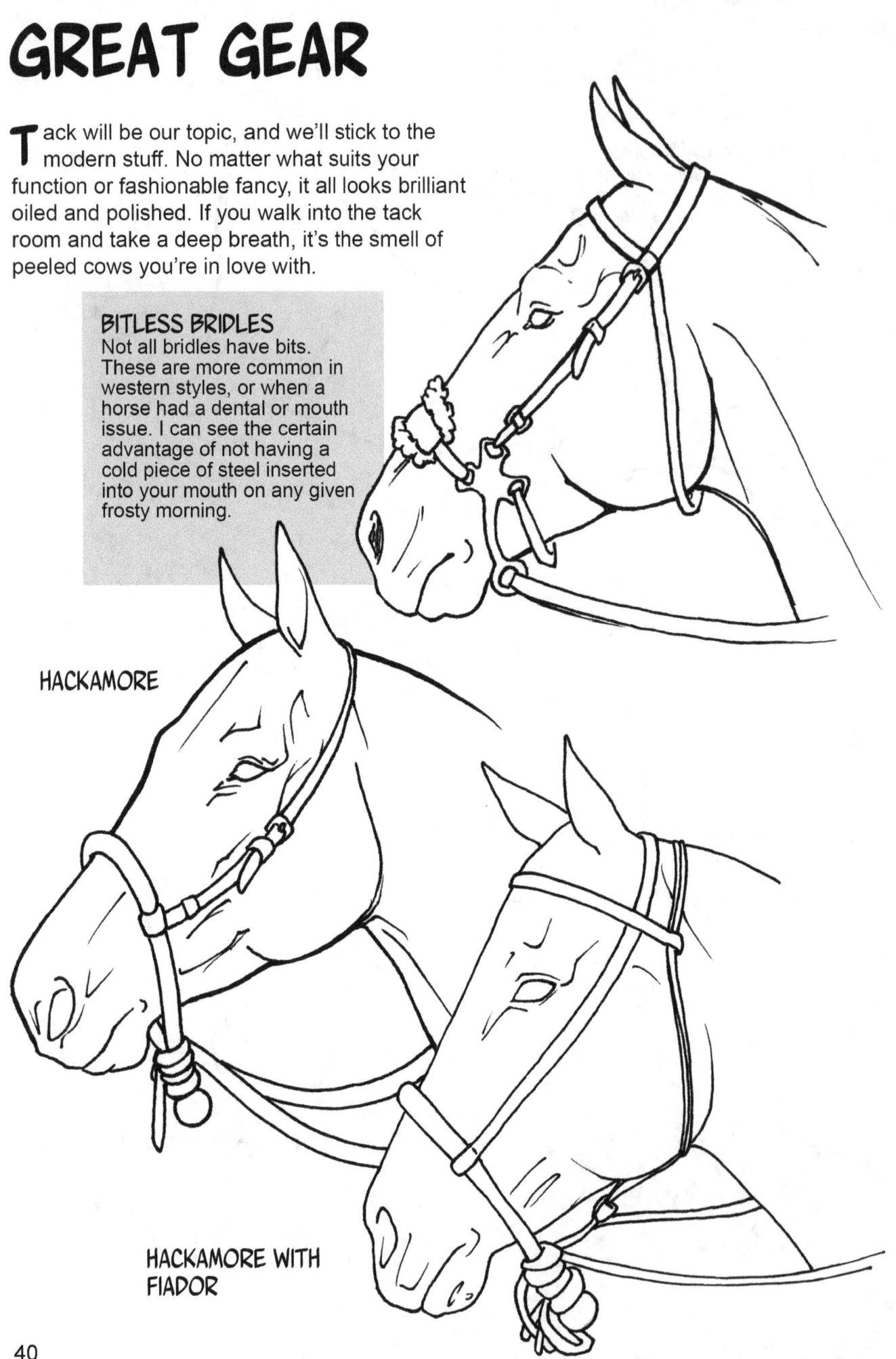

HACKAMORE

HACKAMORE WITH
FIADOR

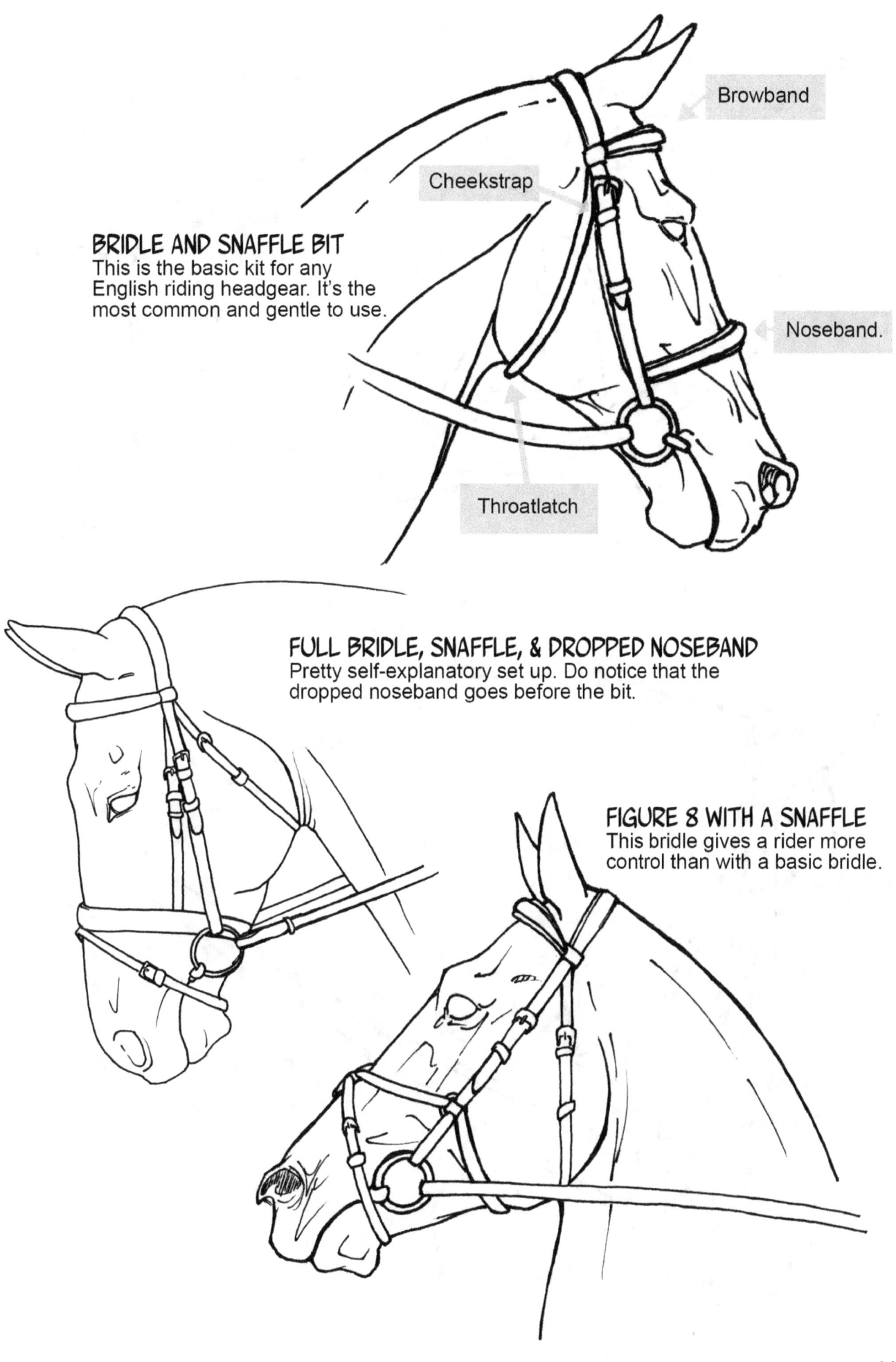

Browband

Cheekstrap

Noseband.

BRIDLE AND SNAFFLE BIT
This is the basic kit for any
English riding headgear. It's the
most common and gentle to use.

Throatlatch

FULL BRIDLE, SNAFFLE, & DROPPED NOSEBAND
Pretty self-explanatory set up. Do notice that the
dropped noseband goes before the bit.

FIGURE 8 WITH A SNAFFLE
This bridle gives a rider more
control than with a basic bridle.

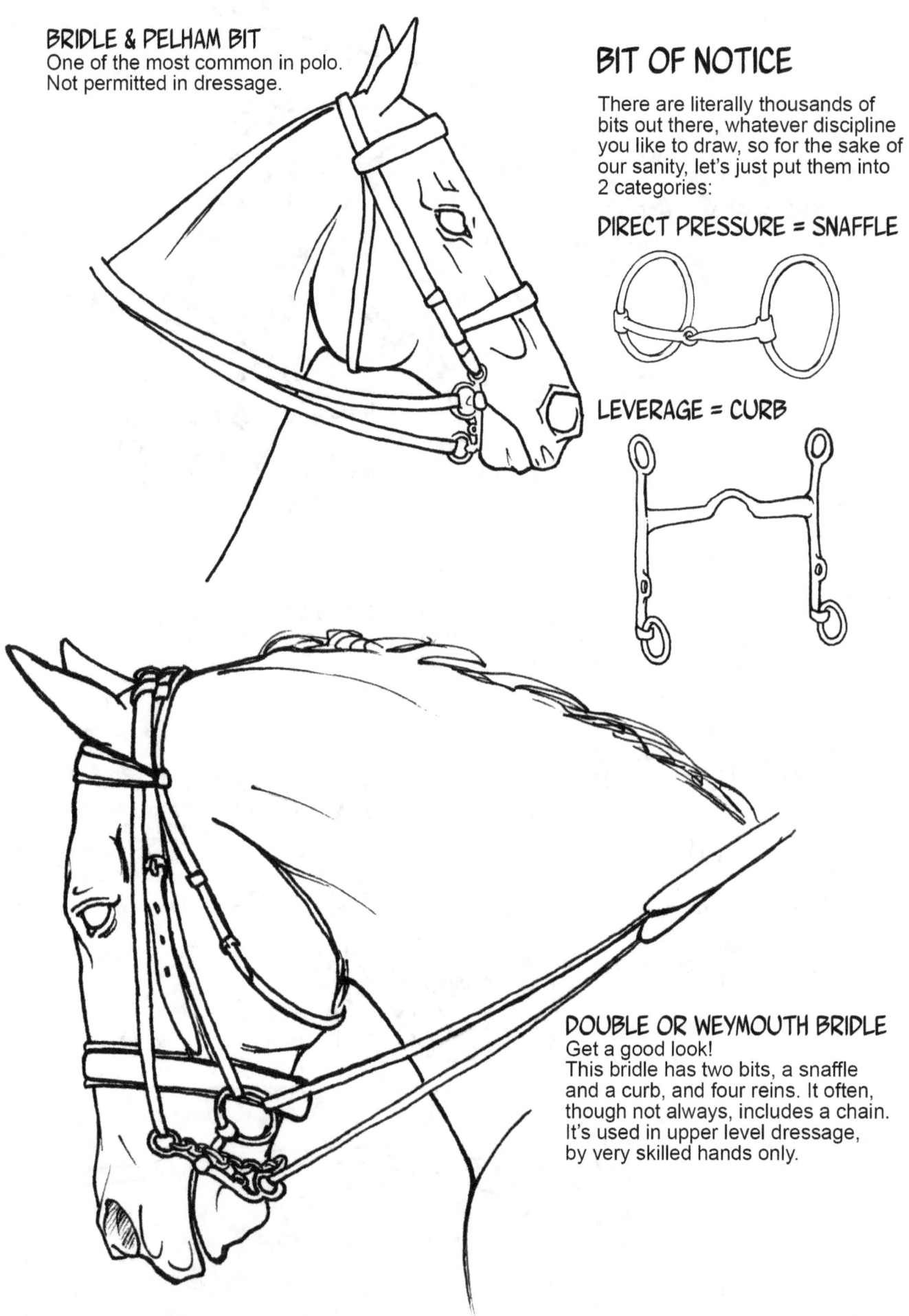

BRIDLE & PELHAM BIT
One of the most common in polo.
Not permitted in dressage.

BIT OF NOTICE

There are literally thousands of
bits out there, whatever discipline
you like to draw, so for the sake of
our sanity, let's just put them into
2 categories:

DIRECT PRESSURE = SNAFFLE

LEVERAGE = CURB

DOUBLE OR WEYMOUTH BRIDLE
Get a good look!
This bridle has two bits, a snaffle
and a curb, and four reins. It often,
though not always, includes a chain.
It's used in upper level dressage,
by very skilled hands only.

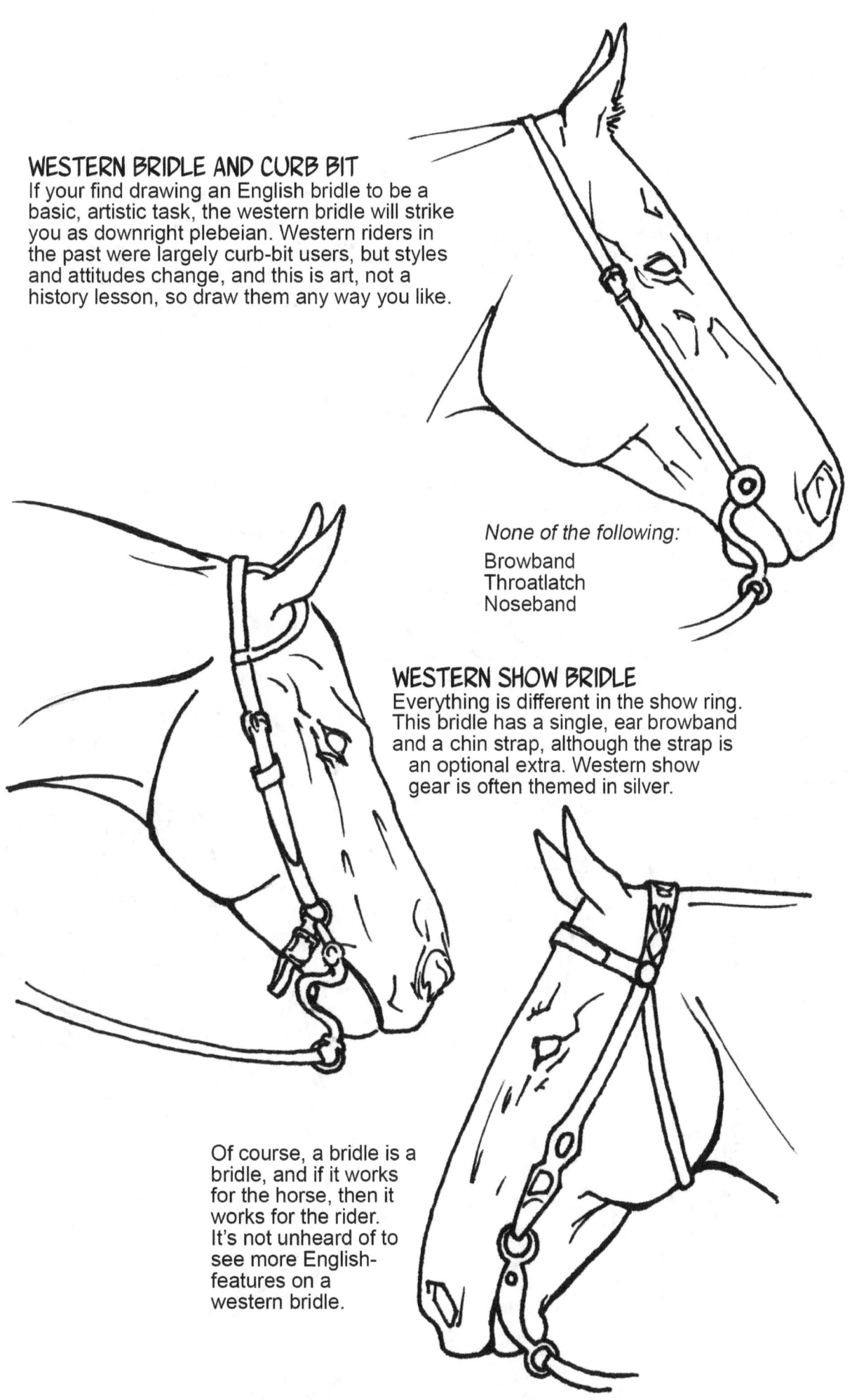

WESTERN BRIDLE AND CURB BIT
If your find drawing an English bridle to be a basic, artistic task, the western bridle will strike you as downright plebeian. Western riders in the past were largely curb-bit users, but styles and attitudes change, and this is art, not a history lesson, so draw them any way you like.

None of the following:
Browband
Throatlatch
Noseband

WESTERN SHOW BRIDLE
Everything is different in the show ring. This bridle has a single, ear browband and a chin strap, although the strap is an optional extra. Western show gear is often themed in silver.

Of course, a bridle is a bridle, and if it works for the horse, then it works for the rider. It's not unheard of to see more English-features on a western bridle.

SADDLES

While "ejector seats," I mean, "saddles," have been around for ages in one shape or another, stirrups have not. The big innovation which made them possible, was the solid saddle tree. If you have no idea what I'm on about, no worries. We'll start with the modern stuff, and break it on down.

ENGLISH SADDLE
Looks pretty Spartan compared to the western style.

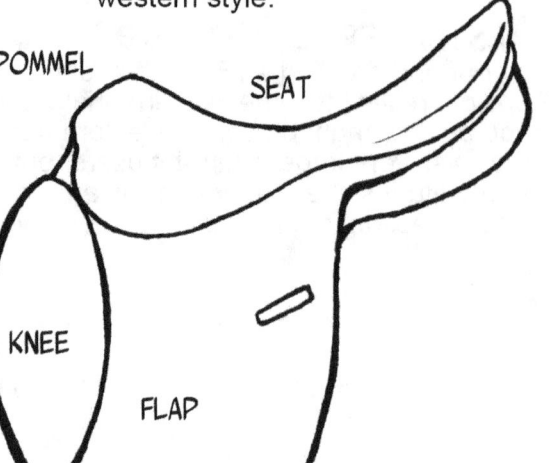

POMMEL

CANTLE

SEAT

KNEE

FLAP

WESTERN SADDLE
You won't win any land speed records with it, but it'll get the job done. Many are highly decorated, if sitting on works of art are your thing.

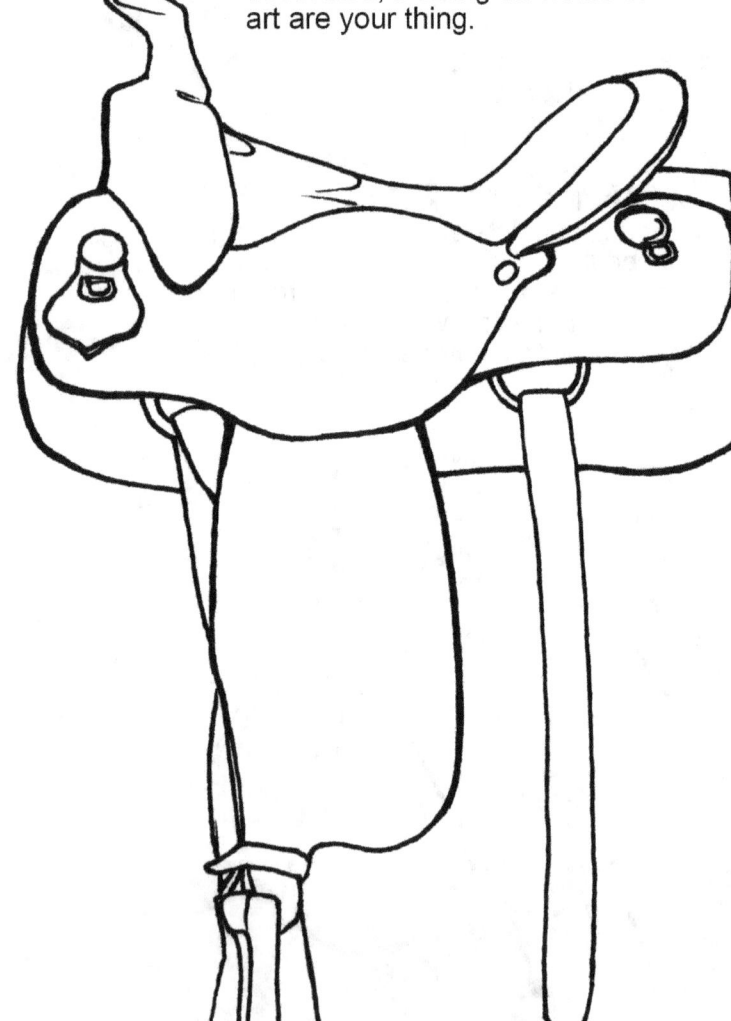

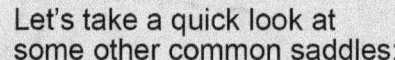
Let's take a quick look at some other common saddles:

DRESSAGE SADDLE
Just what it looks like. An elongated, English saddle with a deep seat.

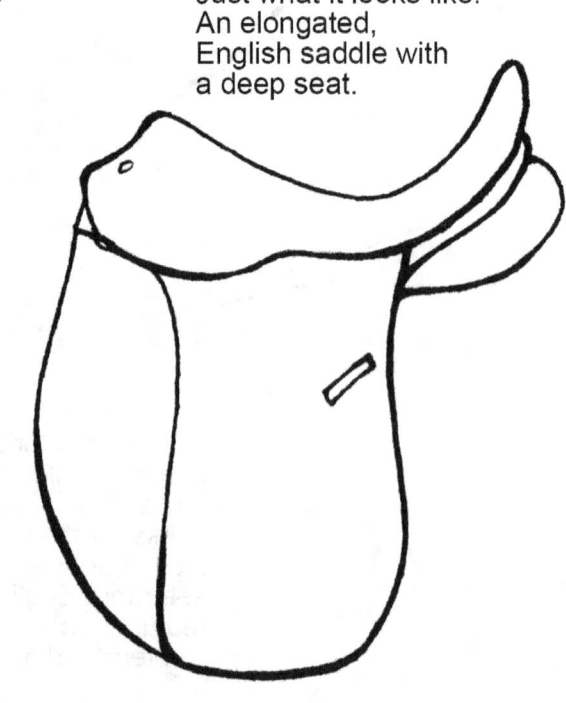

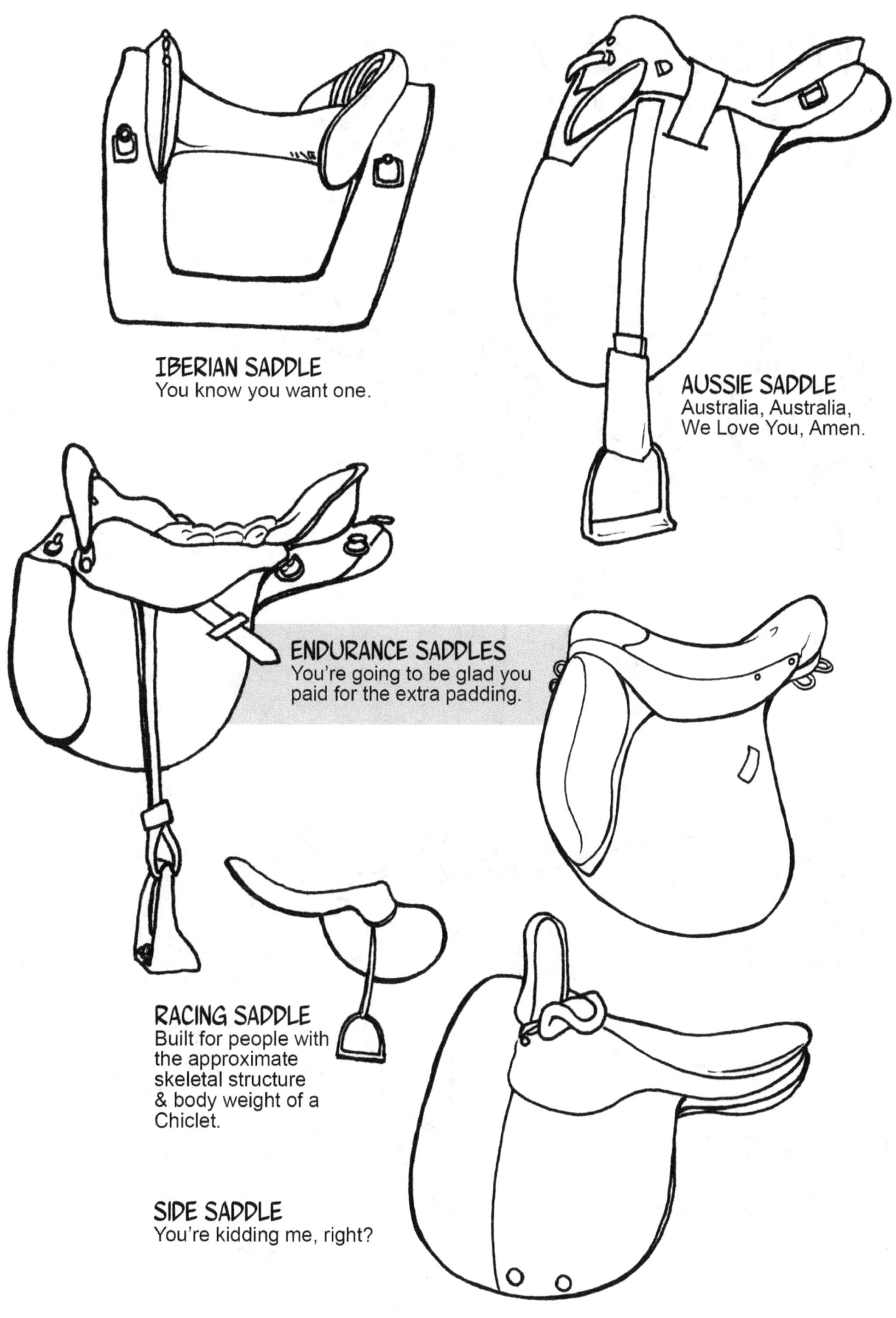

IBERIAN SADDLE
You know you want one.

AUSSIE SADDLE
Australia, Australia,
We Love You, Amen.

ENDURANCE SADDLES
You're going to be glad you
paid for the extra padding.

RACING SADDLE
Built for people with
the approximate
skeletal structure
& body weight of a
Chiclet.

SIDE SADDLE
You're kidding me, right?

HOW DOES IT GO TOGETHER?

Well, you only use an apostrophe when the pronoun "it" is being used as a contraction to combine the words "it is" or "it has". Oh wait. You meant the saddle and bridle thing. My mistake.

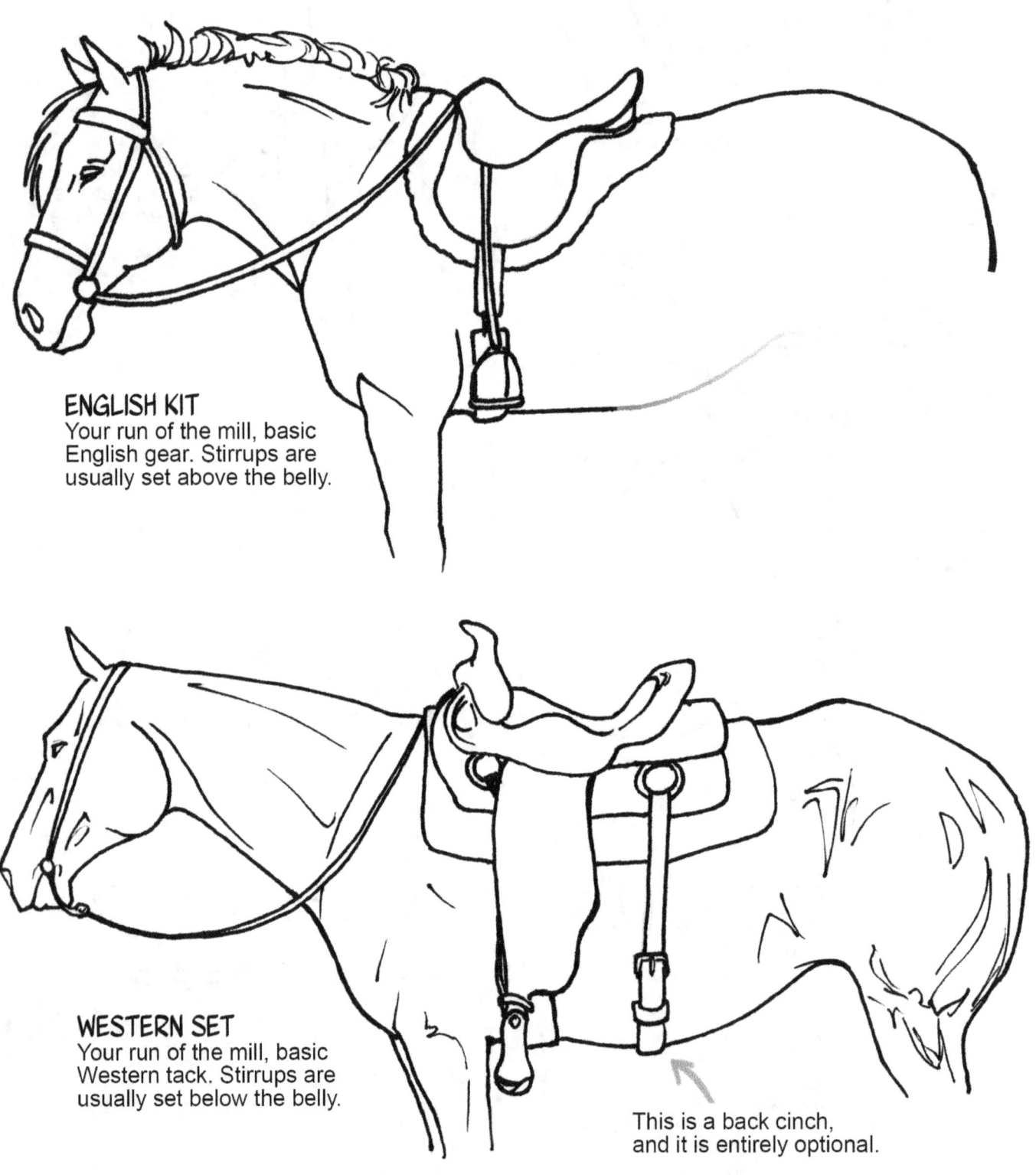

ENGLISH KIT
Your run of the mill, basic English gear. Stirrups are usually set above the belly.

WESTERN SET
Your run of the mill, basic Western tack. Stirrups are usually set below the belly.

This is a back cinch, and it is entirely optional.

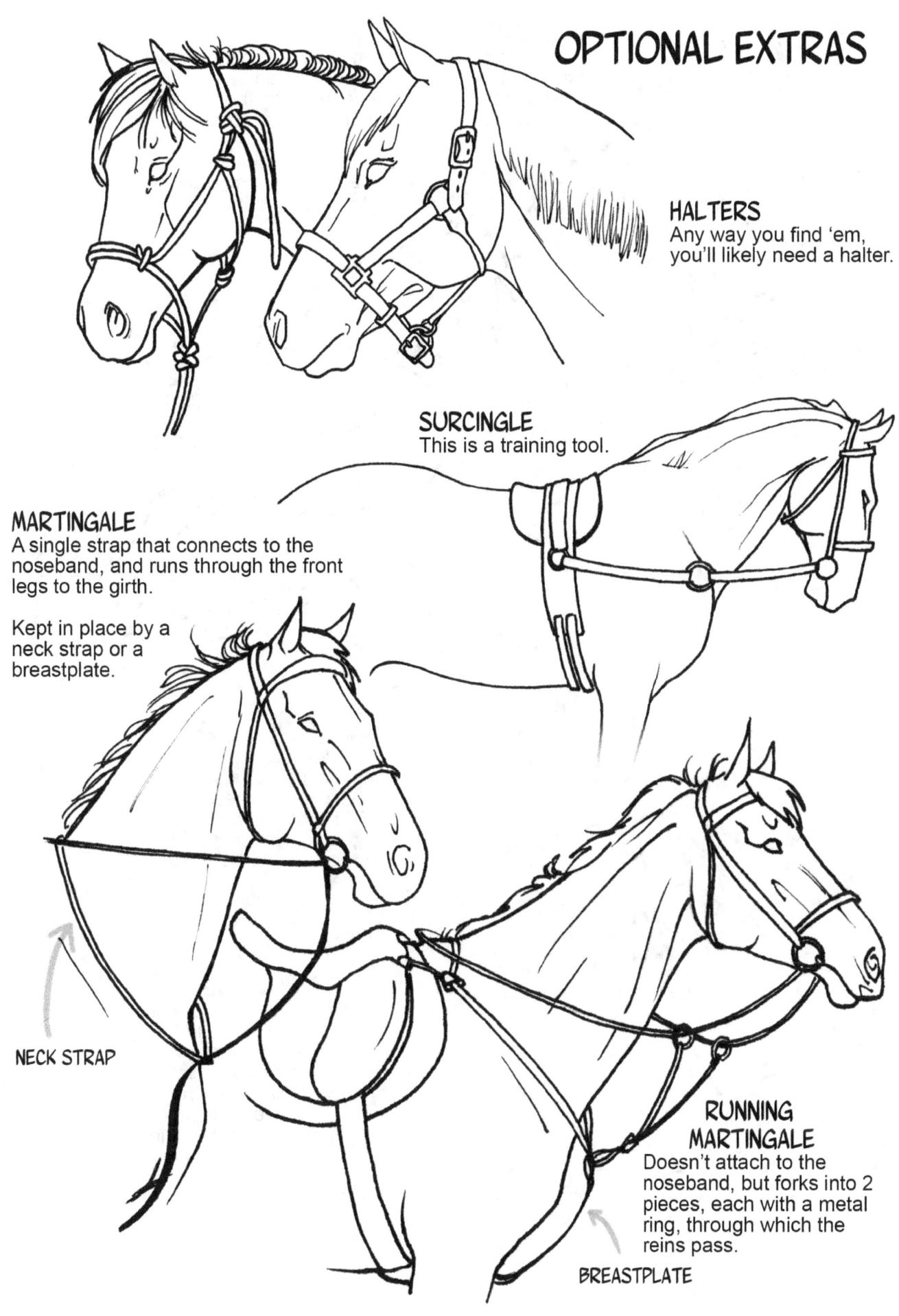

OPTIONAL EXTRAS

HALTERS
Any way you find 'em, you'll likely need a halter.

SURCINGLE
This is a training tool.

MARTINGALE
A single strap that connects to the noseband, and runs through the front legs to the girth.

Kept in place by a neck strap or a breastplate.

NECK STRAP

RUNNING MARTINGALE
Doesn't attach to the noseband, but forks into 2 pieces, each with a metal ring, through which the reins pass.

BREASTPLATE

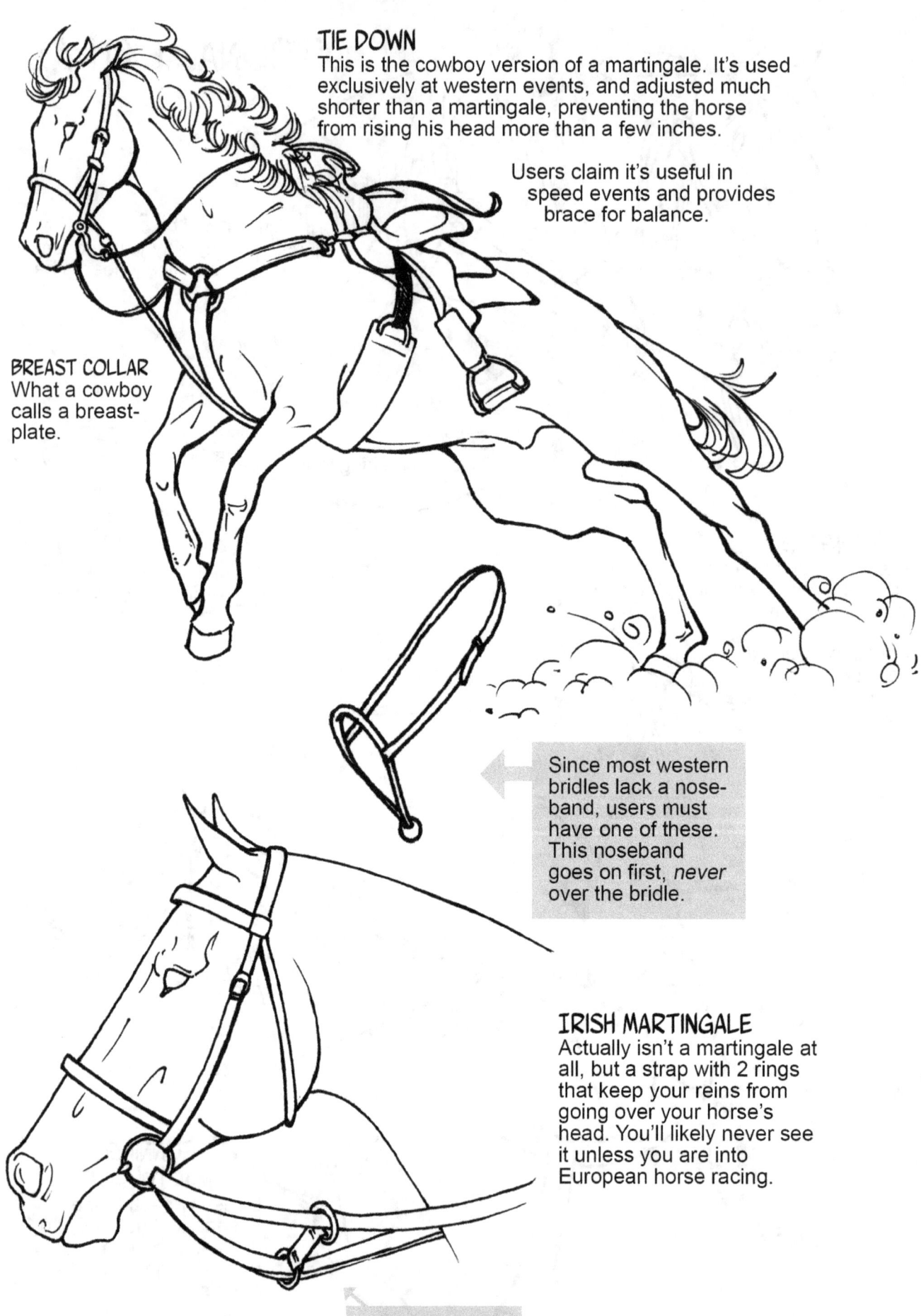

TIE DOWN
This is the cowboy version of a martingale. It's used exclusively at western events, and adjusted much shorter than a martingale, preventing the horse from rising his head more than a few inches.

Users claim it's useful in speed events and provides brace for balance.

BREAST COLLAR
What a cowboy calls a breast-plate.

Since most western bridles lack a nose-band, users must have one of these. This noseband goes on first, *never* over the bridle.

IRISH MARTINGALE
Actually isn't a martingale at all, but a strap with 2 rings that keep your reins from going over your horse's head. You'll likely never see it unless you are into European horse racing.

Yep. That's it.

LEG WRAPS, & SKID BOOTS, & BELL BOOTS, OH MY!

Leg wear comes in two types: Impact Protection and Support.
Generally, all boots are known as brushing or splint boots, the terms being rather interchangeable. If your horse is dealing with speed, it likely has some sort of leg protection.

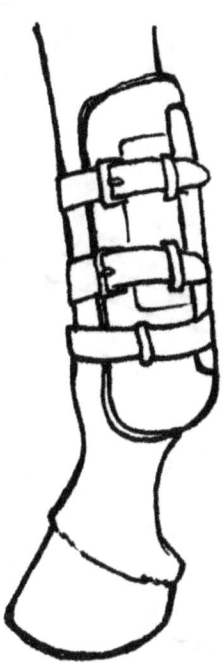 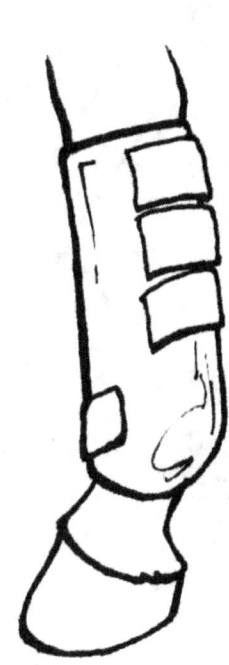 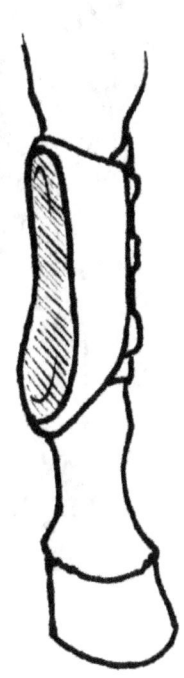 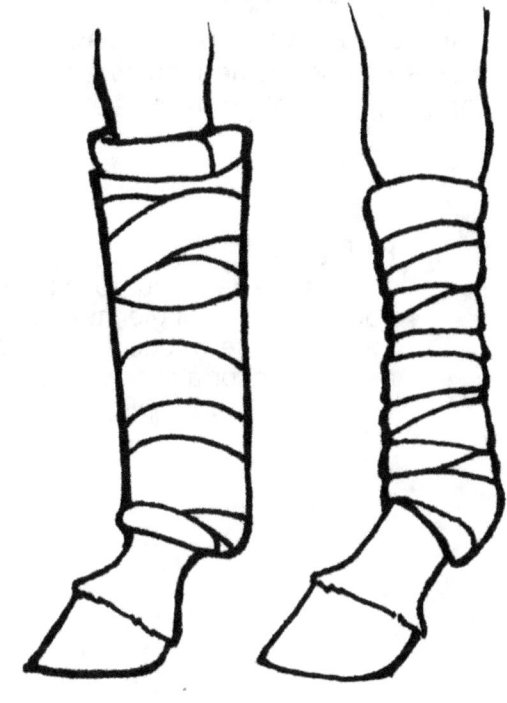

JUMPING
Provides some support, but used mostly for stadium jumping, due to the open front.

SMB
Sports Medicine Boots go all the way around the fetlock. Works similar to an ankle or a knee brace.

SPLINT
Offer only impact protection. These are very common in daily riding.

STABLE WRAPS
A leg wrap wound about some padding. Used only for injury, trailering, or in the stalls.

POLO WRAPS
Doesn't provide any leg support, but does give impact protection while riding.

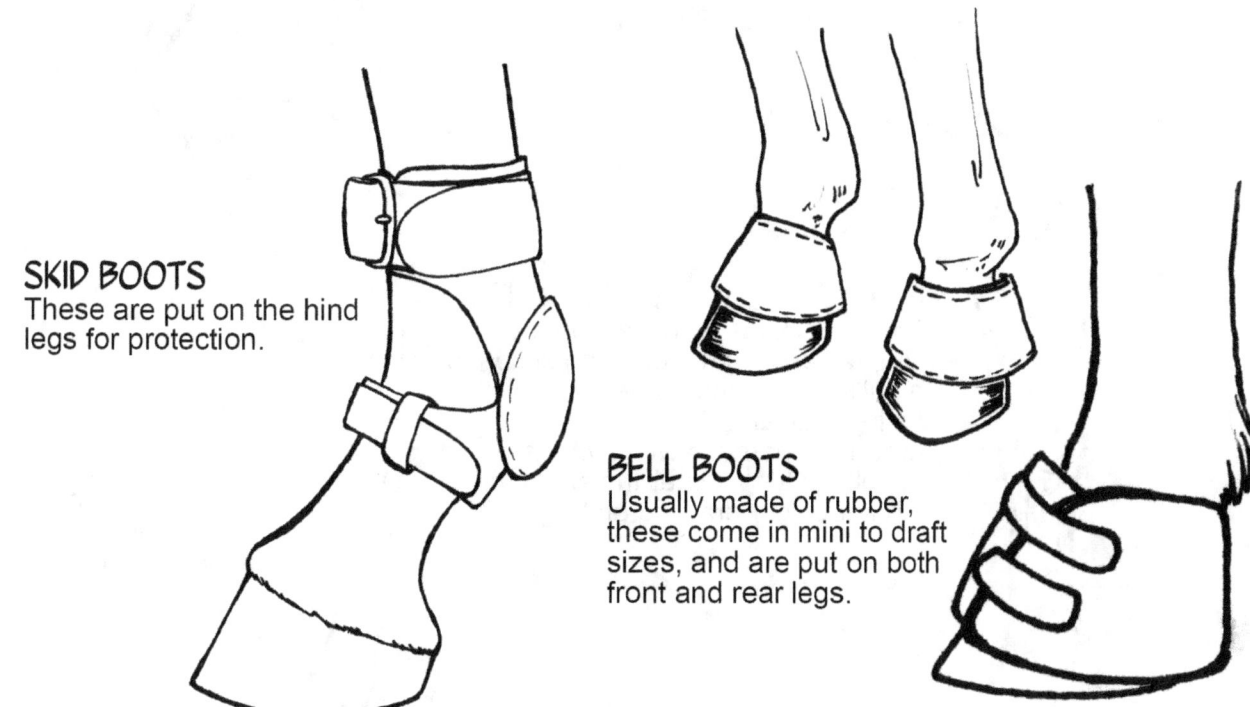

SKID BOOTS
These are put on the hind legs for protection.

BELL BOOTS
Usually made of rubber, these come in mini to draft sizes, and are put on both front and rear legs.

HARNESS

This author loves harnesses. If you've found them artistically intimidating, you're in good company. There really isn't room to look at their full history, but we will cover most modern, western-type harnesses, which account for 99% of what you will see.

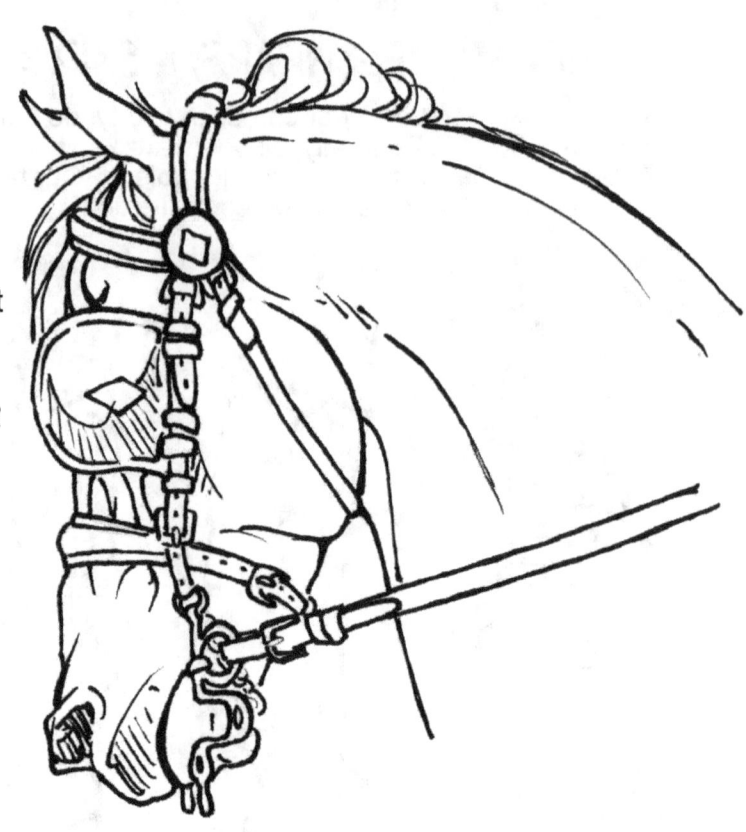

BLINDER

BRIDLE

Serves the same purpose as when you're riding, using either snaffle or curb bits. A few added extras, such as blinders, or a check rein, are common, though optional, extras.

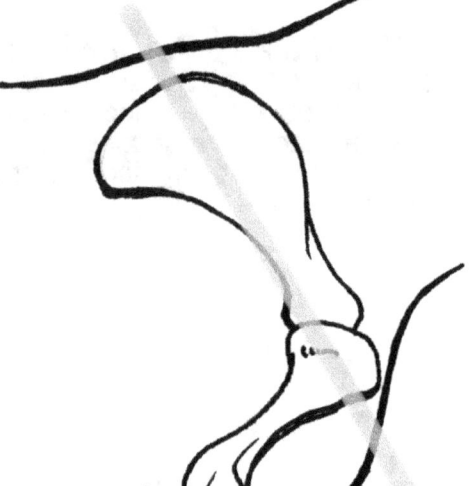

COLLAR

GREAT FIT!
This collar is drawn right over the shoulder and is ready for action.

Brilliant!

PUT YOUR SHOULDER INTO IT
The mechanics of this action are simply translating a pushing action to a pulling one, and horses *push* with their shoulders. So whether you're drawing a harness with a breast strap or collar, fitting it over the shoulder will keep your drawing on target.

(Draw your collar too high, and it'll look as though the horse is trying to move the load with its windpipe.)

HARNESS STYLES

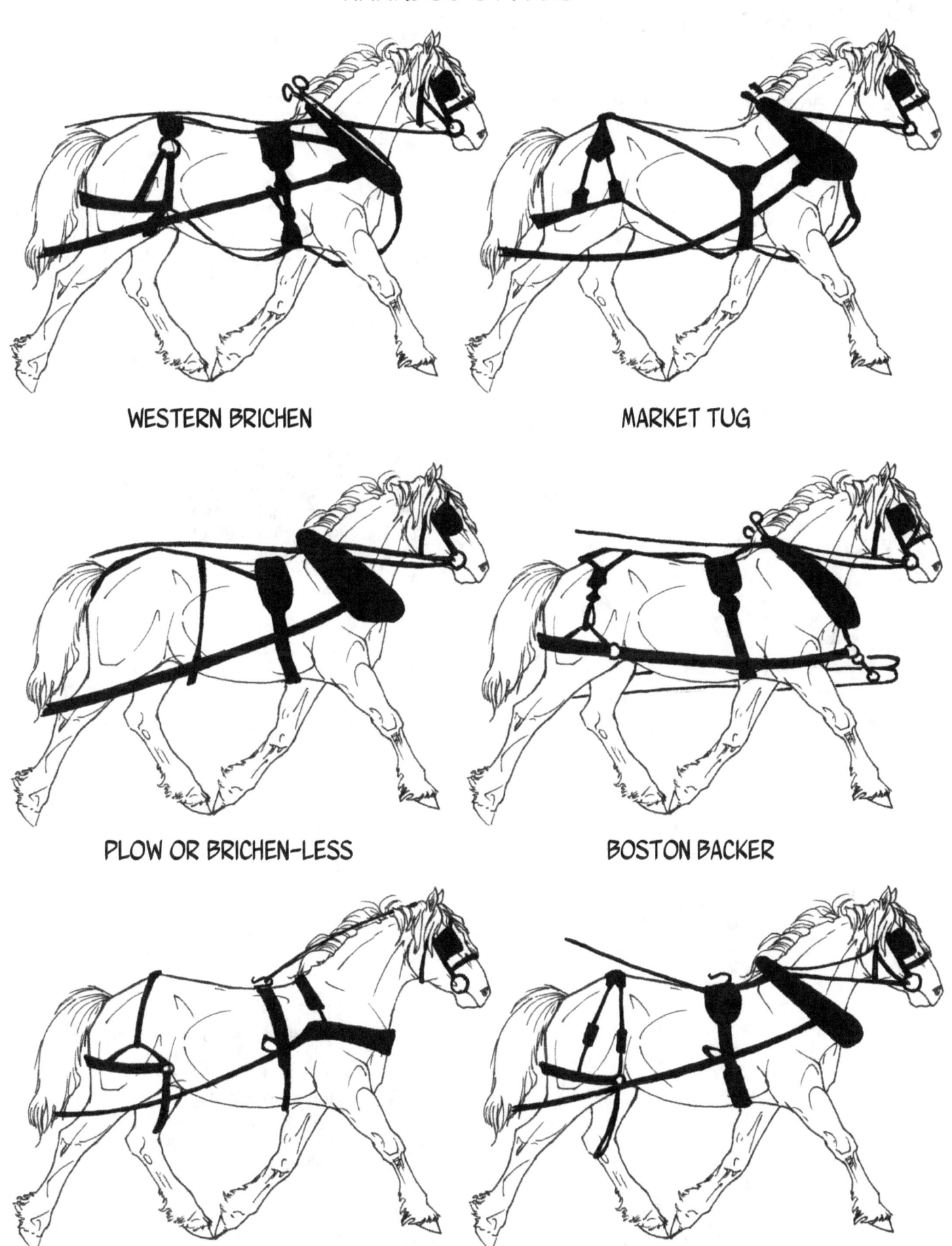

WESTERN BRICHEN

MARKET TUG

PLOW OR BRICHEN-LESS

BOSTON BACKER

BREAST STRAP BUGGY

COLLAR BUGGY

51

HARNESS STEP-BY-STEP

Harness may look really intimidating,
but I promise, looks are often deceiving.
We'll go through it step by step with the
most common of gear, a western brichen.

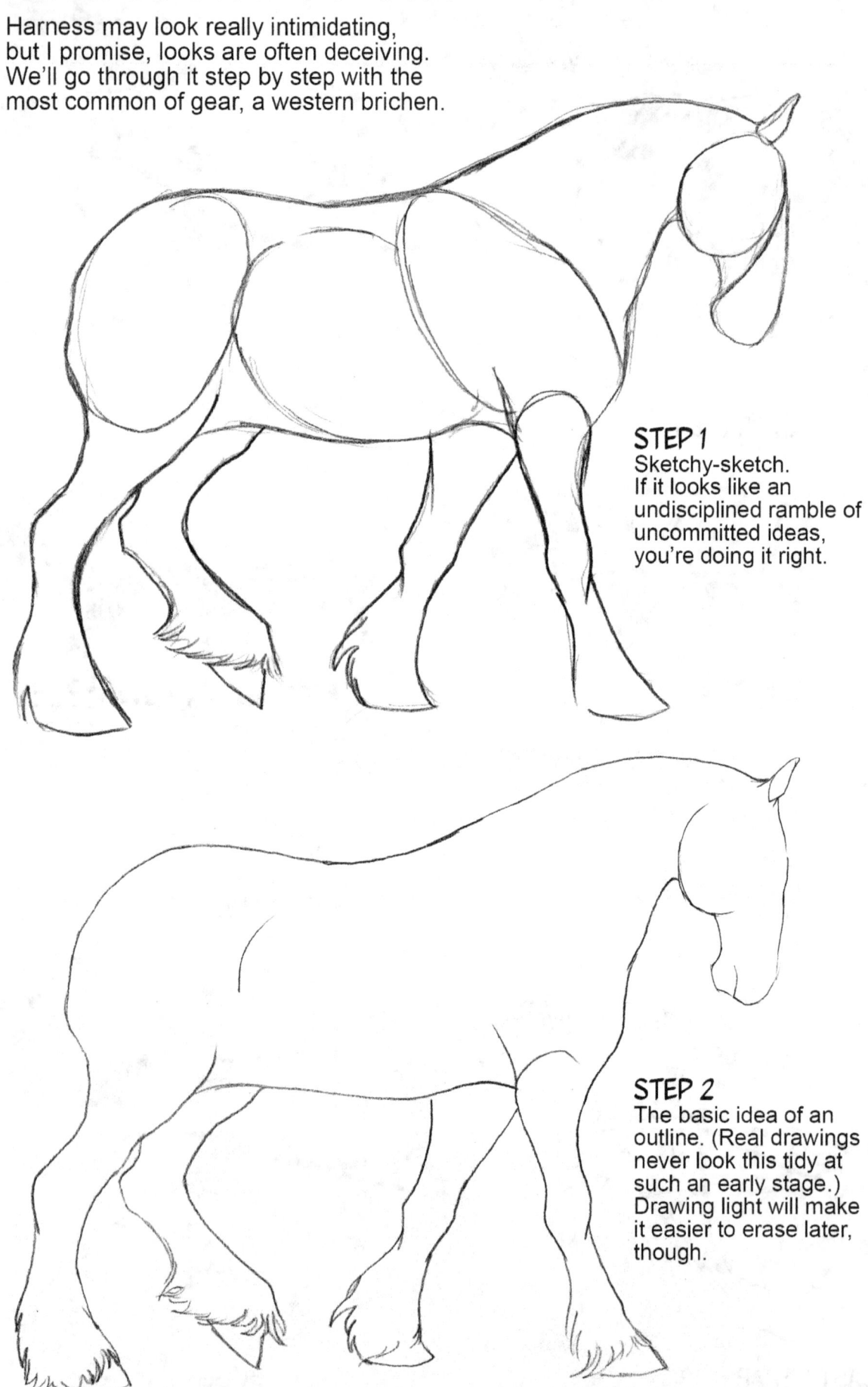

STEP 1
Sketchy-sketch.
If it looks like an
undisciplined ramble of
uncommitted ideas,
you're doing it right.

STEP 2
The basic idea of an
outline. (Real drawings
never look this tidy at
such an early stage.)
Drawing light will make
it easier to erase later,
though.

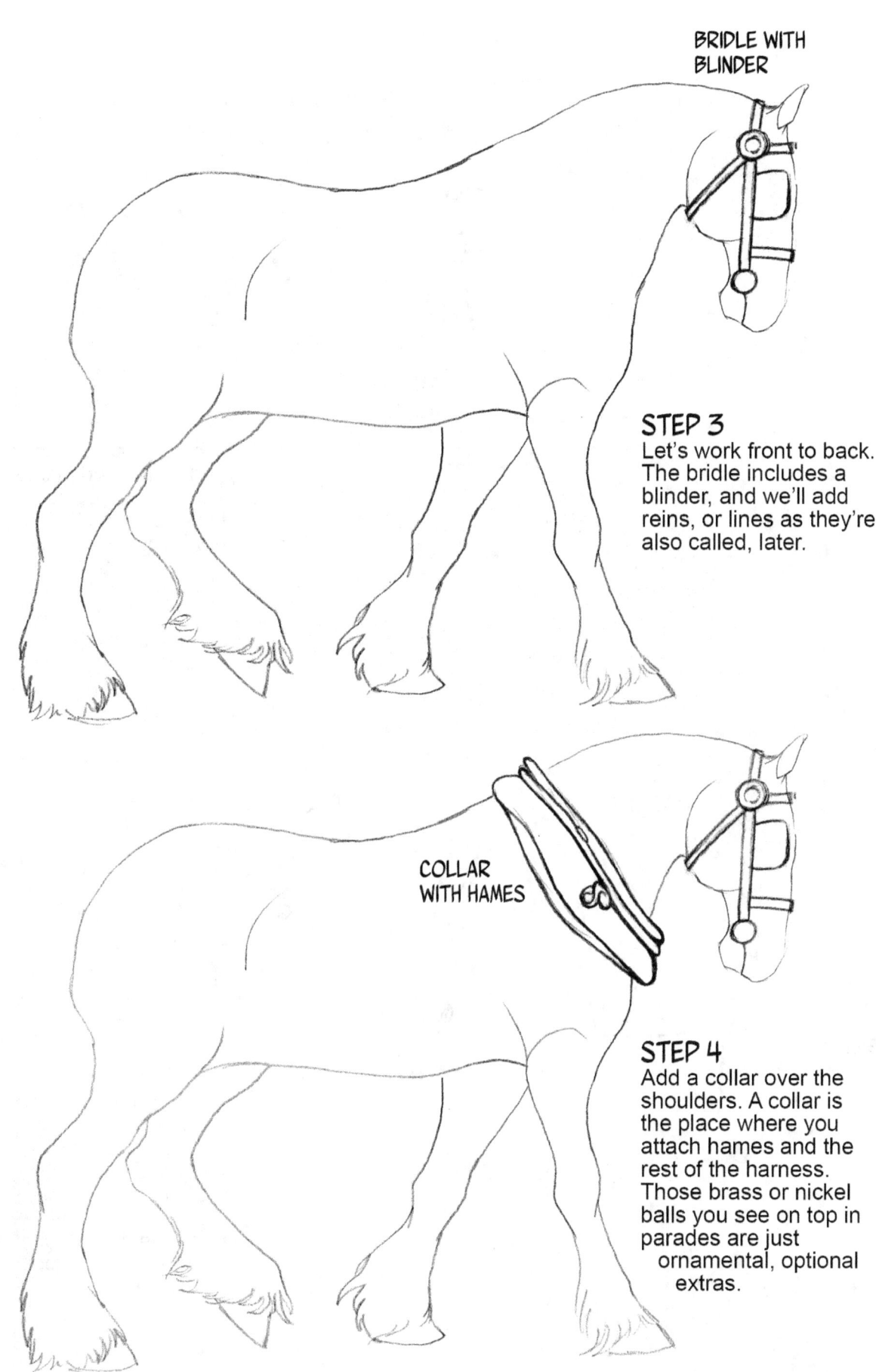

BRIDLE WITH BLINDER

STEP 3
Let's work front to back. The bridle includes a blinder, and we'll add reins, or lines as they're also called, later.

COLLAR WITH HAMES

STEP 4
Add a collar over the shoulders. A collar is the place where you attach hames and the rest of the harness. Those brass or nickel balls you see on top in parades are just ornamental, optional extras.

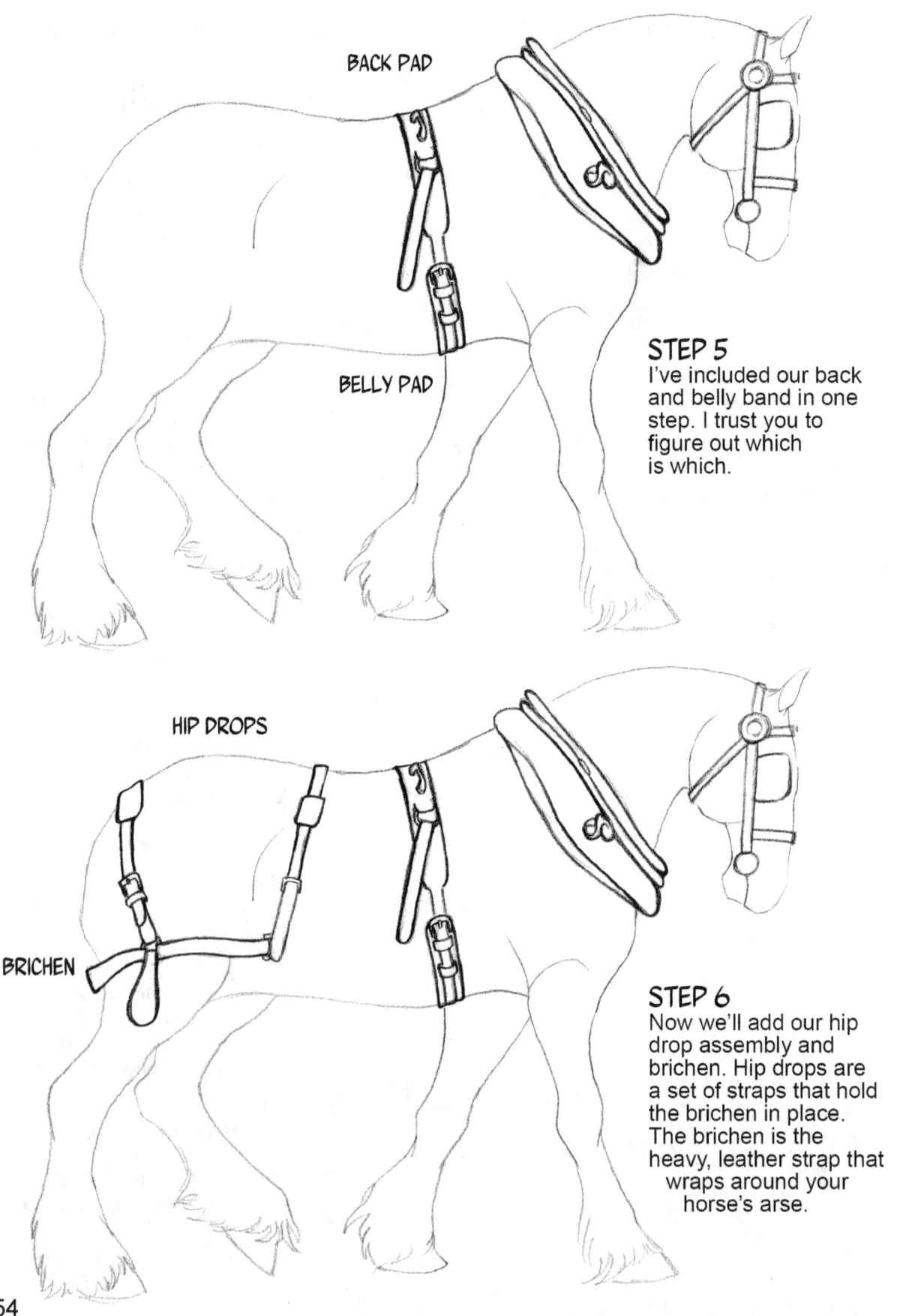

BACK PAD

BELLY PAD

STEP 5
I've included our back
and belly band in one
step. I trust you to
figure out which
is which.

HIP DROPS

BRICHEN

STEP 6
Now we'll add our hip
drop assembly and
brichen. Hip drops are
a set of straps that hold
the brichen in place.
The brichen is the
heavy, leather strap that
wraps around your
horse's arse.

STEP 7

Now all we have to do, is connect it up. Pole strap runs through the front legs. Reins, (Lines,) connect through the hames and back pad, the back straps along the back to the cruper, and the collar, back to the load, by the tug. Got that? There'll be a quiz later.

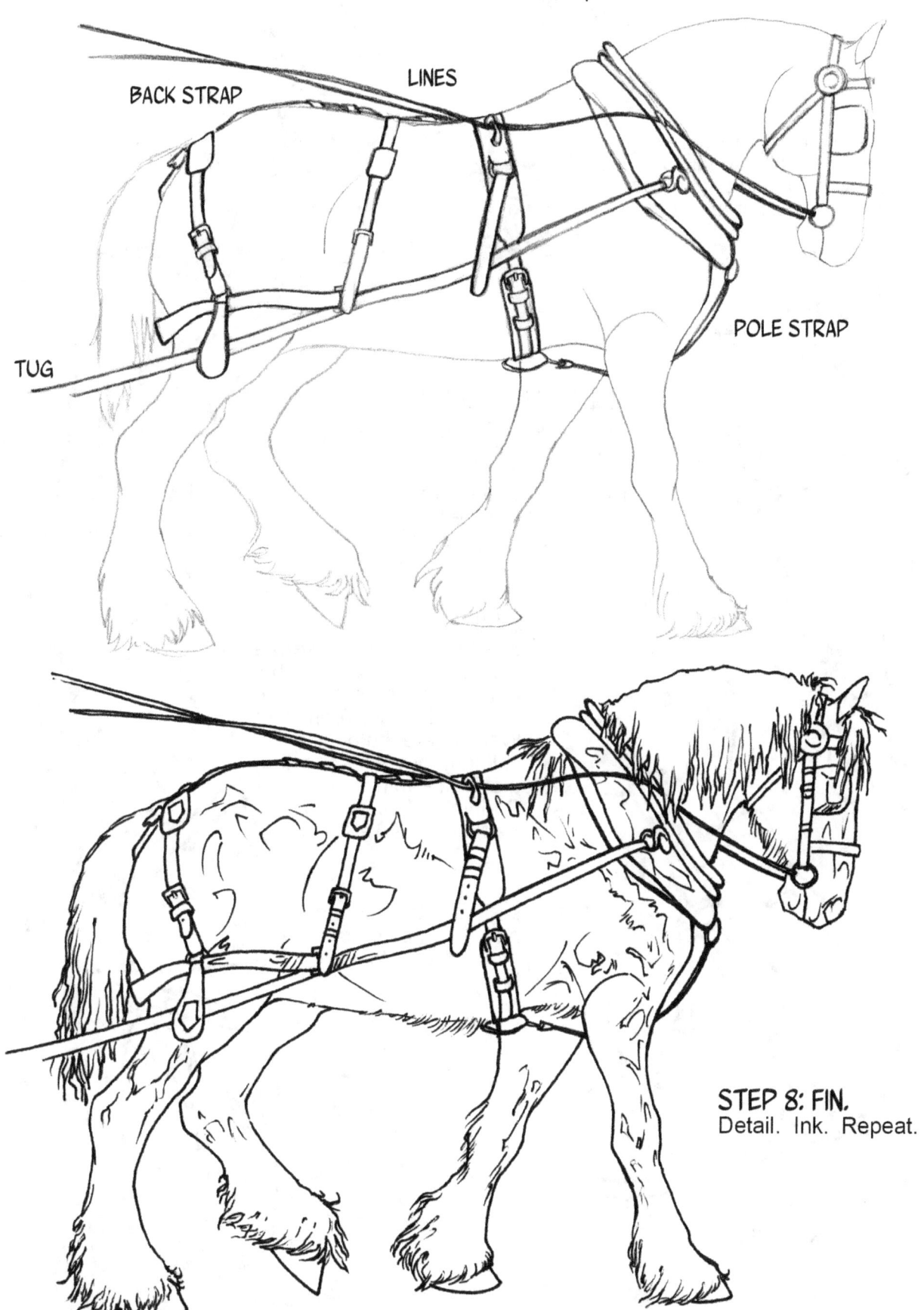

LINES

BACK STRAP

POLE STRAP

TUG

STEP 8: FIN.
Detail. Ink. Repeat.

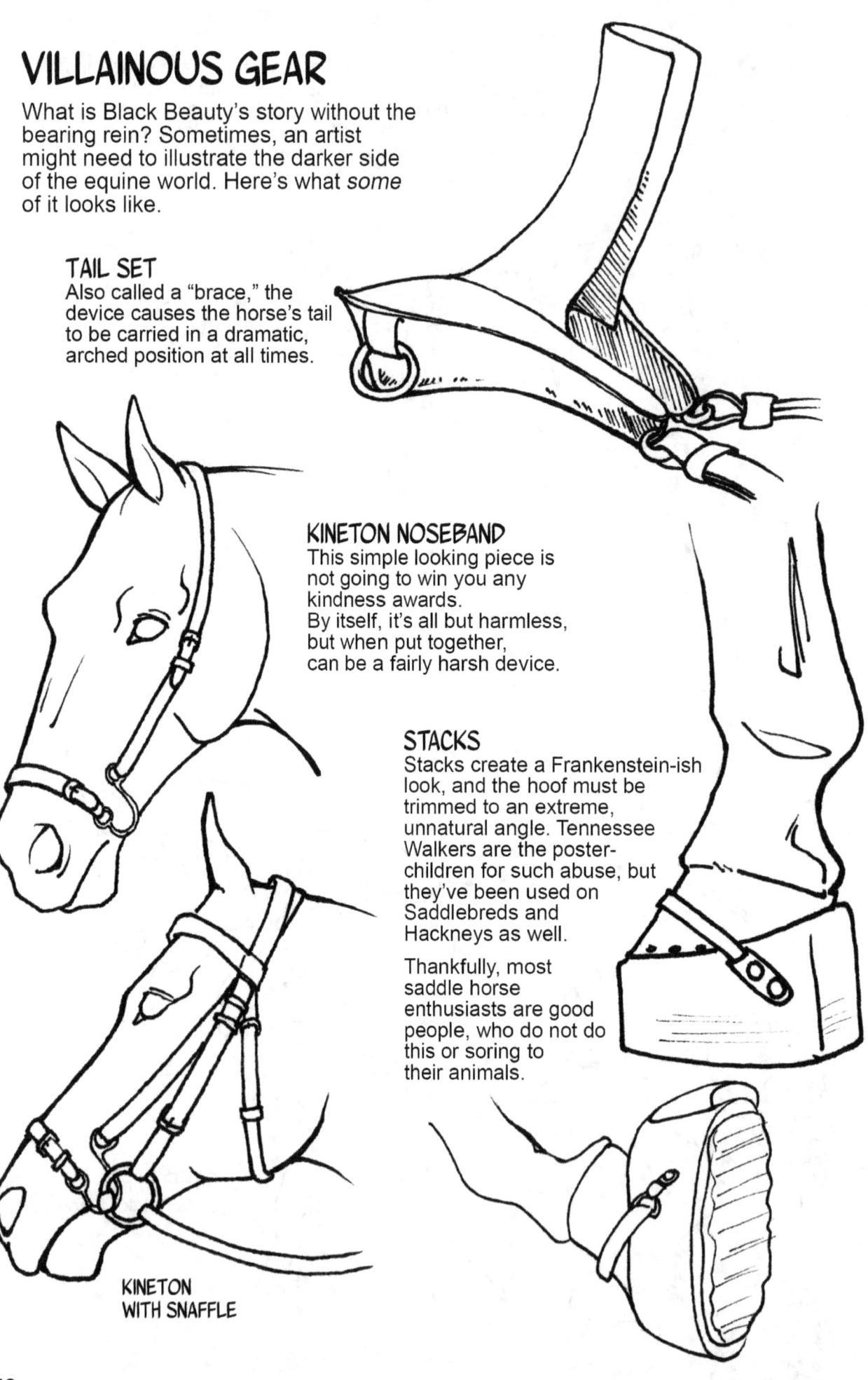

VILLAINOUS GEAR

What is Black Beauty's story without the bearing rein? Sometimes, an artist might need to illustrate the darker side of the equine world. Here's what *some* of it looks like.

TAIL SET
Also called a "brace," the device causes the horse's tail to be carried in a dramatic, arched position at all times.

KINETON NOSEBAND
This simple looking piece is not going to win you any kindness awards.
By itself, it's all but harmless, but when put together, can be a fairly harsh device.

STACKS
Stacks create a Frankenstein-ish look, and the hoof must be trimmed to an extreme, unnatural angle. Tennessee Walkers are the poster-children for such abuse, but they've been used on Saddlebreds and Hackneys as well.

Thankfully, most saddle horse enthusiasts are good people, who do not do this or soring to their animals.

KINETON
WITH SNAFFLE

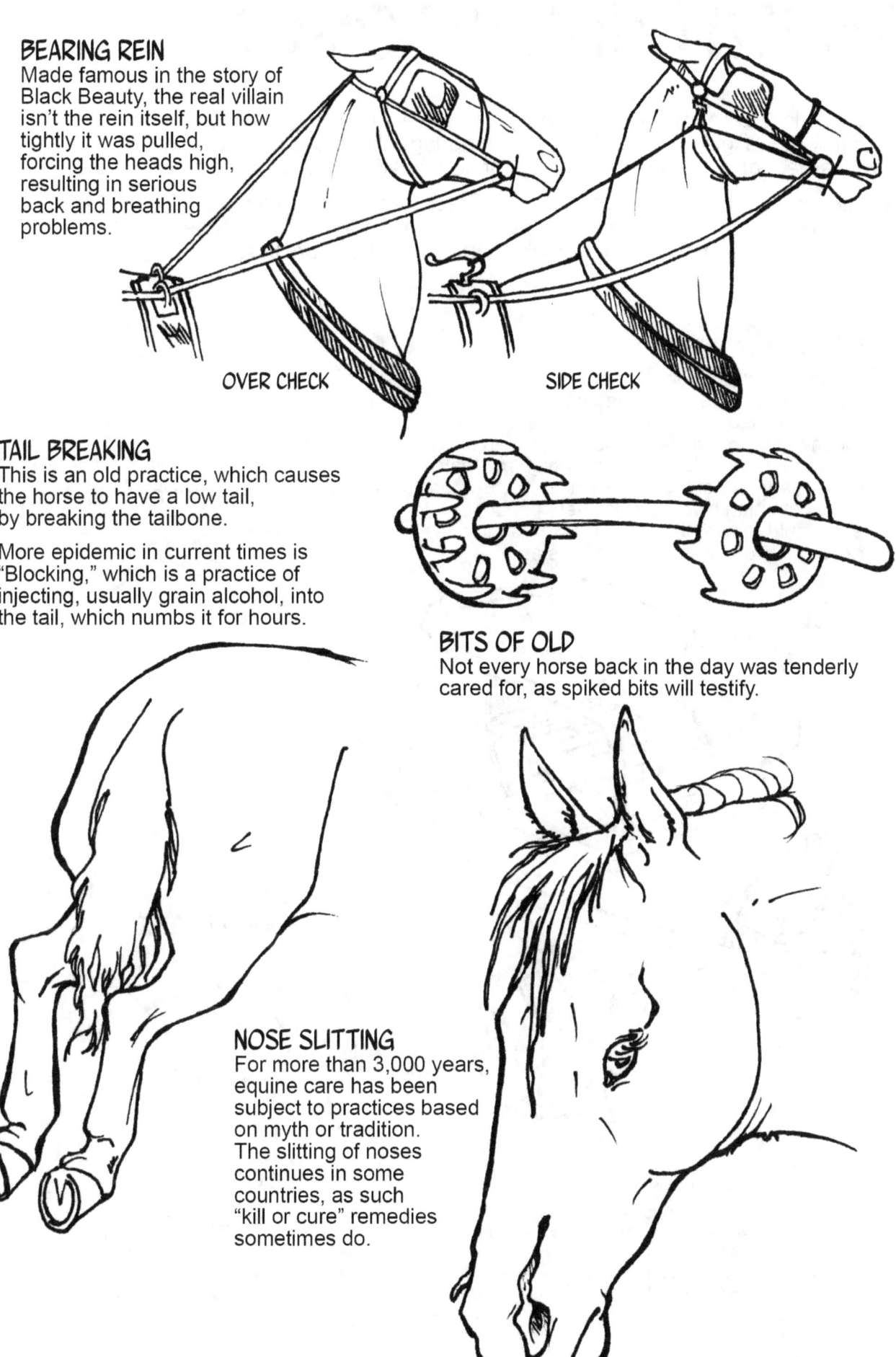

BEARING REIN
Made famous in the story of Black Beauty, the real villain isn't the rein itself, but how tightly it was pulled, forcing the heads high, resulting in serious back and breathing problems.

OVER CHECK

SIDE CHECK

TAIL BREAKING
This is an old practice, which causes the horse to have a low tail, by breaking the tailbone.

More epidemic in current times is "Blocking," which is a practice of injecting, usually grain alcohol, into the tail, which numbs it for hours.

BITS OF OLD
Not every horse back in the day was tenderly cared for, as spiked bits will testify.

NOSE SLITTING
For more than 3,000 years, equine care has been subject to practices based on myth or tradition. The slitting of noses continues in some countries, as such "kill or cure" remedies sometimes do.

ANCIENT HORSEPOWER

From Africa, Europe, and across Asia, you have a melting pot of several major world religions, ancient empires, languages, and peoples, all of which have learned, after the last 6,000 years of cohabitation, to hate each other.

Despite this, Egyptians, Mesopotamians, Greeks and others built many large, broken objects that you should definitely see, if the armies of Japanese tourists ever move. In the meantime, let's look at ancient equine transport.

CHARIOTS

An ancient chariot is made of four basic parts: **car**, **wheels**, **axle**, and **pole**. In several models, it also involved a yoke. Most are rudimentary, consisting of little more than a floor on two wheels, and a waist-high rail that looks made out of brittle twigs and spit. But the Mesopotamian invention was very popular, and would remain the set of wheels for any prestigious person of high social status.

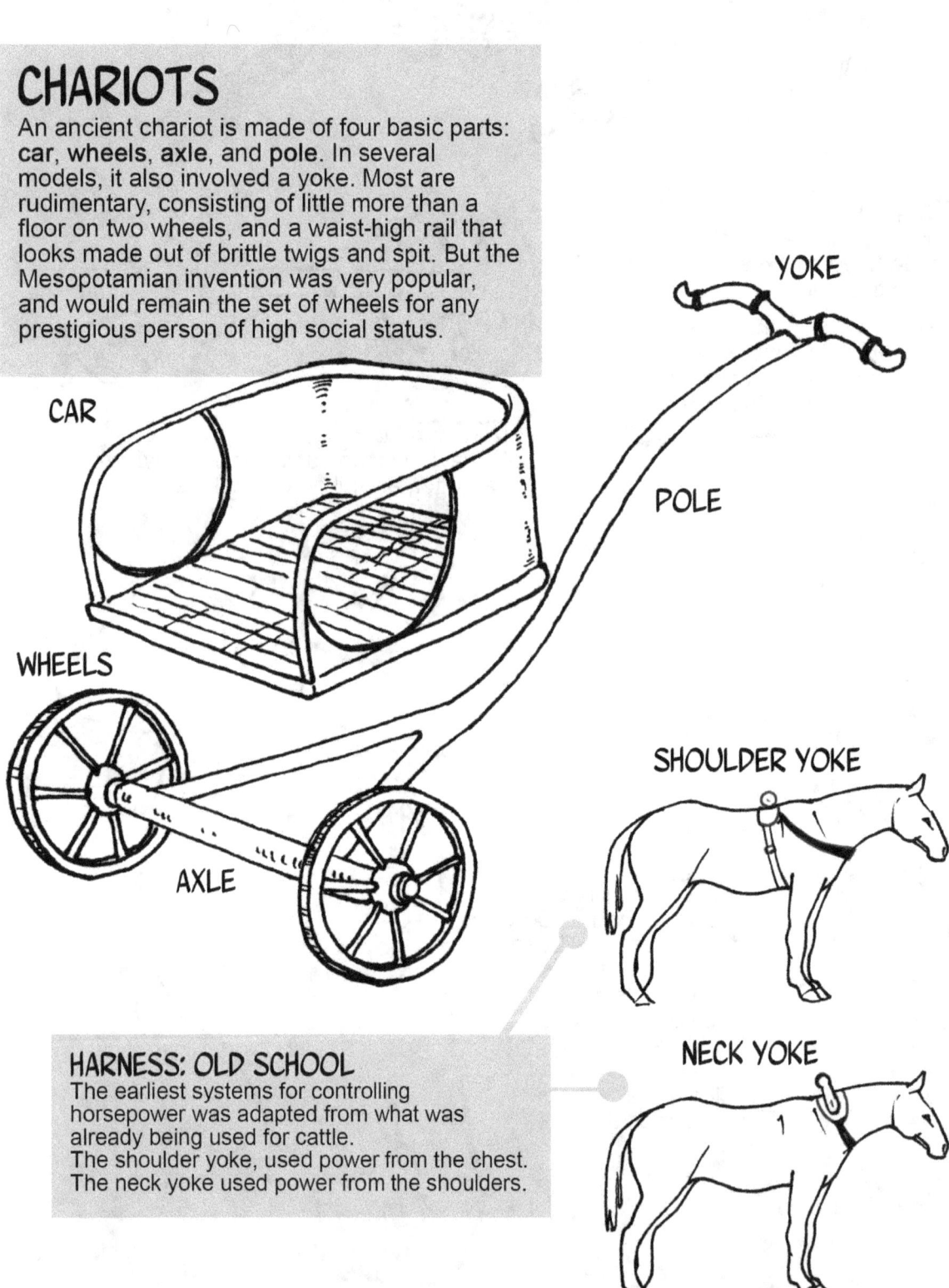

YOKE

CAR

POLE

WHEELS

AXLE

SHOULDER YOKE

NECK YOKE

HARNESS: OLD SCHOOL
The earliest systems for controlling horsepower was adapted from what was already being used for cattle.
The shoulder yoke, used power from the chest.
The neck yoke used power from the shoulders.

EGYPTIAN CHARIOT

They may not have invented it, but wow, did they put it to good use. Egyptians took their chariots to war, used them to hunt, even had their chariots buried with them. The handling wasn't terrific, and the ride would have jolted your spine into dust, but if you could afford it, you had to have one. It was the Cadillac Escalade of 2000 BCE.

Egyptians were very fond of their chariots, and they get more elaborate and extravagant as the dynasties go on.

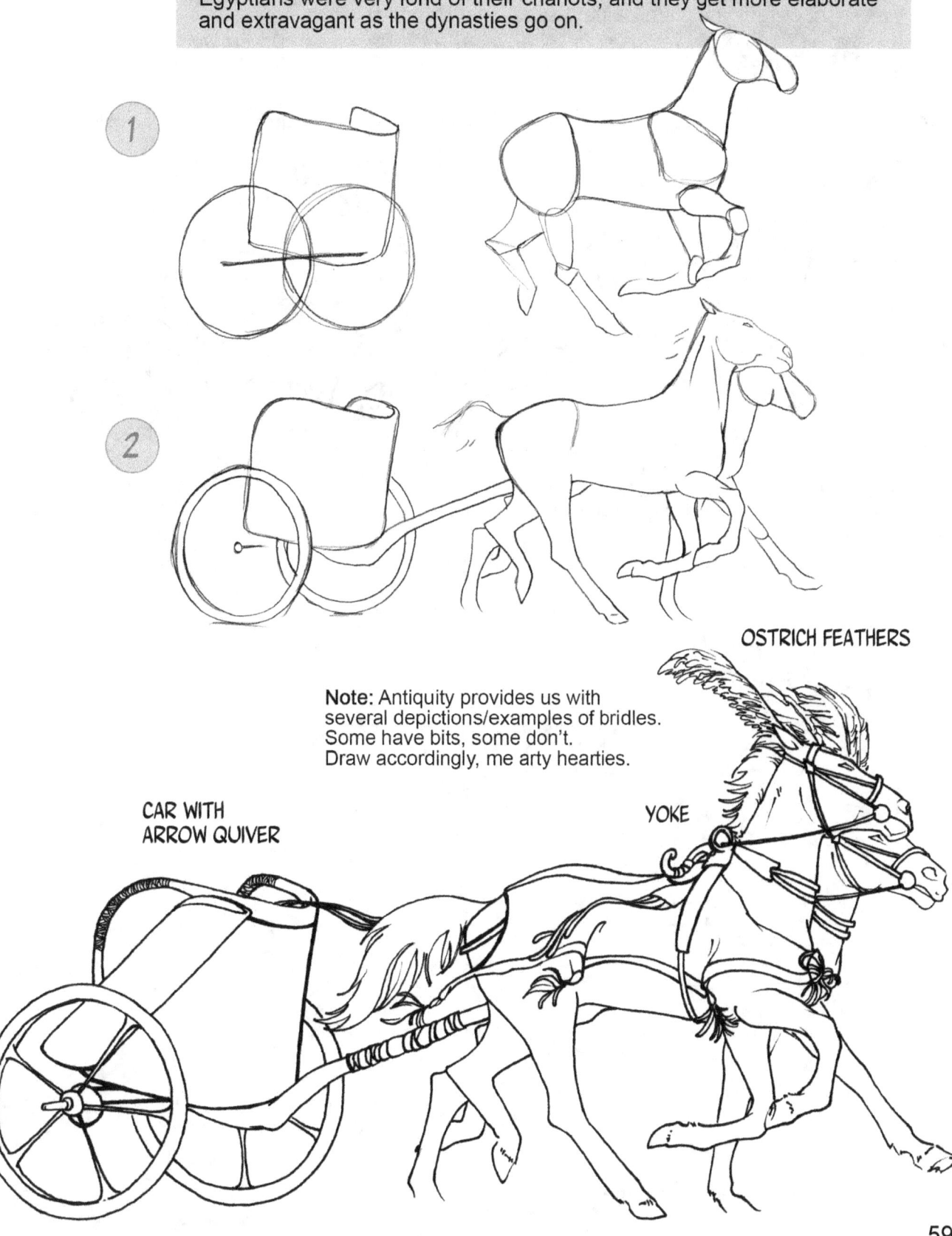

OSTRICH FEATHERS

Note: Antiquity provides us with several depictions/examples of bridles. Some have bits, some don't. Draw accordingly, me arty hearties.

CAR WITH
ARROW QUIVER

YOKE

GREEK CHARIOT

The most popular sport in the Greek Olympics was the chariot racing. Which isn't such high praise when you consider the rest of the games mostly consisted of naked guys.

The Greek tale of the Battle of Marathon, wherein a messenger runs the 26 miles back to Athens, shouted, "Nike!*", and then fell down dead, clearly illustrates the need for horses. Also... to avoid running marathons.

CEREMONIAL CAR

A racing car would be similar, but lighter. Drivers would be teenage males, and the car makes for a bone-shattering ride because it lays right on the axle.

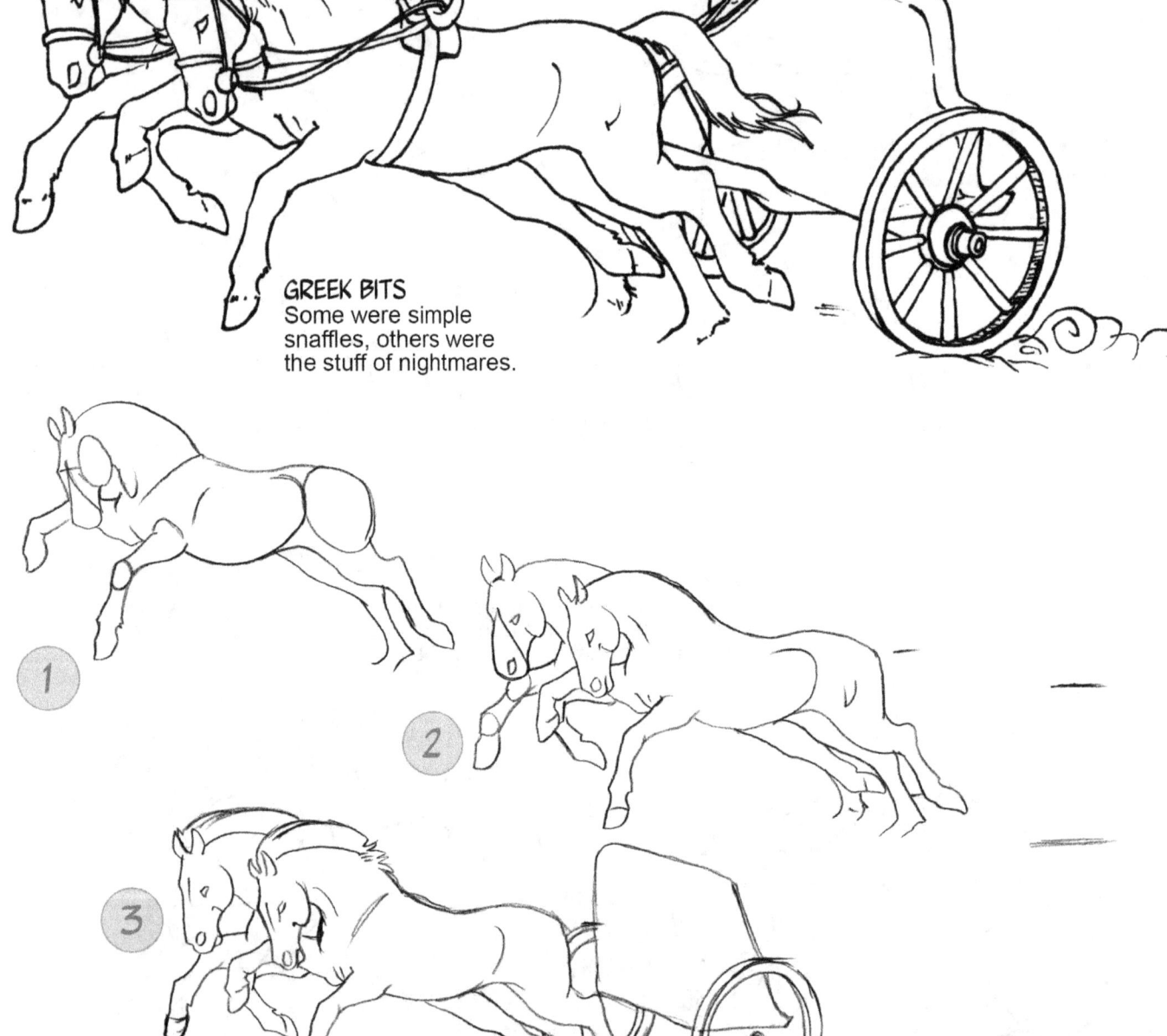

GREEK BITS
Some were simple snaffles, others were the stuff of nightmares.

* translated, "My feet are *killing* me!"

OVERHEAD VIEW

ROMAN CHARIOT

By Greek and then Roman times, the chariot was no longer used in practical warfare. Racing however, was as popular as ever.

Romans had nearly religious devotion for their racing colors/teams, and drivers, who were mostly slaves, *could* attain mass fame and wealth from winning, *most* however, didn't have a long life expectancy.

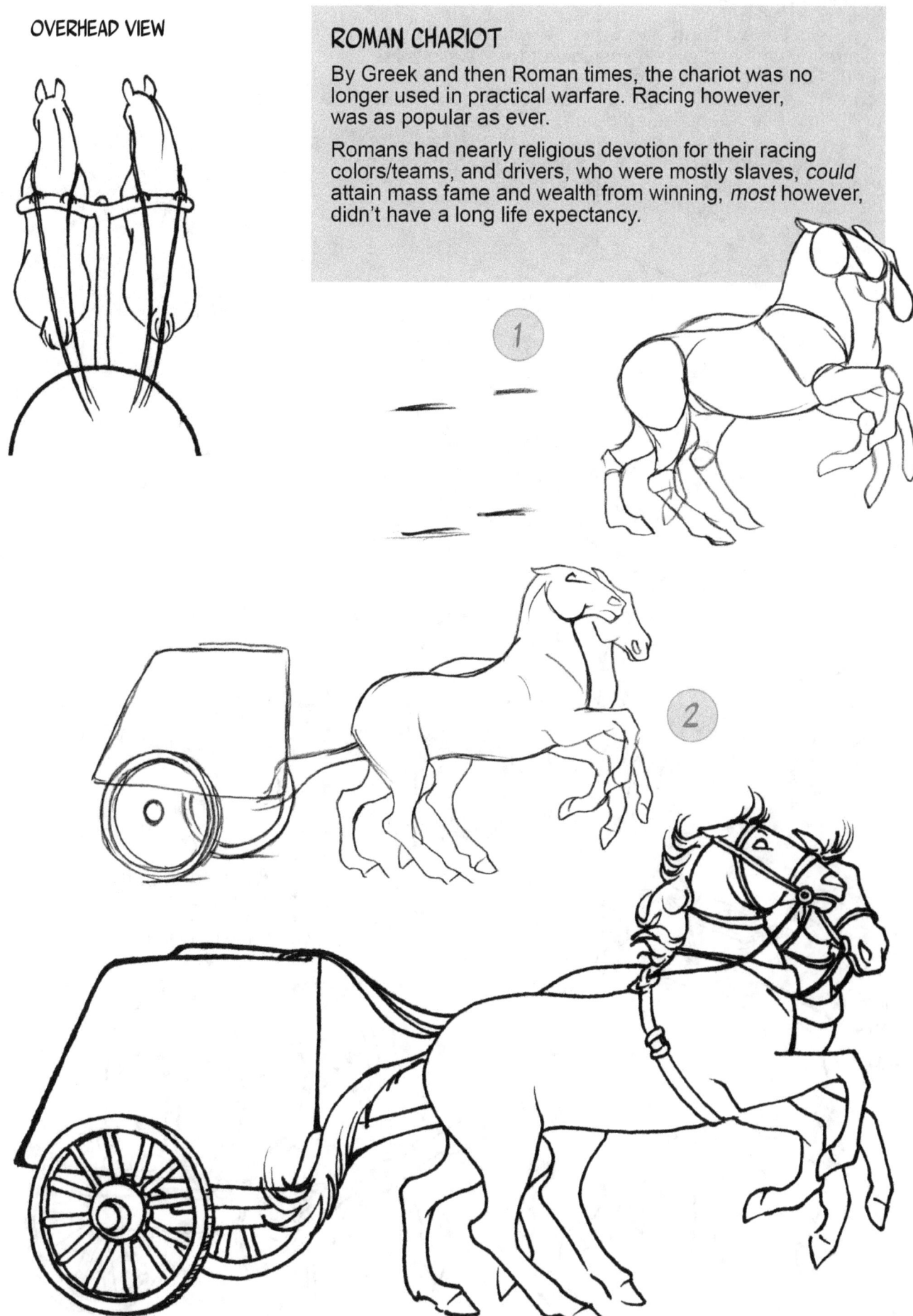

CELTIC CHARIOT

The Celts were a pretty handy people with horses and hammers. One of the main sources for their exploits is Julius Caesar himself, which, even allowing for his tendency to "remember bigger" than most people, paints a pretty impressive equestrian picture of the Celtic people.

Unfortunately for the Celts, they were up against Romans. Who knew a civilization so decent at building roads would be mighty fine at logistics?

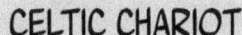

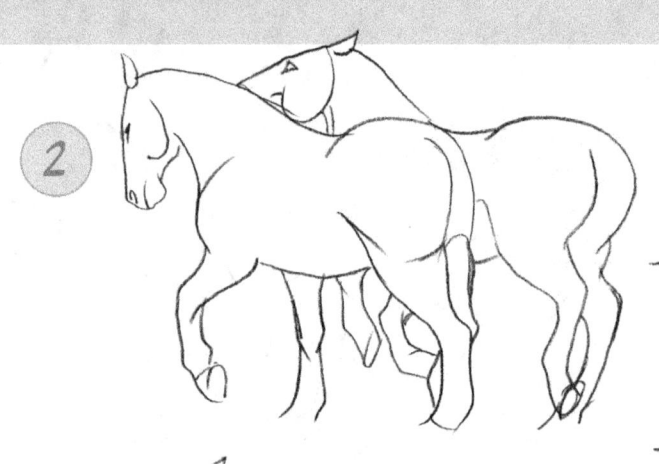

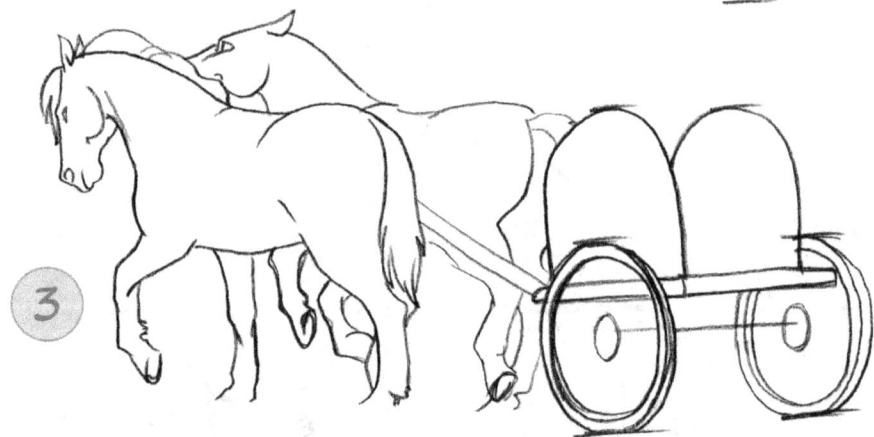

CAR WITH SUSPENSION
Chains or leather straps were used to give some relief from the jolting ride.

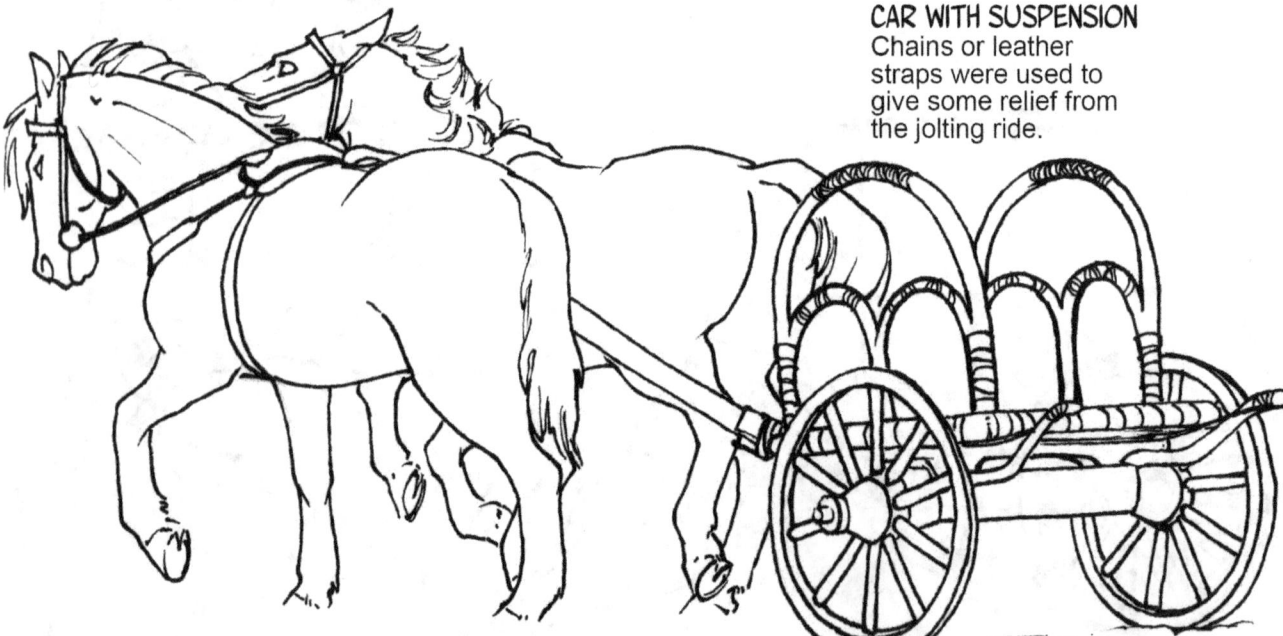

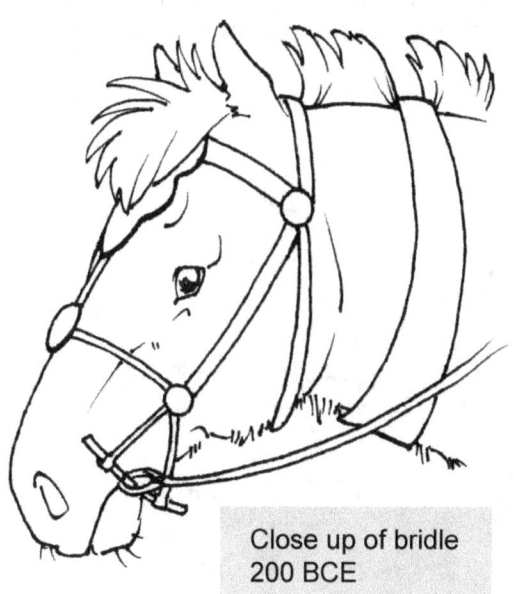

Close up of bridle
200 BCE

CHINESE CHARIOT

Ancient Chinese chariots were typically two wheeled vehicles drawn by two or four horses with a single pole down the middle. They were ultra-lightweight, but the trade-off does mean you have to charge into battle with all the engineering protection of wicker.

Larger horses, which are introduced later, and the double shaft chariot, which is both light and easy to use, mean that you don't have to take the wheels off every time you park it.

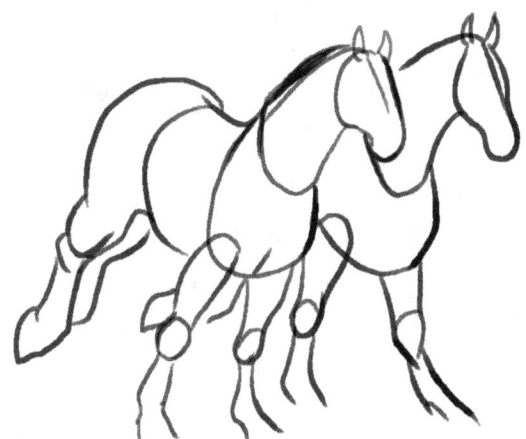

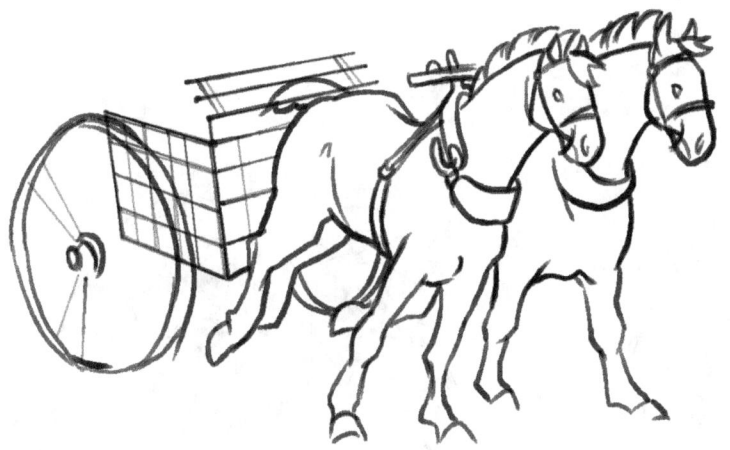

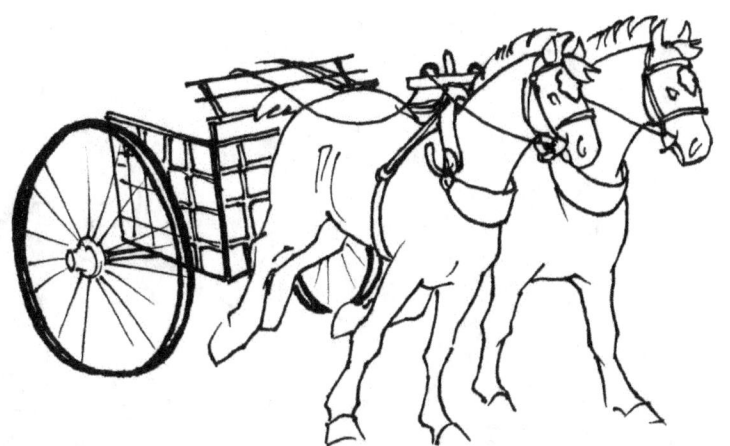

QUADRIGAS were chariots of four horses. They were symbols of power and fame. Not to be confused with the quagga, which is an extinct sub-species of zebra. Althought a quadriga of quaggas would be internet-worthy-watching.

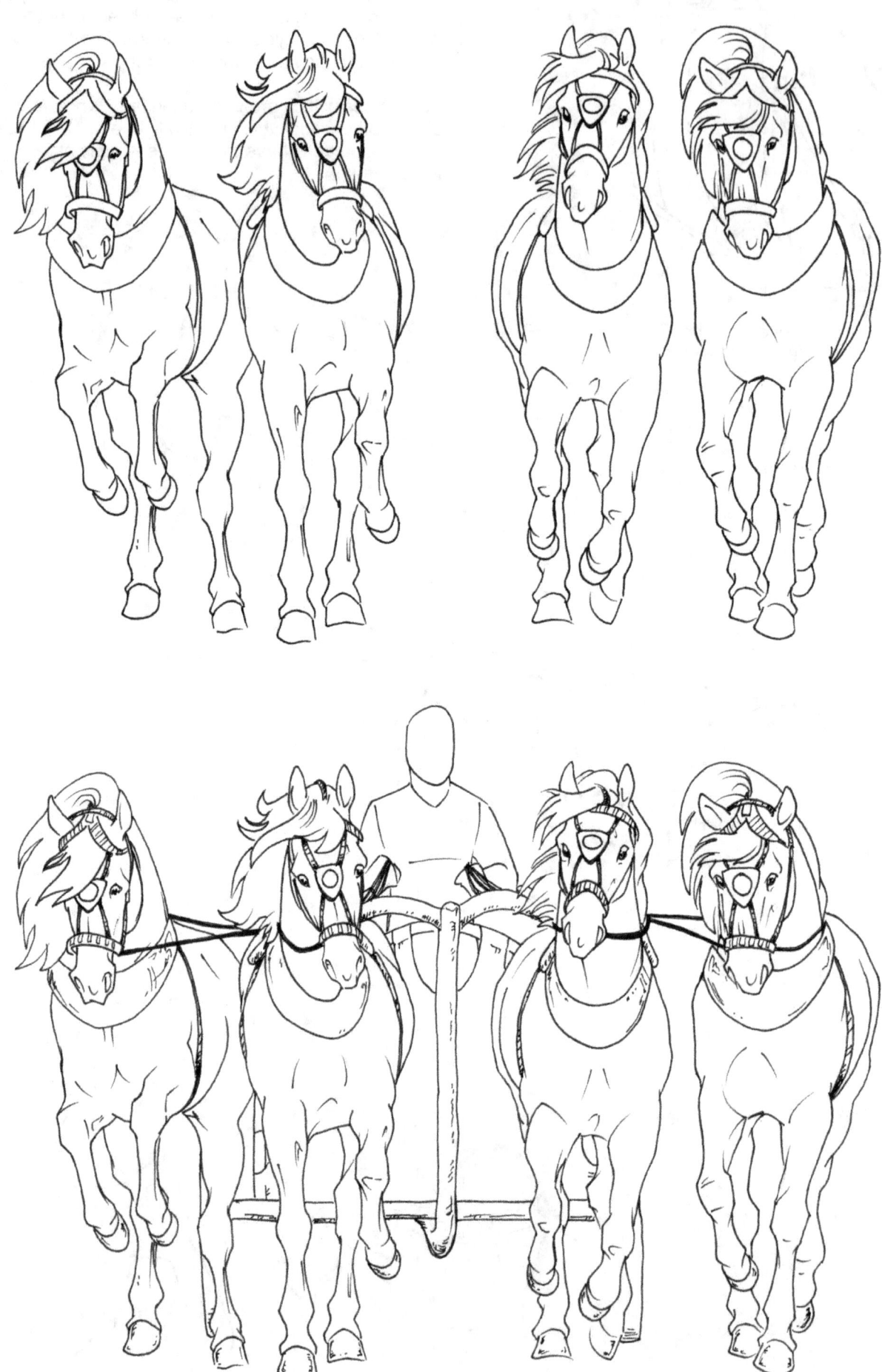

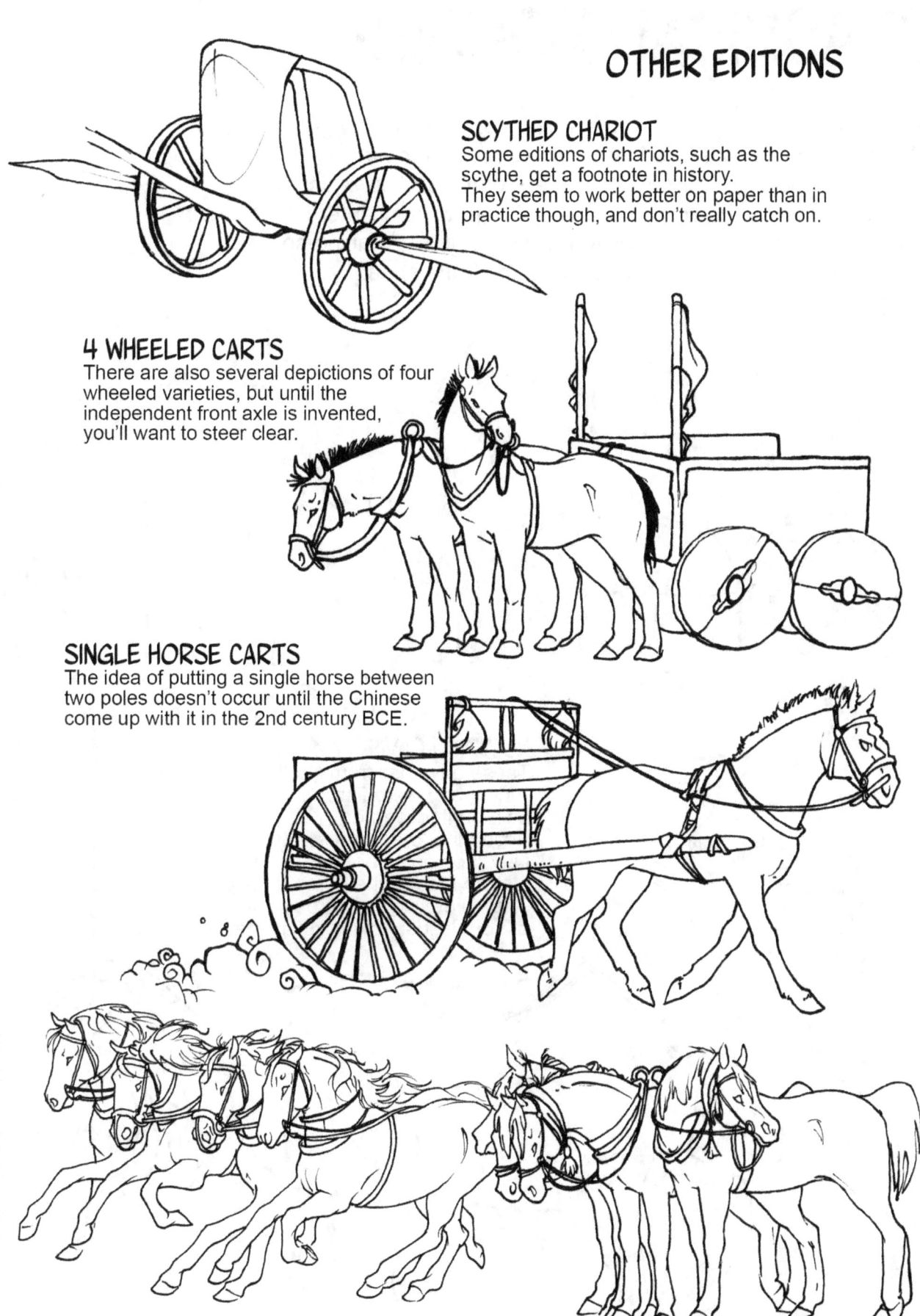

OTHER EDITIONS

SCYTHED CHARIOT
Some editions of chariots, such as the scythe, get a footnote in history.
They seem to work better on paper than in practice though, and don't really catch on.

4 WHEELED CARTS
There are also several depictions of four wheeled varieties, but until the independent front axle is invented, you'll want to steer clear.

SINGLE HORSE CARTS
The idea of putting a single horse between two poles doesn't occur until the Chinese come up with it in the 2nd century BCE.

4 OR MORE
Four-horse teams were very common in the classical world.
Despite what you see in films, the most common rig consisted of the two, central horses yoked together, and the two outside used to steer.
This takes advantage of the horse's pulling power, and herd mentality.

CLASSICAL HORSES

By 1000 BCE, people agree that riding horses is a fairly good way to get around. This forward thinking movement was followed by the not-so-overnight success of the saddle, which was improved upon by the you-wouldn't-believe-how-much later invention of the stirrup, and finally, the we-got-bored-waiting-so-we-invented-the-Middle Ages technology of the horseshoe.

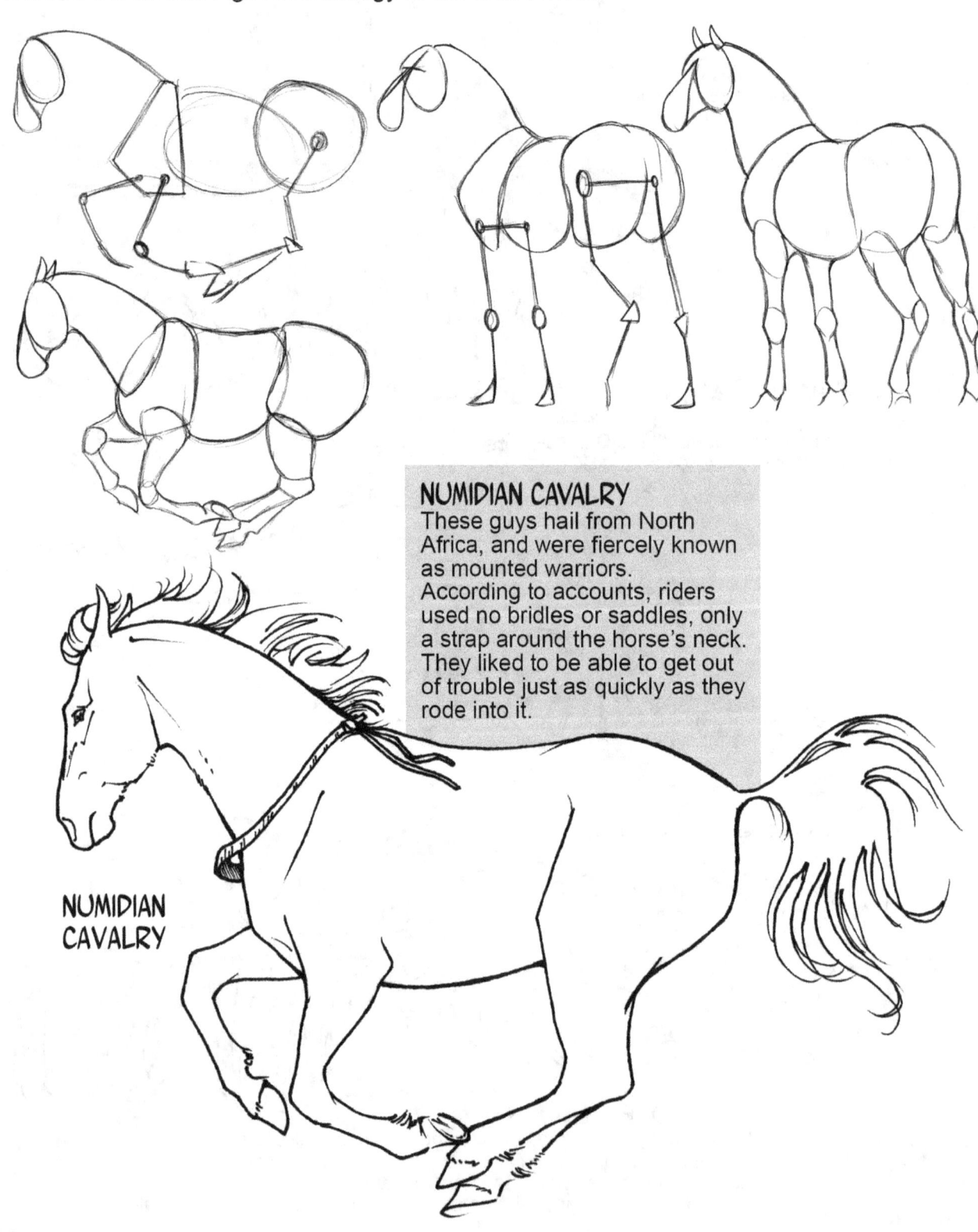

NUMIDIAN CAVALRY
These guys hail from North Africa, and were fiercely known as mounted warriors.
According to accounts, riders used no bridles or saddles, only a strap around the horse's neck. They liked to be able to get out of trouble just as quickly as they rode into it.

NUMIDIAN CAVALRY

GREEKS

The famous Greek* founder of horsemanship, Xenophon, wrote treatises on horse training. The first, "Horse Training: Difficult and Impossible," was followed up by the best seller, "Horses: With a Minimum of Unpleasantness & Death."

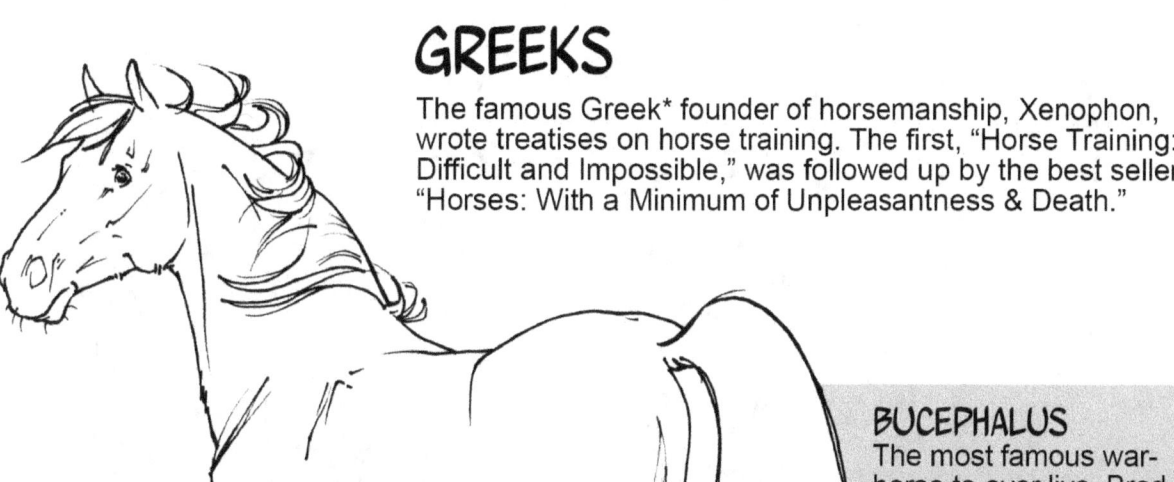

BUCEPHALUS

The most famous war-horse to ever live. Bred in Thessaly, black, reportedly very afraid of his own shadow, Bucephalus, which means "Ox-head," I am totally not making that up, would take Alex T. Great on to conquer the lands from Greece to Pakistan.

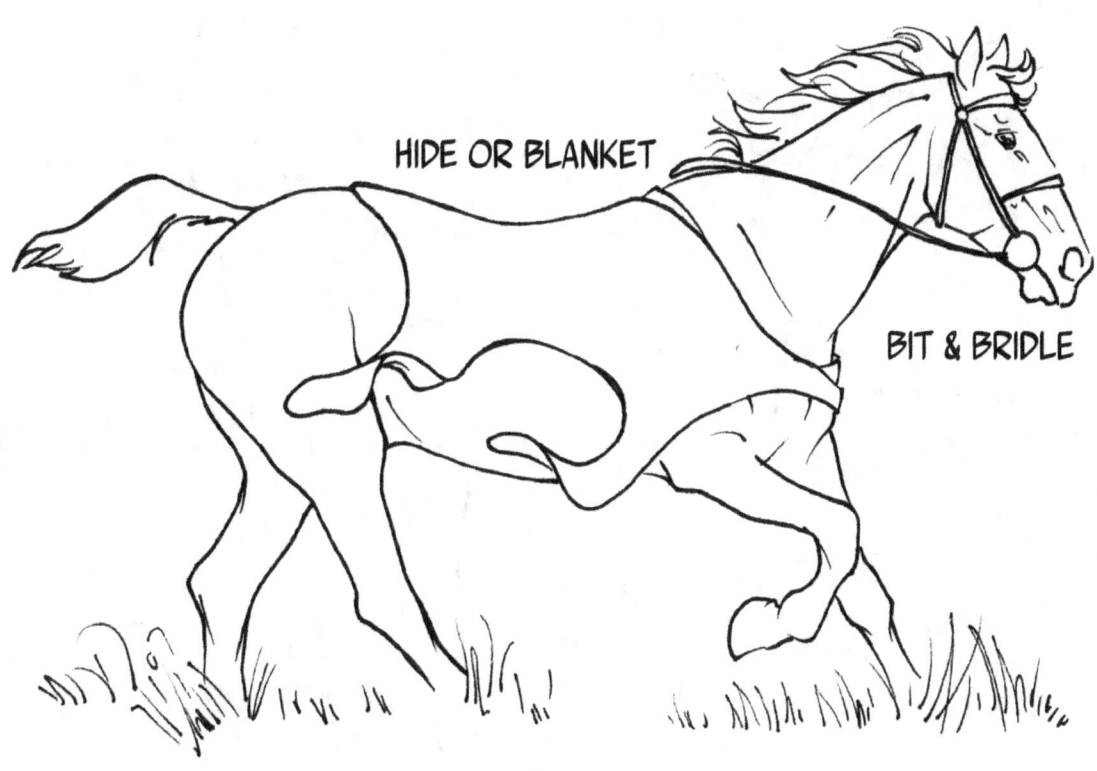

HIDE OR BLANKET

BIT & BRIDLE

*Official Motto: Where the democracy comes from!

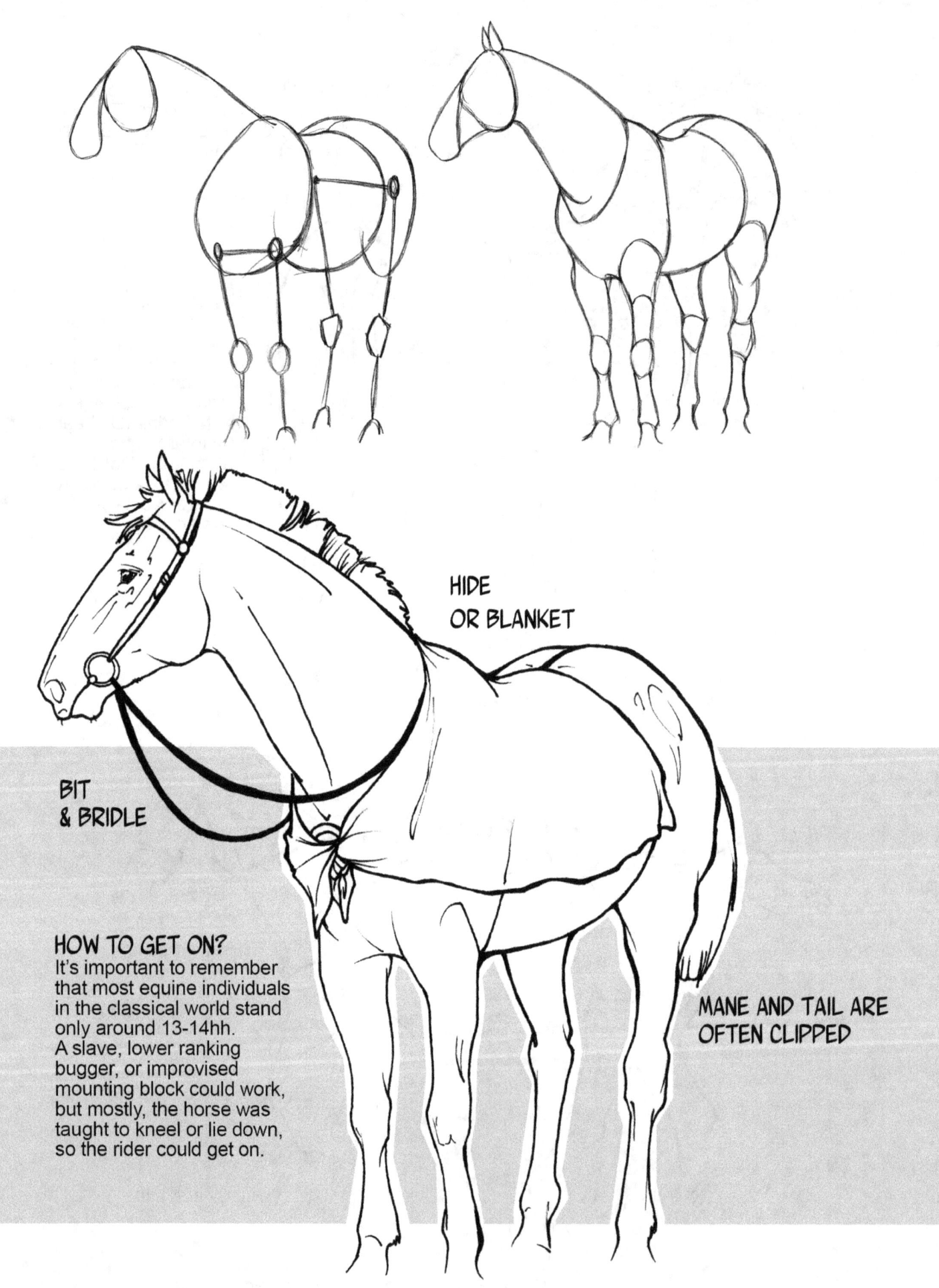

HIDE
OR BLANKET

BIT
& BRIDLE

HOW TO GET ON?
It's important to remember
that most equine individuals
in the classical world stand
only around 13-14hh.
A slave, lower ranking
bugger, or improvised
mounting block could work,
but mostly, the horse was
taught to kneel or lie down,
so the rider could get on.

MANE AND TAIL ARE
OFTEN CLIPPED

PERSIANS

The Persians were horse-crazy people who were very adept at the "Parthian Shot," a brilliant move, wherein a rider, while retreating at full gallop, turns around to fire arrows at the pursuing enemy.

It could be said that the Greeks were not fans.

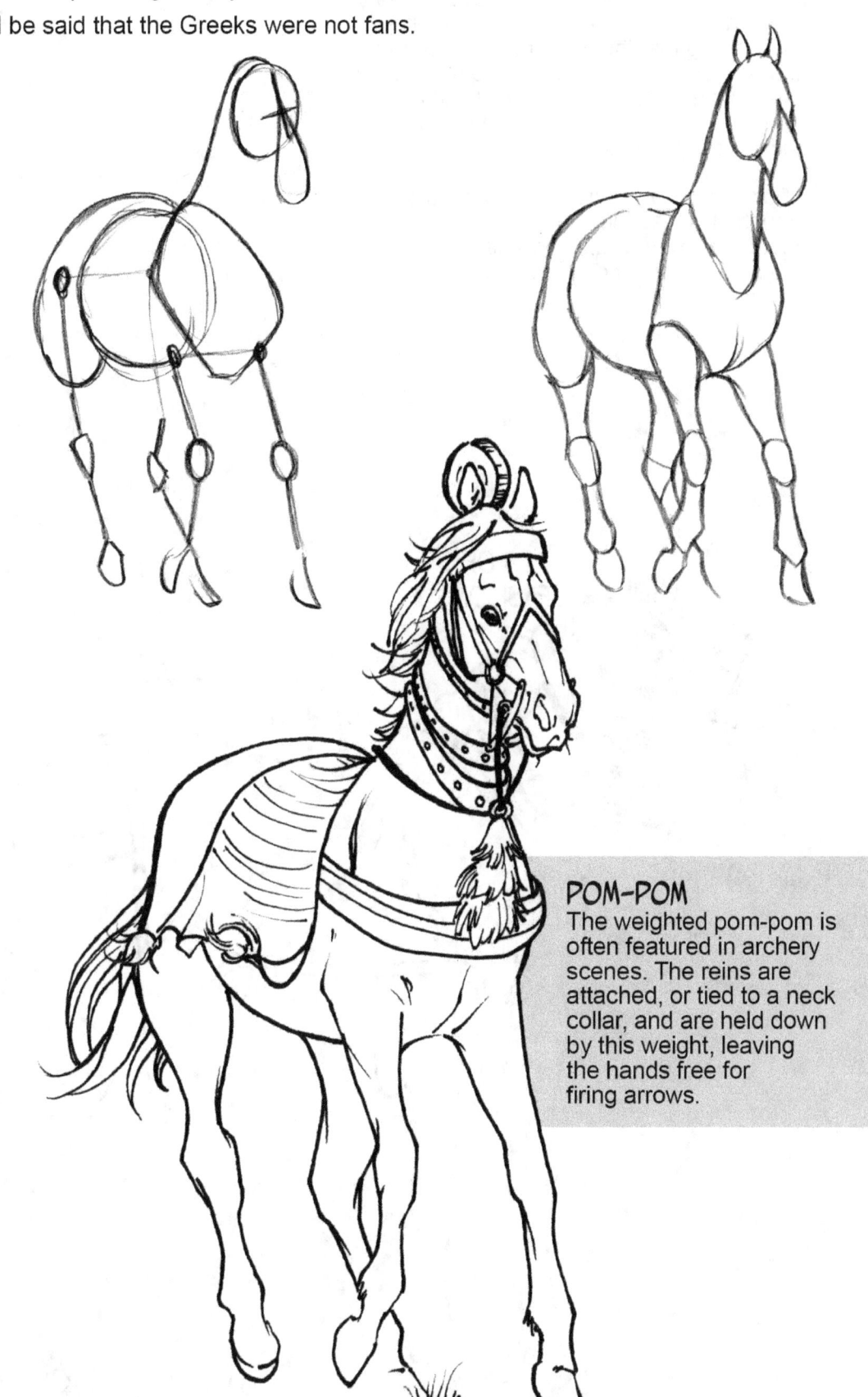

POM-POM
The weighted pom-pom is often featured in archery scenes. The reins are attached, or tied to a neck collar, and are held down by this weight, leaving the hands free for firing arrows.

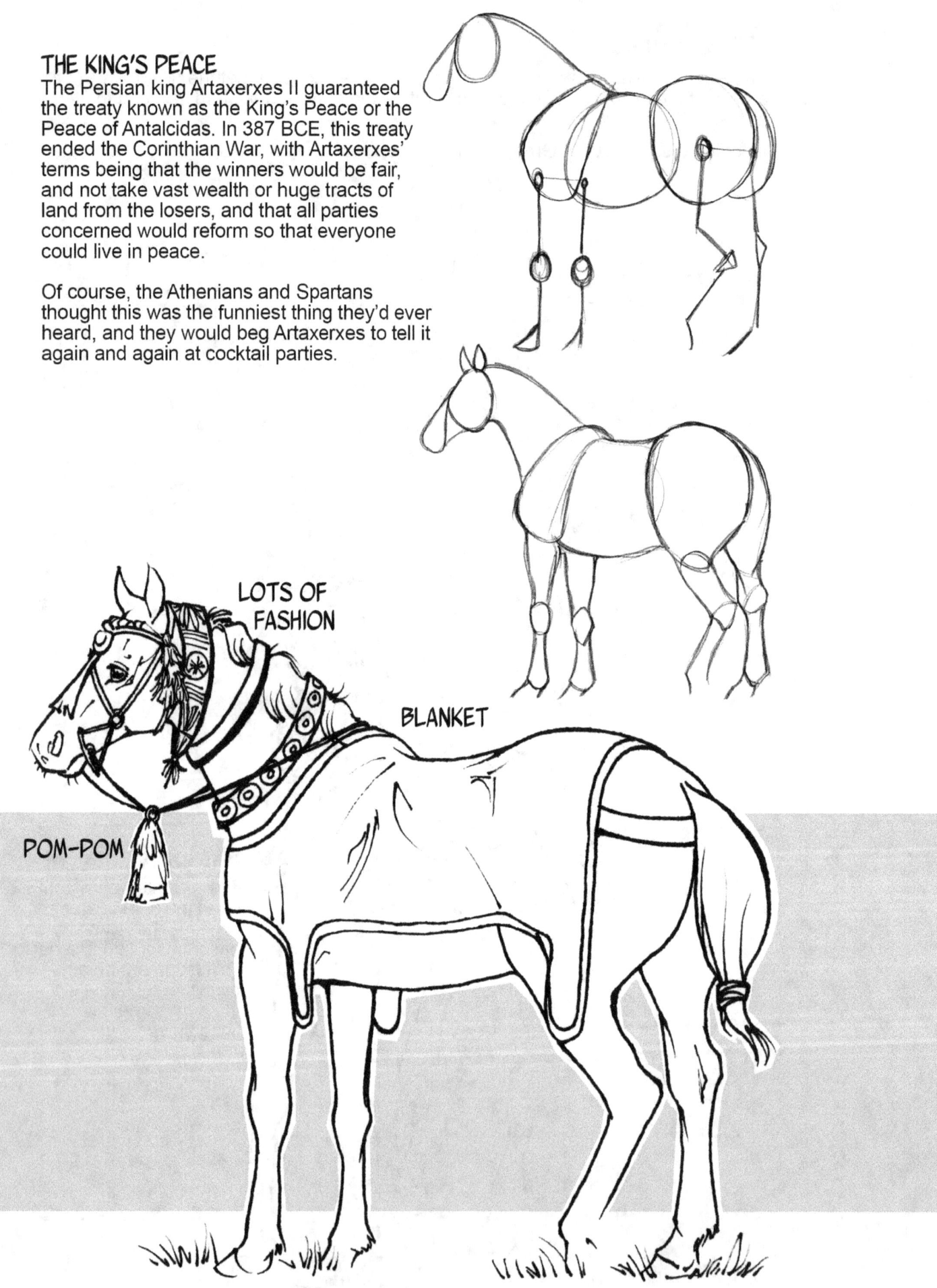

THE KING'S PEACE

The Persian king Artaxerxes II guaranteed the treaty known as the King's Peace or the Peace of Antalcidas. In 387 BCE, this treaty ended the Corinthian War, with Artaxerxes' terms being that the winners would be fair, and not take vast wealth or huge tracts of land from the losers, and that all parties concerned would reform so that everyone could live in peace.

Of course, the Athenians and Spartans thought this was the funniest thing they'd ever heard, and they would beg Artaxerxes to tell it again and again at cocktail parties.

LOTS OF FASHION

BLANKET

POM-POM

SCYTHIAN

The biggest Scythian contribution to the equine world was early development of the saddle. These initial designs involve two cushions, one on either side of the spine, connected by a wooden arch.

These show up roughly around in the 4th century, BCE, so the saddle, as we know it, still has a long way to go.

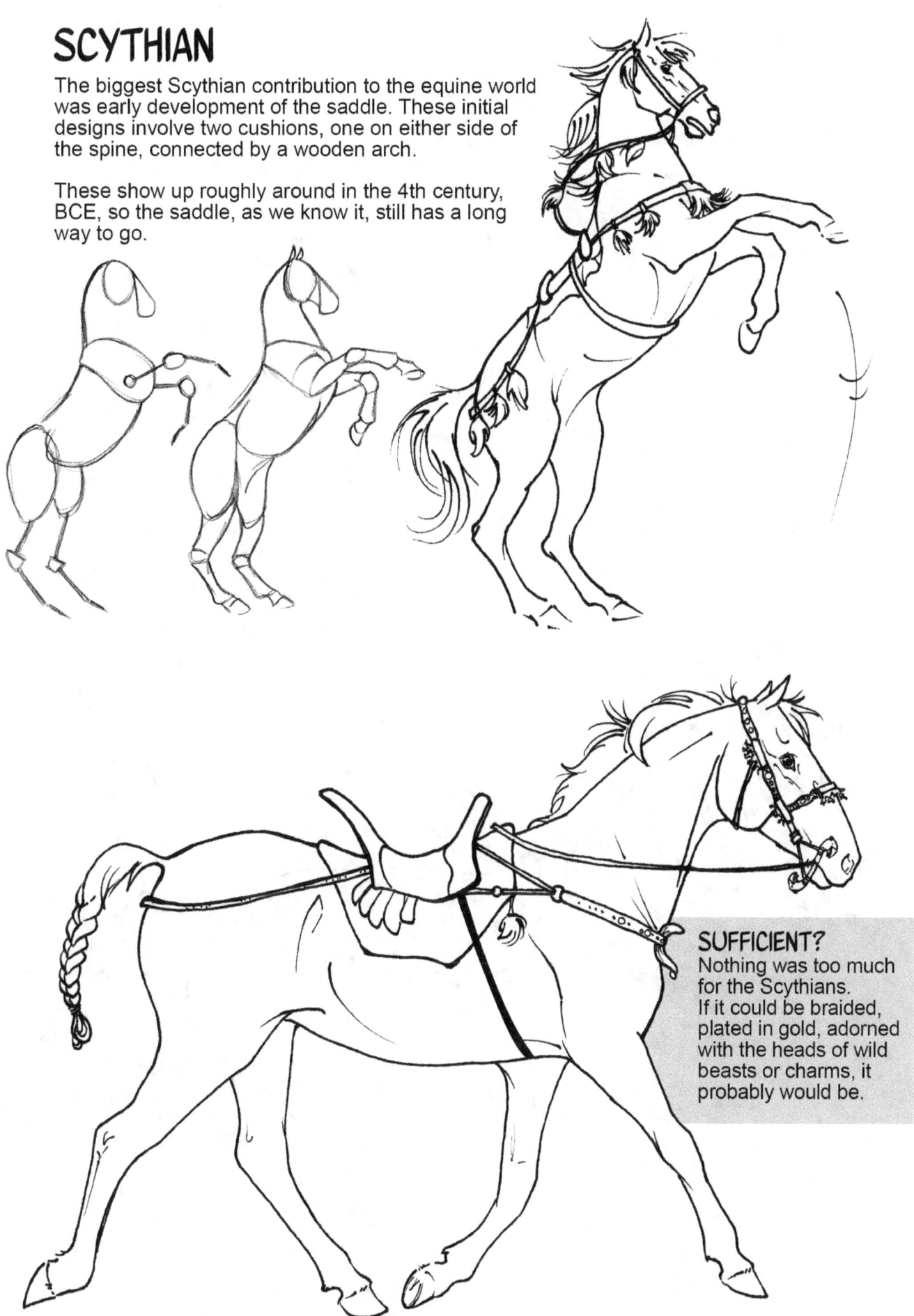

SUFFICIENT?
Nothing was too much for the Scythians. If it could be braided, plated in gold, adorned with the heads of wild beasts or charms, it probably would be.

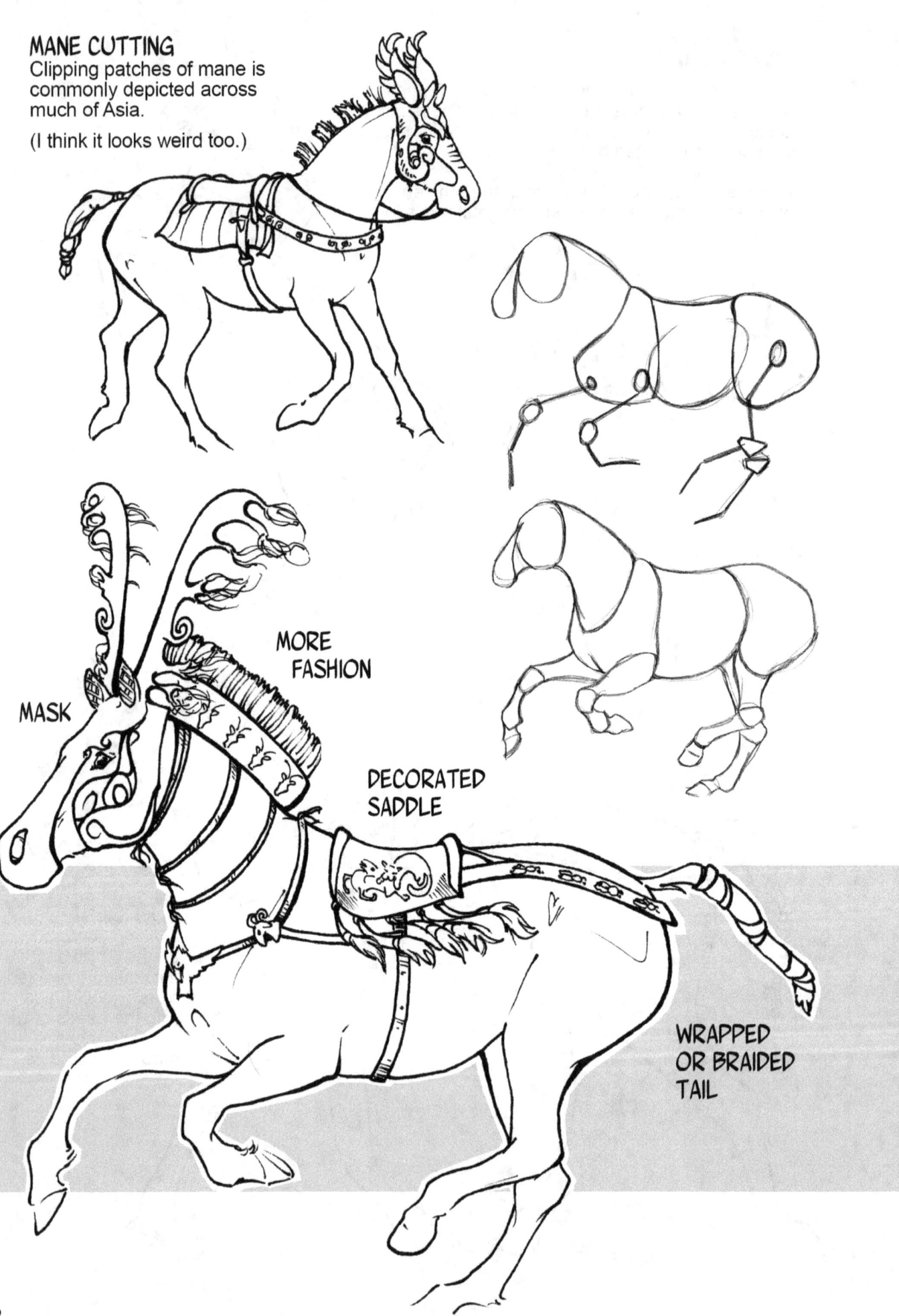

MANE CUTTING
Clipping patches of mane is commonly depicted across much of Asia.

(I think it looks weird too.)

MASK

MORE FASHION

DECORATED SADDLE

WRAPPED OR BRAIDED TAIL

ROMAN

Rome was a great empire, and is famously known for being portrayed by British actors. This empire created several, important structures that revolutionized art, architecture, and culture.

Which you are welcome to chip off little pieces of.

Italians just love that sort of thing.

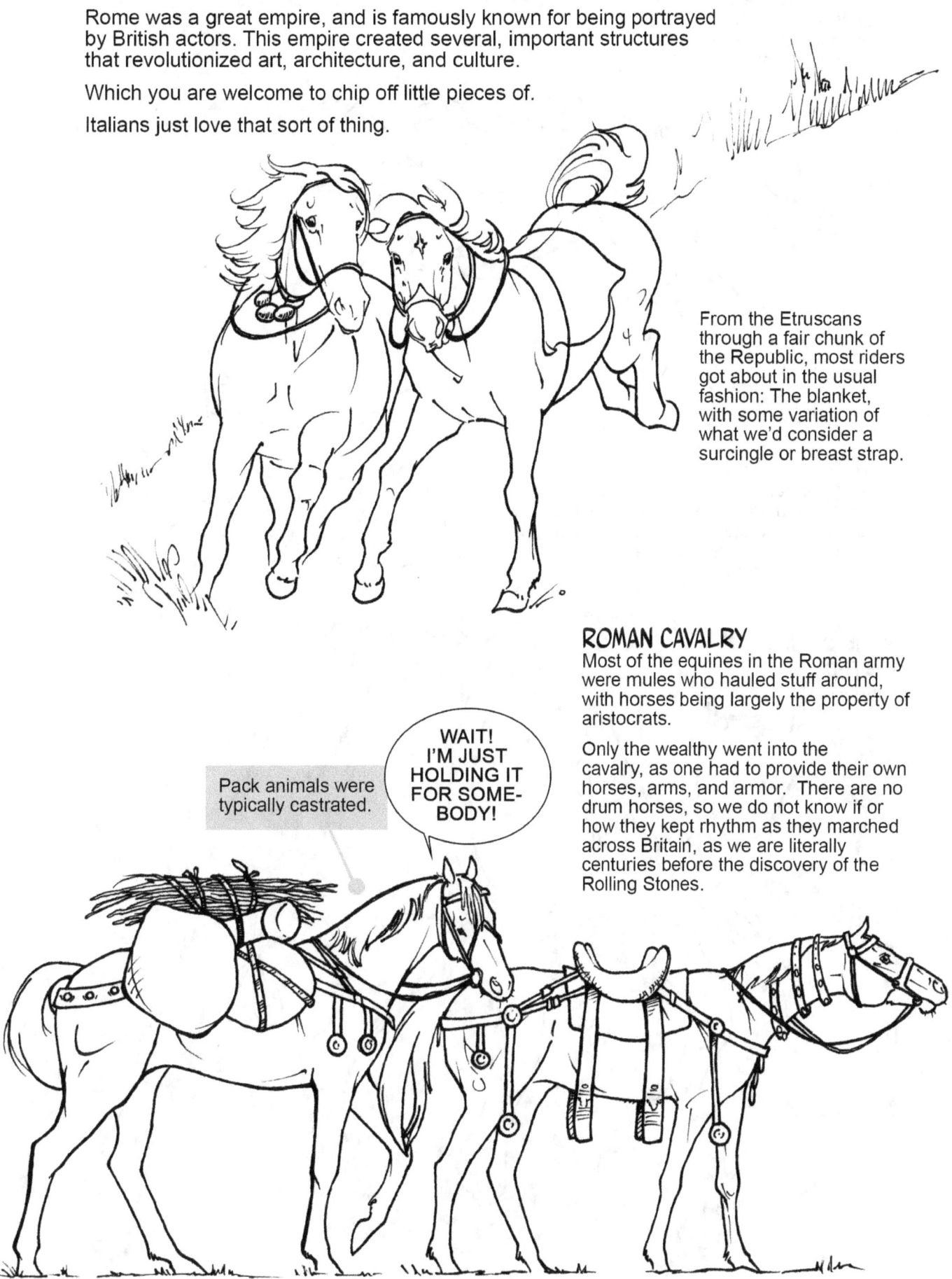

From the Etruscans through a fair chunk of the Republic, most riders got about in the usual fashion: The blanket, with some variation of what we'd consider a surcingle or breast strap.

ROMAN CAVALRY

Most of the equines in the Roman army were mules who hauled stuff around, with horses being largely the property of aristocrats.

Only the wealthy went into the cavalry, as one had to provide their own horses, arms, and armor. There are no drum horses, so we do not know if or how they kept rhythm as they marched across Britain, as we are literally centuries before the discovery of the Rolling Stones.

Pack animals were typically castrated.

WAIT! I'M JUST HOLDING IT FOR SOME-BODY!

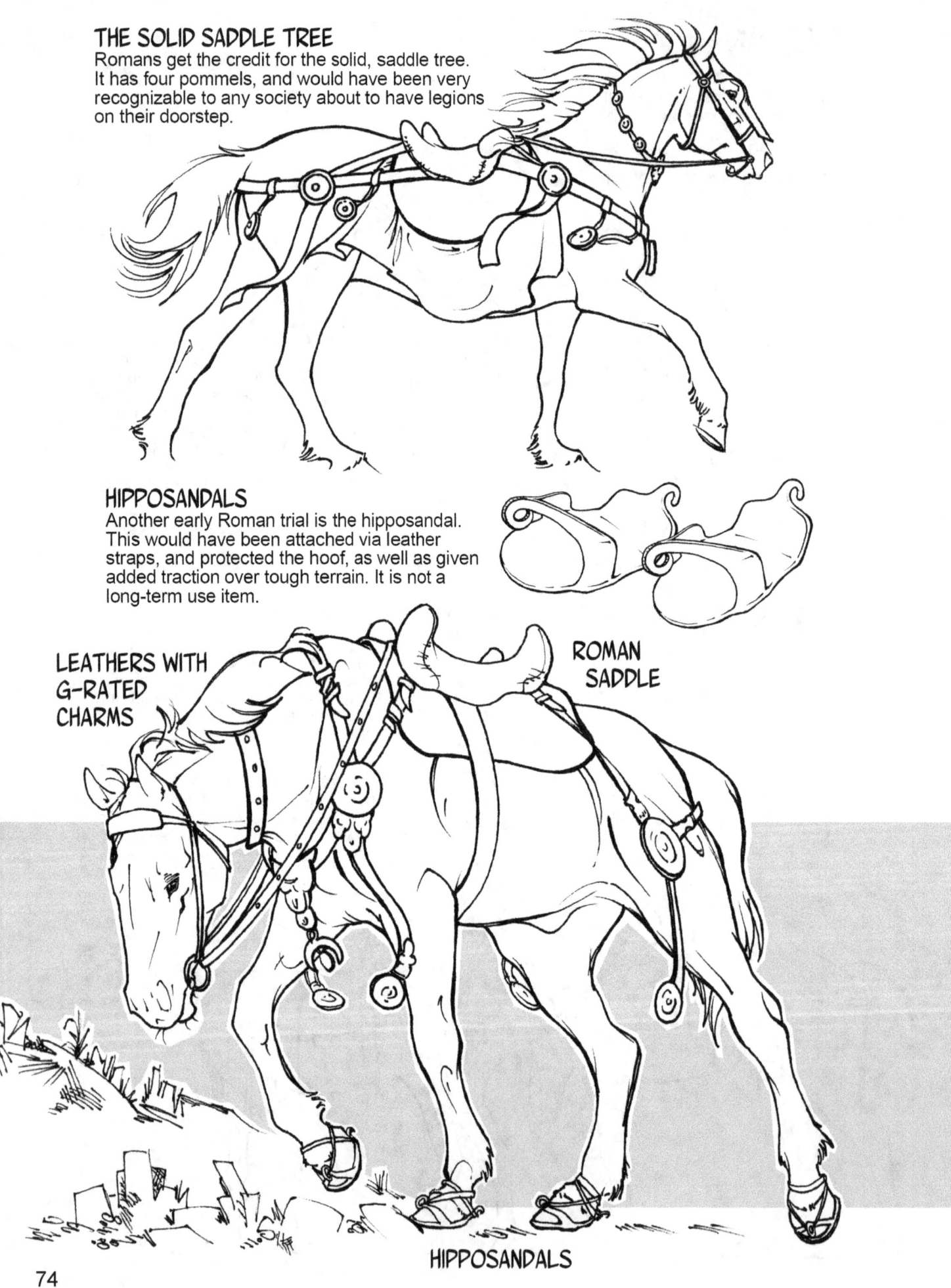

THE SOLID SADDLE TREE
Romans get the credit for the solid, saddle tree.
It has four pommels, and would have been very
recognizable to any society about to have legions
on their doorstep.

HIPPOSANDALS
Another early Roman trial is the hipposandal.
This would have been attached via leather
straps, and protected the hoof, as well as given
added traction over tough terrain. It is not a
long-term use item.

LEATHERS WITH
G-RATED
CHARMS

ROMAN
SADDLE

HIPPOSANDALS

MIX + MATCH

Hellenistic culture represents a fusion of the Ancient Greek world with that of the Near East, Middle East, and Southwest Asia.
A visit to the museum, or their website, will explain what I'm on about - and ask away! Museum people are really awesome like that.
Maybe not normal human beings, but awesome people.

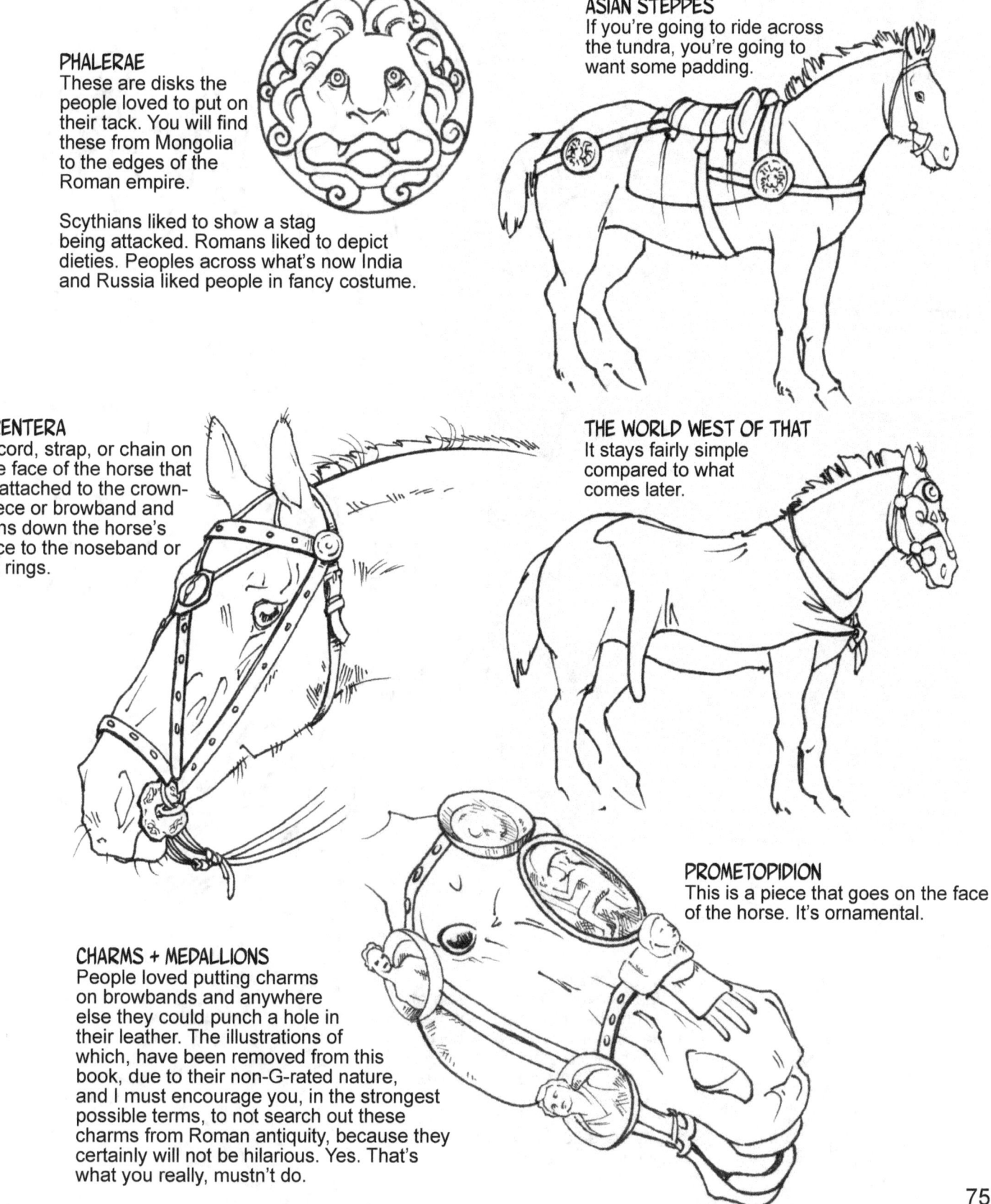

PHALERAE
These are disks the people loved to put on their tack. You will find these from Mongolia to the edges of the Roman empire.

Scythians liked to show a stag being attacked. Romans liked to depict dieties. Peoples across what's now India and Russia liked people in fancy costume.

ASIAN STEPPES
If you're going to ride across the tundra, you're going to want some padding.

FRENTERA
A cord, strap, or chain on the face of the horse that is attached to the crown-piece or browband and runs down the horse's face to the noseband or bit rings.

THE WORLD WEST OF THAT
It stays fairly simple compared to what comes later.

PROMETOPIDION
This is a piece that goes on the face of the horse. It's ornamental.

CHARMS + MEDALLIONS
People loved putting charms on browbands and anywhere else they could punch a hole in their leather. The illustrations of which, have been removed from this book, due to their non-G-rated nature, and I must encourage you, in the strongest possible terms, to not search out these charms from Roman antiquity, because they certainly will not be hilarious. Yes. That's what you really, mustn't do.

75

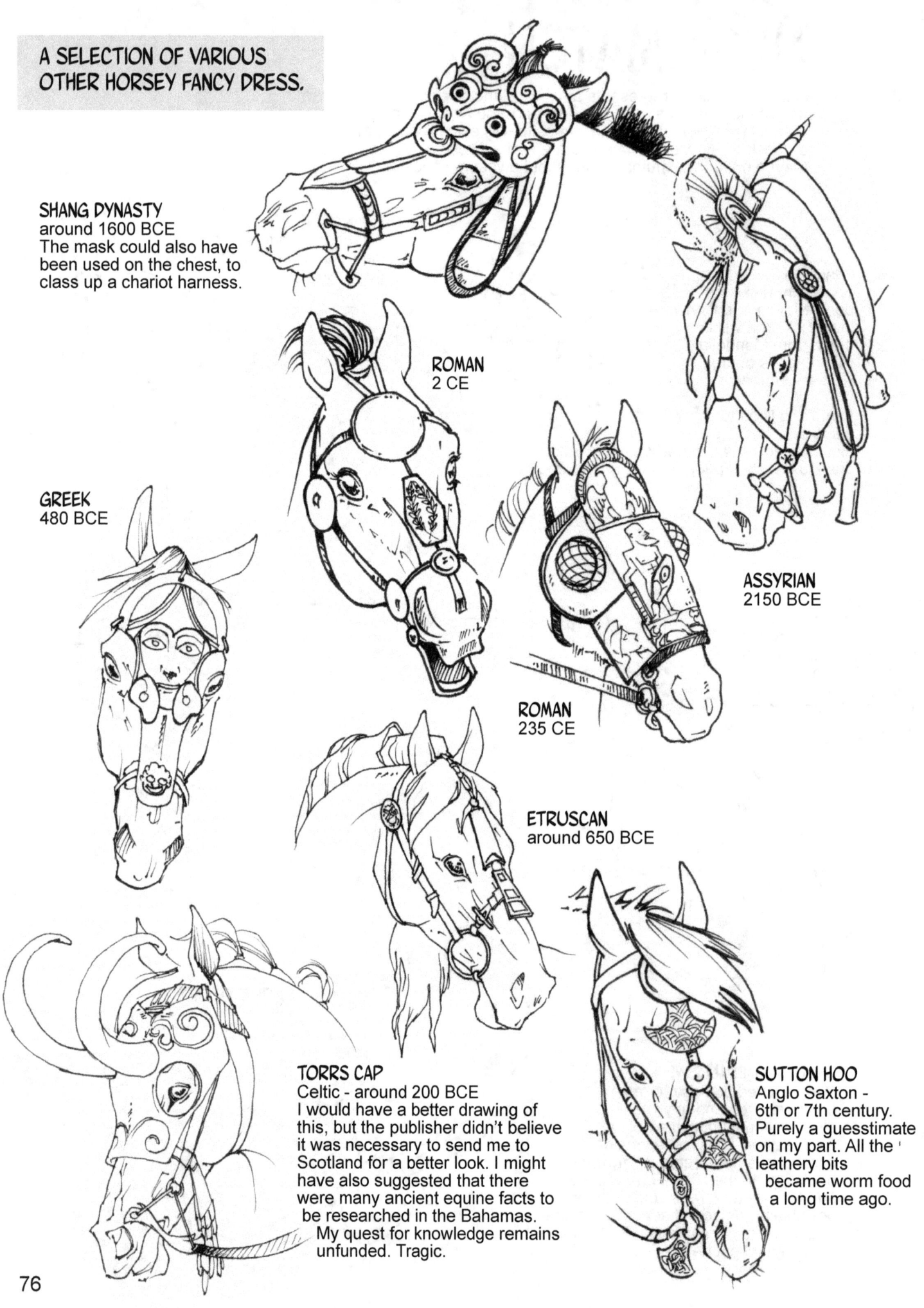

A SELECTION OF VARIOUS OTHER HORSEY FANCY DRESS.

SHANG DYNASTY
around 1600 BCE
The mask could also have been used on the chest, to class up a chariot harness.

ROMAN
2 CE

GREEK
480 BCE

ASSYRIAN
2150 BCE

ROMAN
235 CE

ETRUSCAN
around 650 BCE

TORRS CAP
Celtic - around 200 BCE
I would have a better drawing of this, but the publisher didn't believe it was necessary to send me to Scotland for a better look. I might have also suggested that there were many ancient equine facts to be researched in the Bahamas. My quest for knowledge remains unfunded. Tragic.

SUTTON HOO
Anglo Saxton -
6th or 7th century.
Purely a guesstimate on my part. All the leathery bits became worm food a long time ago.

KOREAN

Once you're through with the non-English speaking ancient empires of the west, you can try not speaking English in the east. The Korean horses likely get the prize for the smallest steeds of East Asia. Gojoseon through the time of the Three Kingdoms would see a fair amount of tiffs in the ongoing power struggle for control of the little peninsula, and the equines will have an important role.

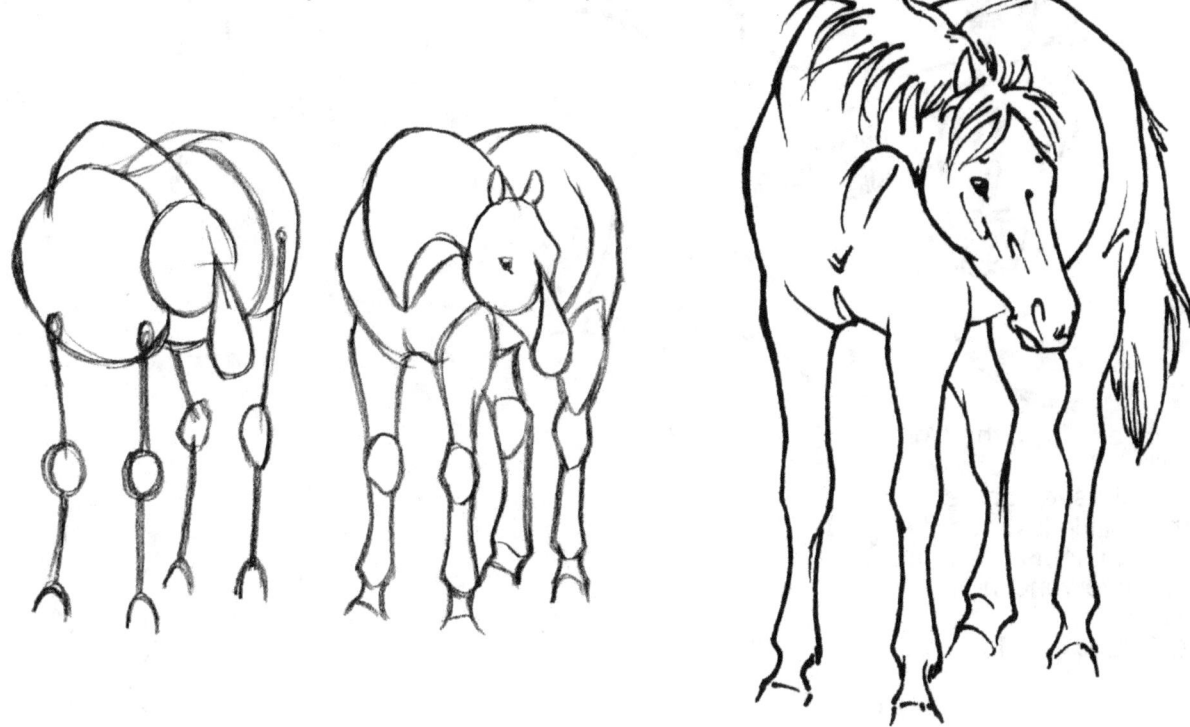

HORSES & PONIES
How we classify horses vs. ponies today is based on conformation. Tough, pretty, and reliable are valuable attributes of equines of any age.

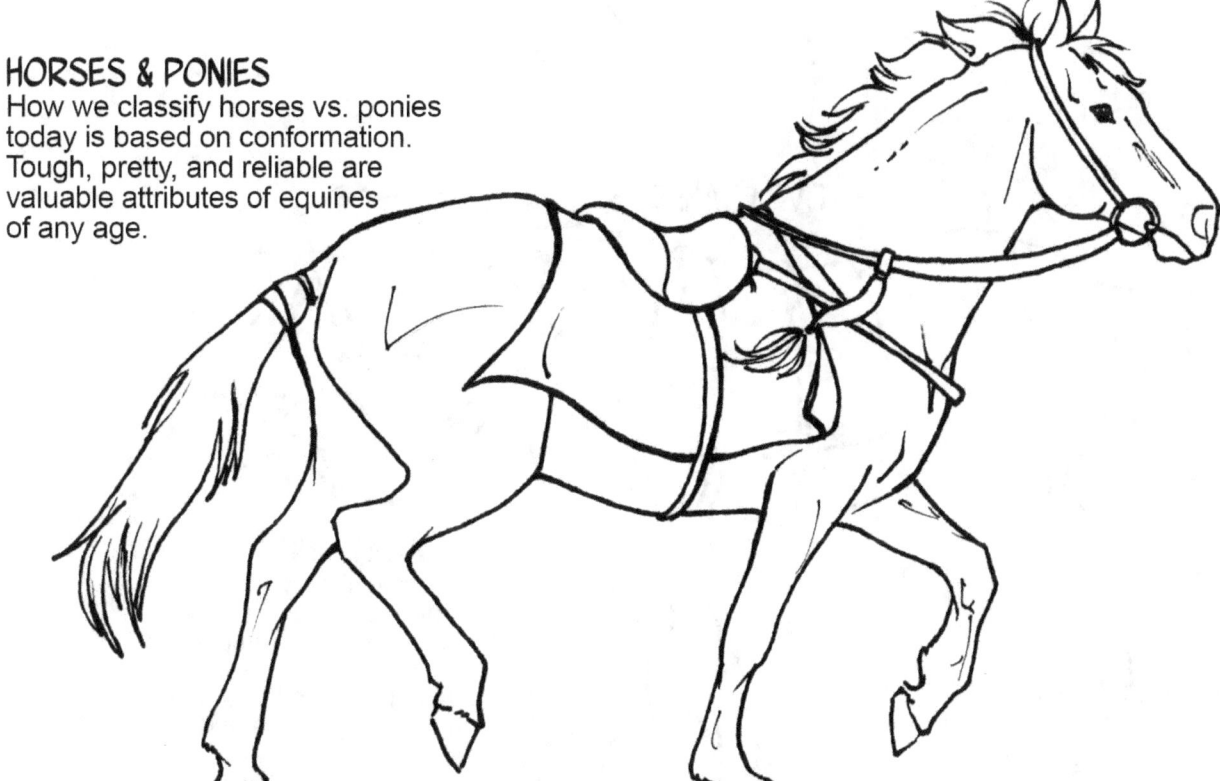

NORTH VS. SOUTH

Today, Korea remains split, with the South having sensational cities and beautiful landscapes, and the North, having the most homicidal dictators who could also win the Elvis-Impersonator-Look-Alike contest.

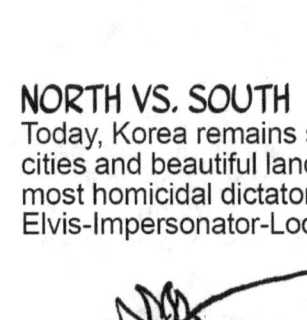

With any luck, the North will ditch nuclear weapons, embrace those little luxuries like human rights and food, and everyone in Korea can ride,...
GANGNAM STYLE!

FESTIVE BLANKETS

BIT & BRIDLE

TRADITIONS

Horses played a meaningful, ceremonial role in Korean tradition. For example, a groom often rides a horse being led with the wedding party, to meet his bride.

CHINA

China has a long love-affair with the horse, as the stout, stocky equines of the life-sized terra-cotta statues from the tomb of Qin Shihuang, first emperor of China, can testify. Thanks to Qin's slight bout of megalomania, we have a peek at what equine life was like in and around 200 BCE.

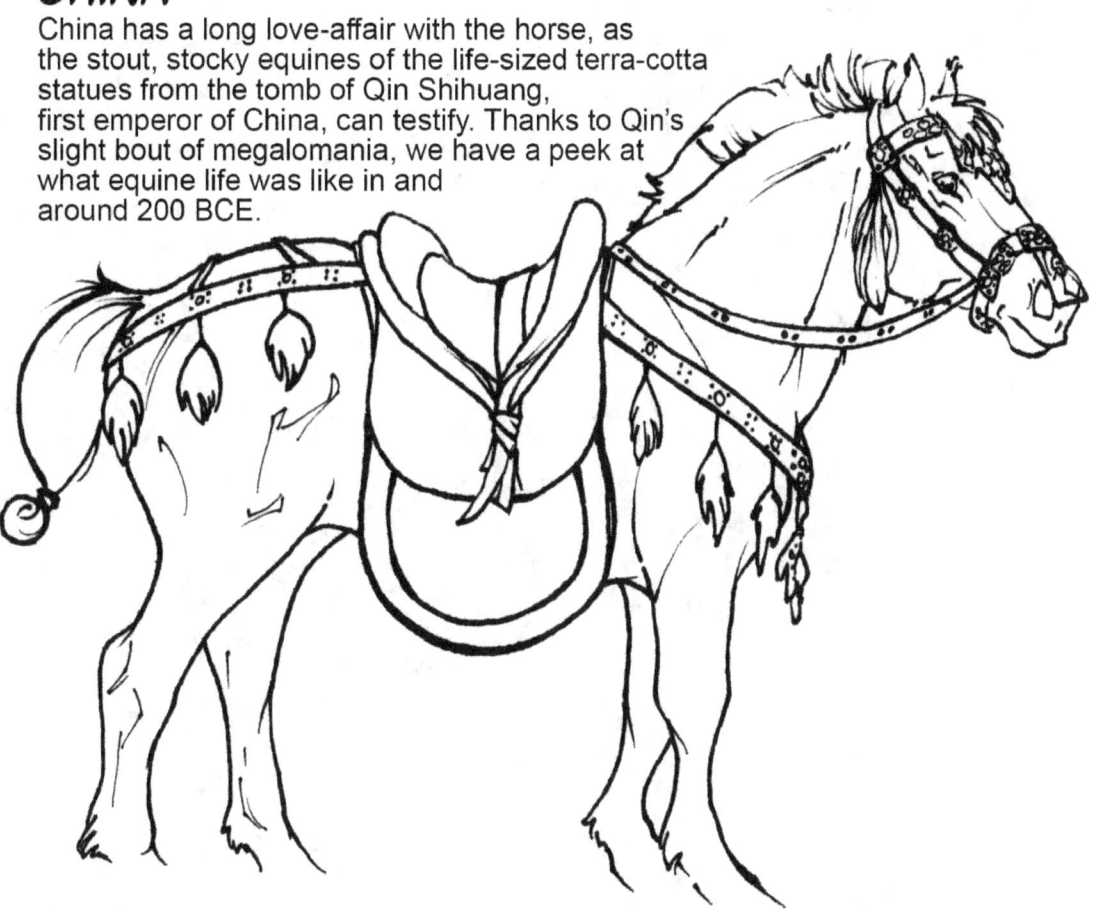

HEAVENLY HORSES

The Ferghana heavenly horses are brought to China around 100 BCE. They are associated with the emperor, and become legendary, often depicted in Chinese art and sculpture.

SADDLE

BIT & BRIDLE

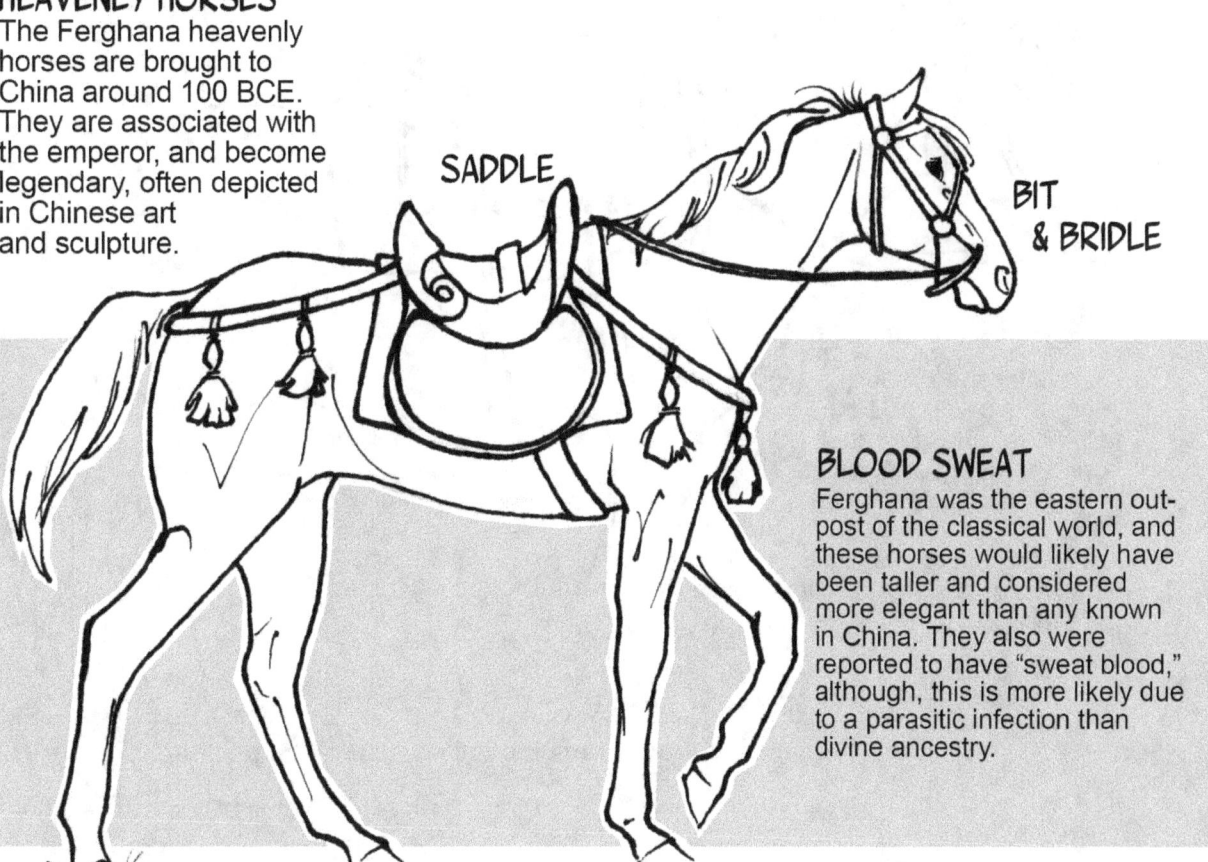

BLOOD SWEAT

Ferghana was the eastern out-post of the classical world, and these horses would likely have been taller and considered more elegant than any known in China. They also were reported to have "sweat blood," although, this is more likely due to a parasitic infection than divine ancestry.

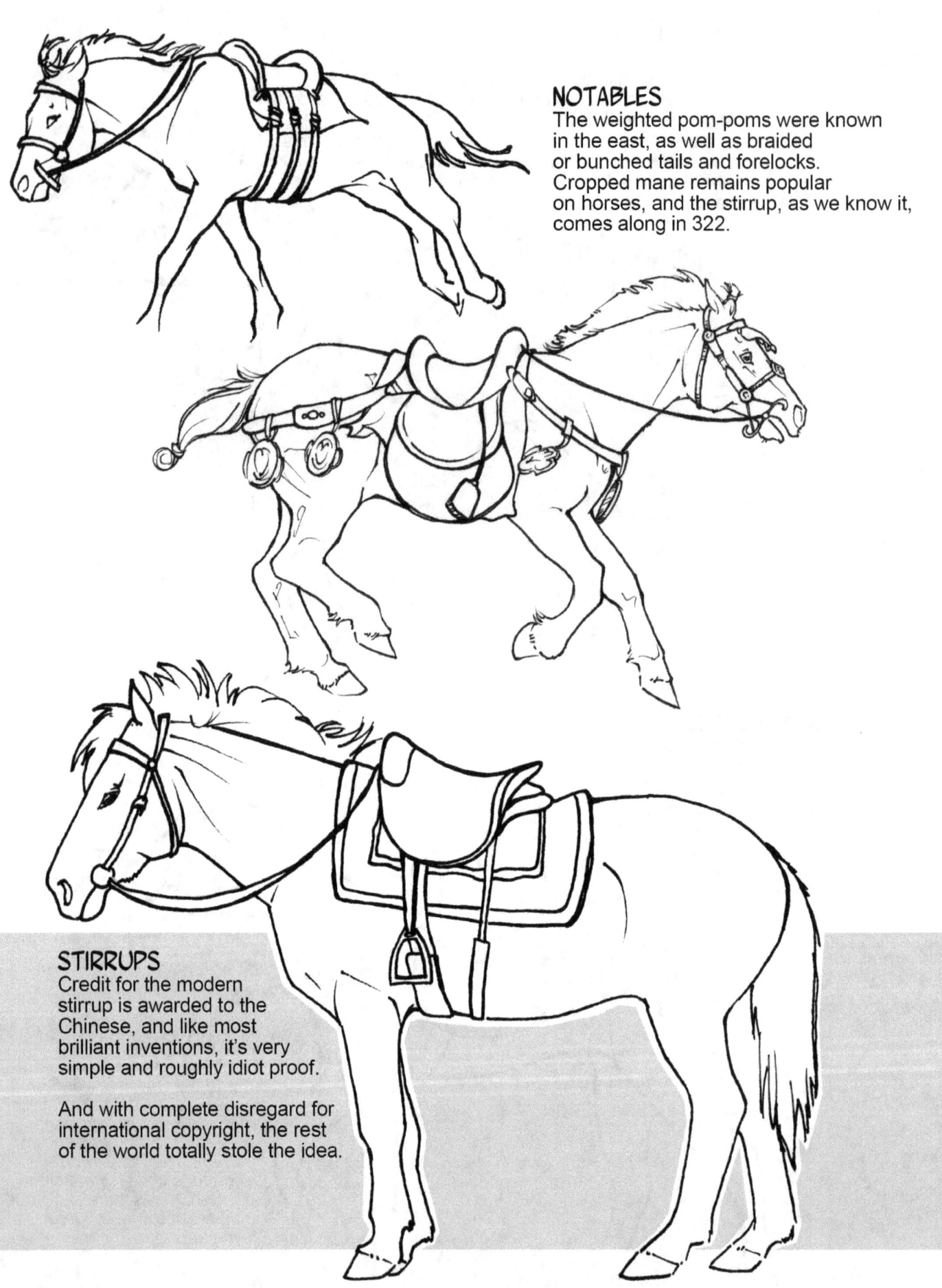

NOTABLES
The weighted pom-poms were known
in the east, as well as braided
or bunched tails and forelocks.
Cropped mane remains popular
on horses, and the stirrup, as we know it,
comes along in 322.

STIRRUPS
Credit for the modern
stirrup is awarded to the
Chinese, and like most
brilliant inventions, it's very
simple and roughly idiot proof.

And with complete disregard for
international copyright, the rest
of the world totally stole the idea.

JAPANESE

"Uma", pronounced "ooo-mah", is the word for horse in Japanese. Although there is evidence for horses earlier, they don't start to factor a role until around the 4th century, with imports coming from China and Korea.

JAPANESE CHEAT-SHEET

KURA - Generic word for saddle

AORI - Leather saddle flaps

CHIKARA-GAWA - Stirrup straps

BAKIN - Padding behind the kura, covers the shirigai

SHIRIGAI - Crupper

ABUMI - Stirrups

KUTSUWA - Bit

KIRITSUKE - Saddle blanket

MUCHI - Whip

MUNAGAI - Breast collar

OMOGAI - Bridle

TAZUNA - Reins

OBUKURO - Tail cover

SHIODE - Tie downs from the four points of the kura

UMA
AGEMAKE - Tassels that attach to the kura

SANJAKUGAWA - Two, leather straps which attach to the bridle. Prevents the bridle from slipping over the ears.

KUFON ERA

Often lumped together with other eras and called the Yamato period, around the 3rd to 7th century, shiploads of immigrants are coming over to Japan from China and Korea, and bringing their stallions, broodmares, trainers, and technology with them. Horses look the part of the stocky-built, steppes until lighter ponies and horses are imported later.

7TH CENTURY STYLE
A brilliant find in Koga, Fukuoka Prefecture,
has given modern eyes the first full set of trappings
and ornaments from a war horse. Buried for centuries,
the bronze pieces and other national treasures are
truly the knees of the bees.

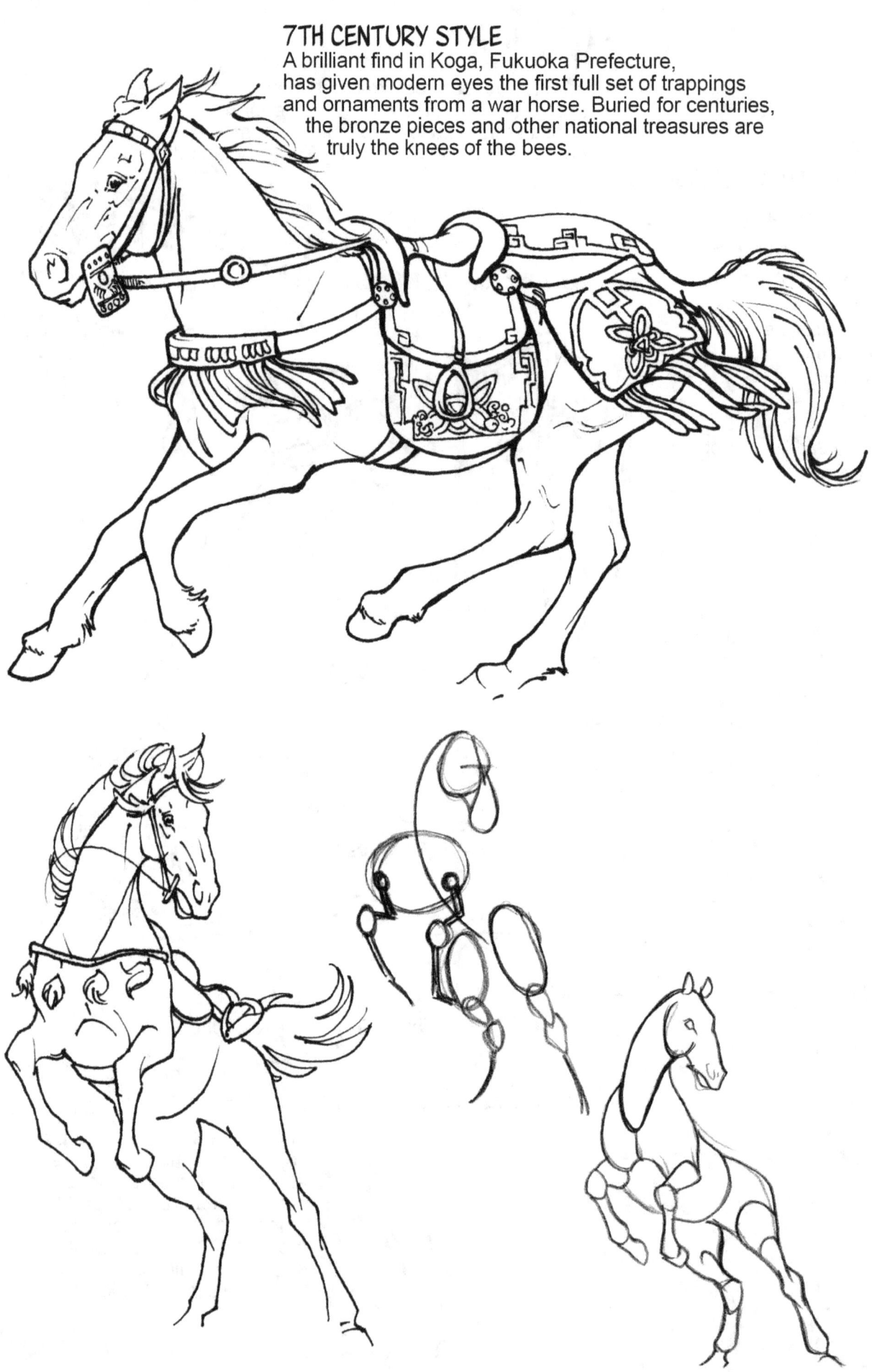

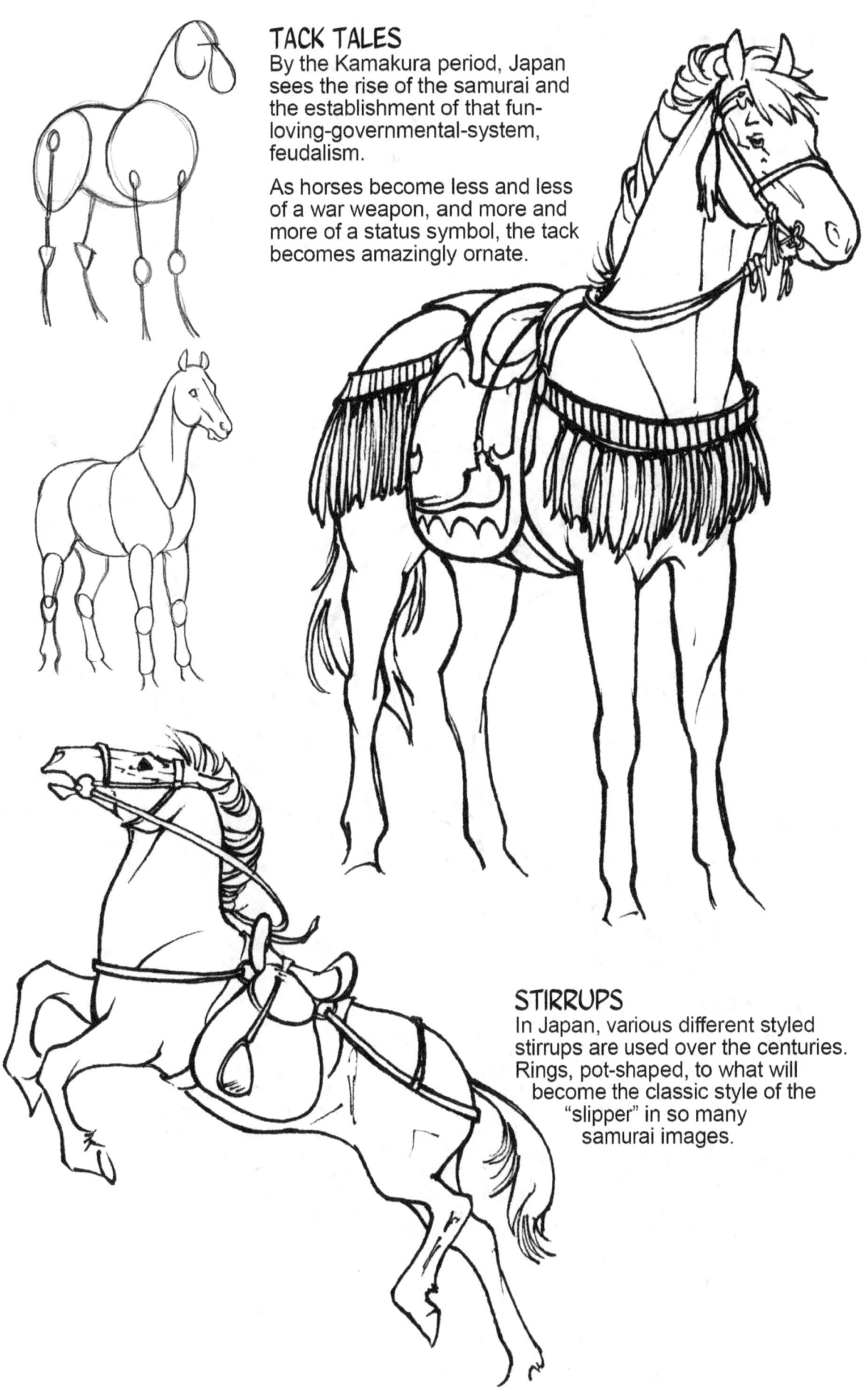

TACK TALES

By the Kamakura period, Japan sees the rise of the samurai and the establishment of that fun-loving-governmental-system, feudalism.

As horses become less and less of a war weapon, and more and more of a status symbol, the tack becomes amazingly ornate.

STIRRUPS

In Japan, various different styled stirrups are used over the centuries. Rings, pot-shaped, to what will become the classic style of the "slipper" in so many samurai images.

MONGOLIA

The nomadic peoples of this area become a unified force under the khan. Khan is a genetically engineered, super-baddie who wants revenge on Kirk, and in the process, steals the Genesis Device... wait. No. That's the plot of Star Trek II. Wrong Khan.

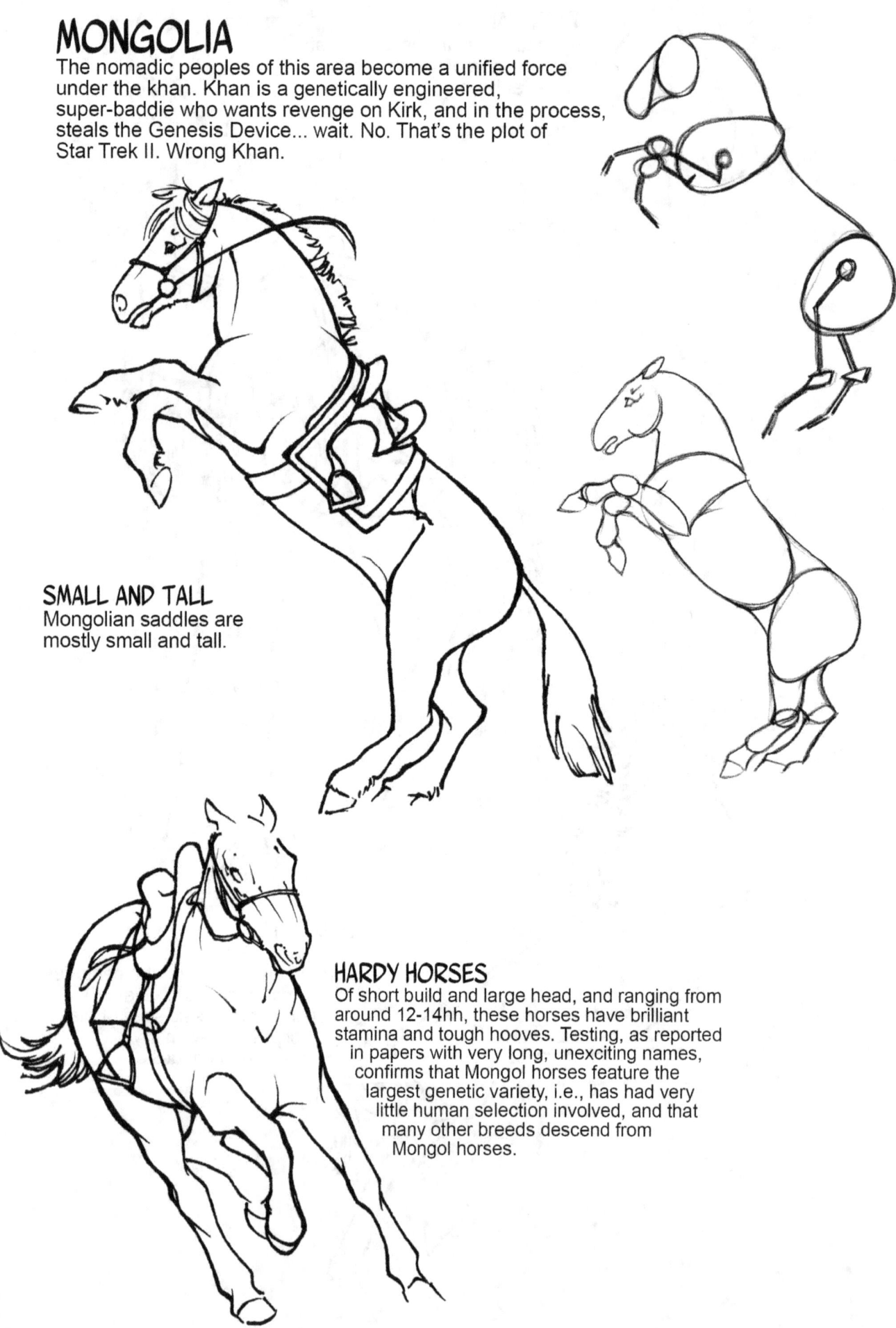

SMALL AND TALL
Mongolian saddles are mostly small and tall.

HARDY HORSES
Of short build and large head, and ranging from around 12-14hh, these horses have brilliant stamina and tough hooves. Testing, as reported in papers with very long, unexciting names, confirms that Mongol horses feature the largest genetic variety, i.e., has had very little human selection involved, and that many other breeds descend from Mongol horses.

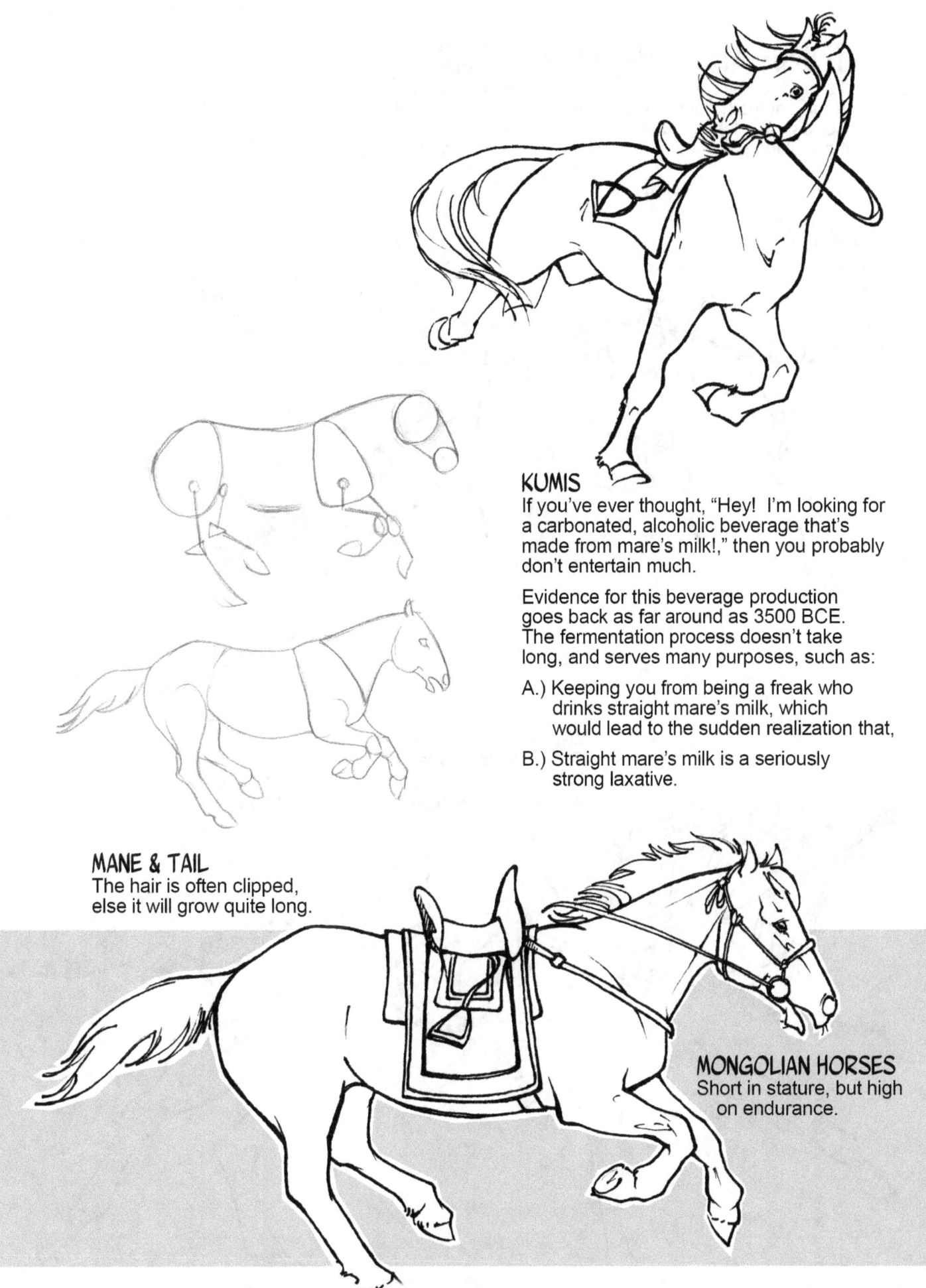

KUMIS

If you've ever thought, "Hey! I'm looking for a carbonated, alcoholic beverage that's made from mare's milk!," then you probably don't entertain much.

Evidence for this beverage production goes back as far around as 3500 BCE. The fermentation process doesn't take long, and serves many purposes, such as:

A.) Keeping you from being a freak who drinks straight mare's milk, which would lead to the sudden realization that,

B.) Straight mare's milk is a seriously strong laxative.

MANE & TAIL
The hair is often clipped, else it will grow quite long.

MONGOLIAN HORSES
Short in stature, but high on endurance.

INDIA AND THE SILK ROAD

It's hard to keep a good thing a secret for long, and while empires
come and go, people always have a taste for the good life.
Goods, peoples, and the ideas that came and went with them make up
the melting pot of miles between Eastern Asia and Western Europe.

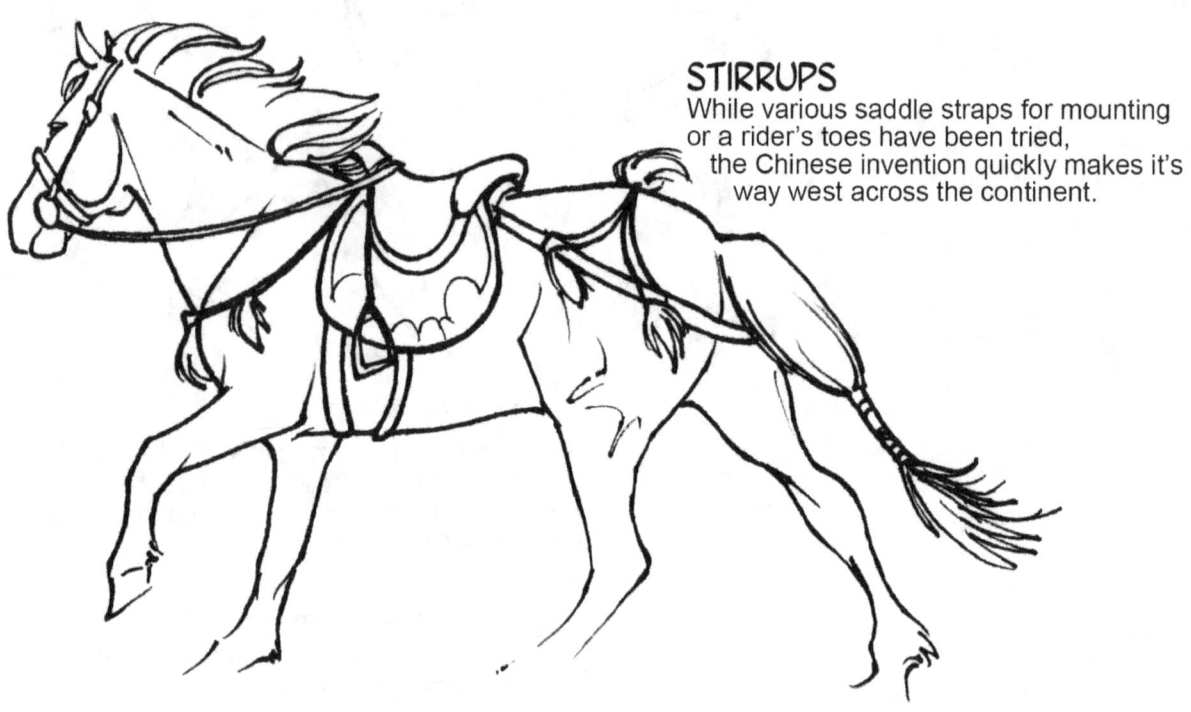

STIRRUPS

While various saddle straps for mounting
or a rider's toes have been tried,
 the Chinese invention quickly makes it's
  way west across the continent.

INDIAN INFLUENCE

Only in a place where riding elephants is the
height of showmanship, could you possibly
argue that keeping a horse was economical.

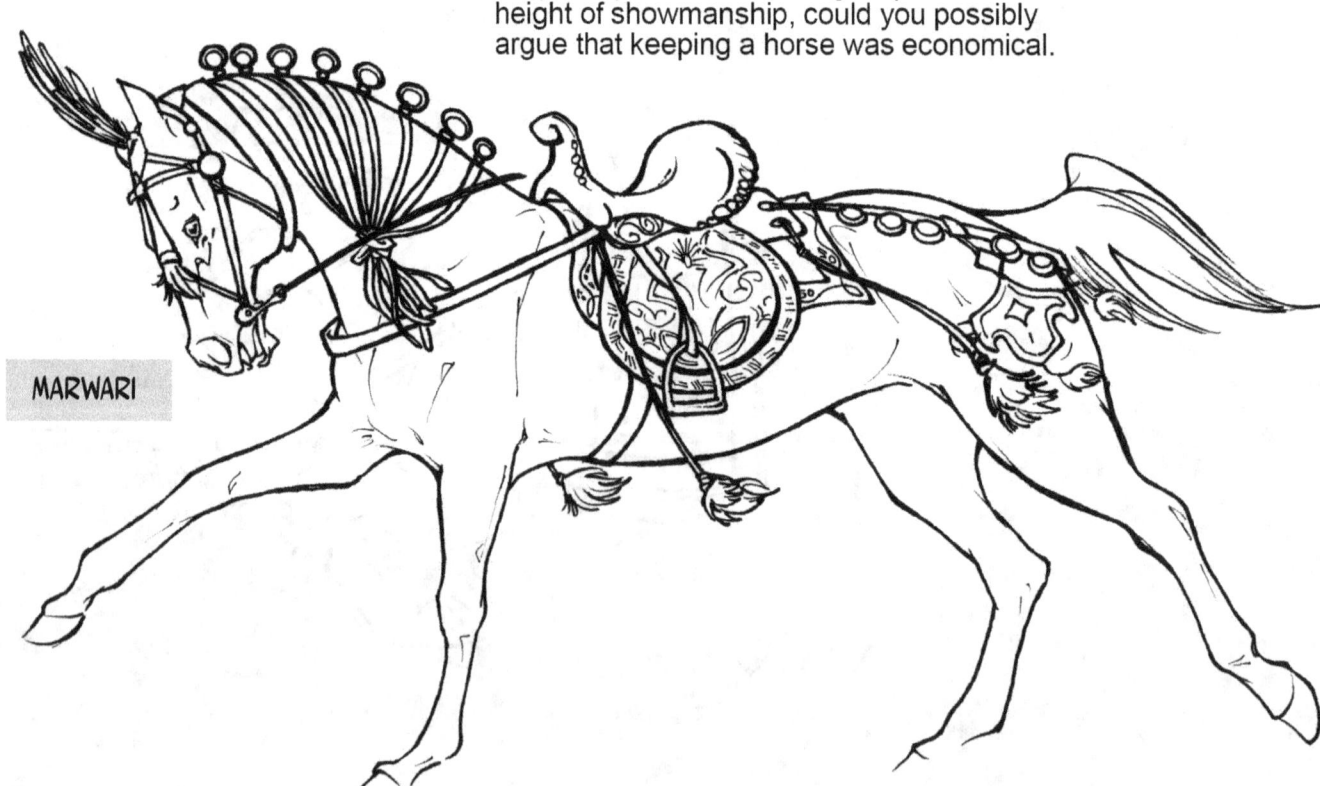

MARWARI

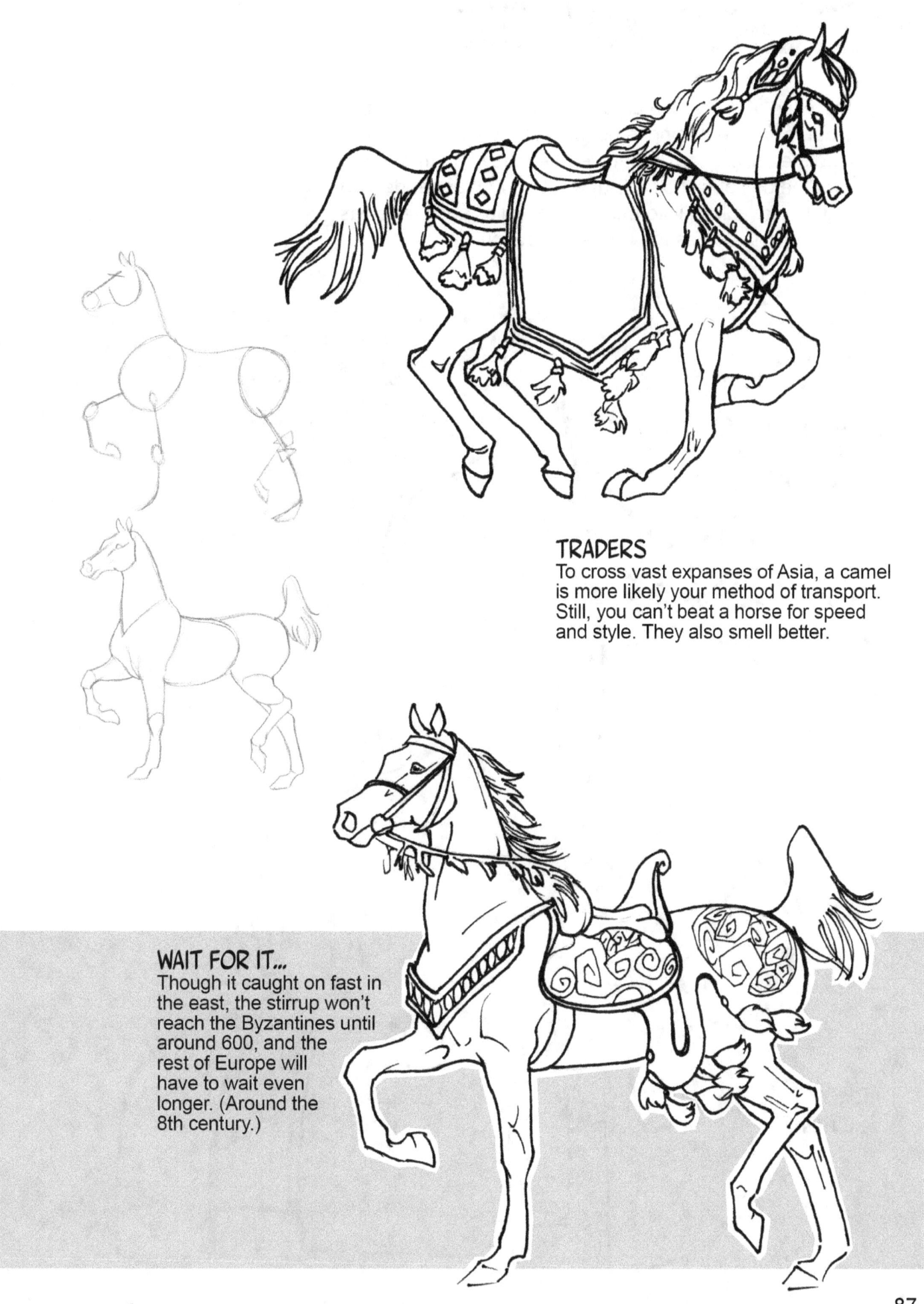

TRADERS
To cross vast expanses of Asia, a camel is more likely your method of transport. Still, you can't beat a horse for speed and style. They also smell better.

WAIT FOR IT...
Though it caught on fast in the east, the stirrup won't reach the Byzantines until around 600, and the rest of Europe will have to wait even longer. (Around the 8th century.)

HISTORIC ARMOR

First accounts of protection amount to amulets and spells, but it turns out that well-wishing is not so effective against arrows, swords, pointed sticks, and whatever else they can throw at you. Armor was the obvious choice. But what sort? It depended on cost, weight, available skill to make it, flexibility, and what was likely to be coming across the battlefield at you.

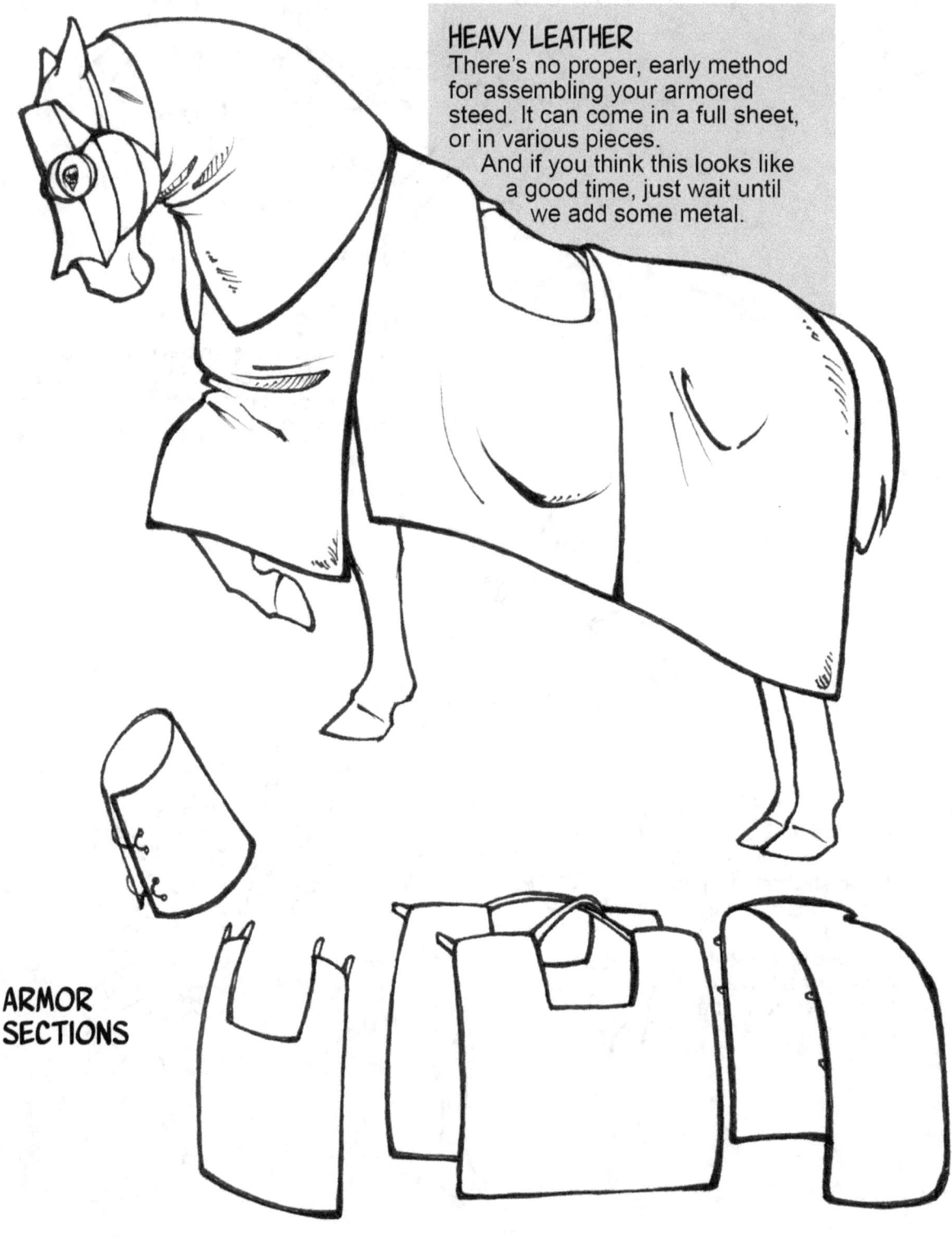

HEAVY LEATHER
There's no proper, early method for assembling your armored steed. It can come in a full sheet, or in various pieces.
 And if you think this looks like a good time, just wait until we add some metal.

ARMOR
SECTIONS

SUIT UP

The best way to put your armor together was a flexible idea. No matter how you choose to mix and match, the intention of the material is to prevent, or at least lessen, serious damage. Leather, historians say, was commonly used, but this is of course nonsense. What the ancients really needed was the most powerful, unmovable force in the universe, as seen from a photograph of my mother in the 1970s: Hair Spray.

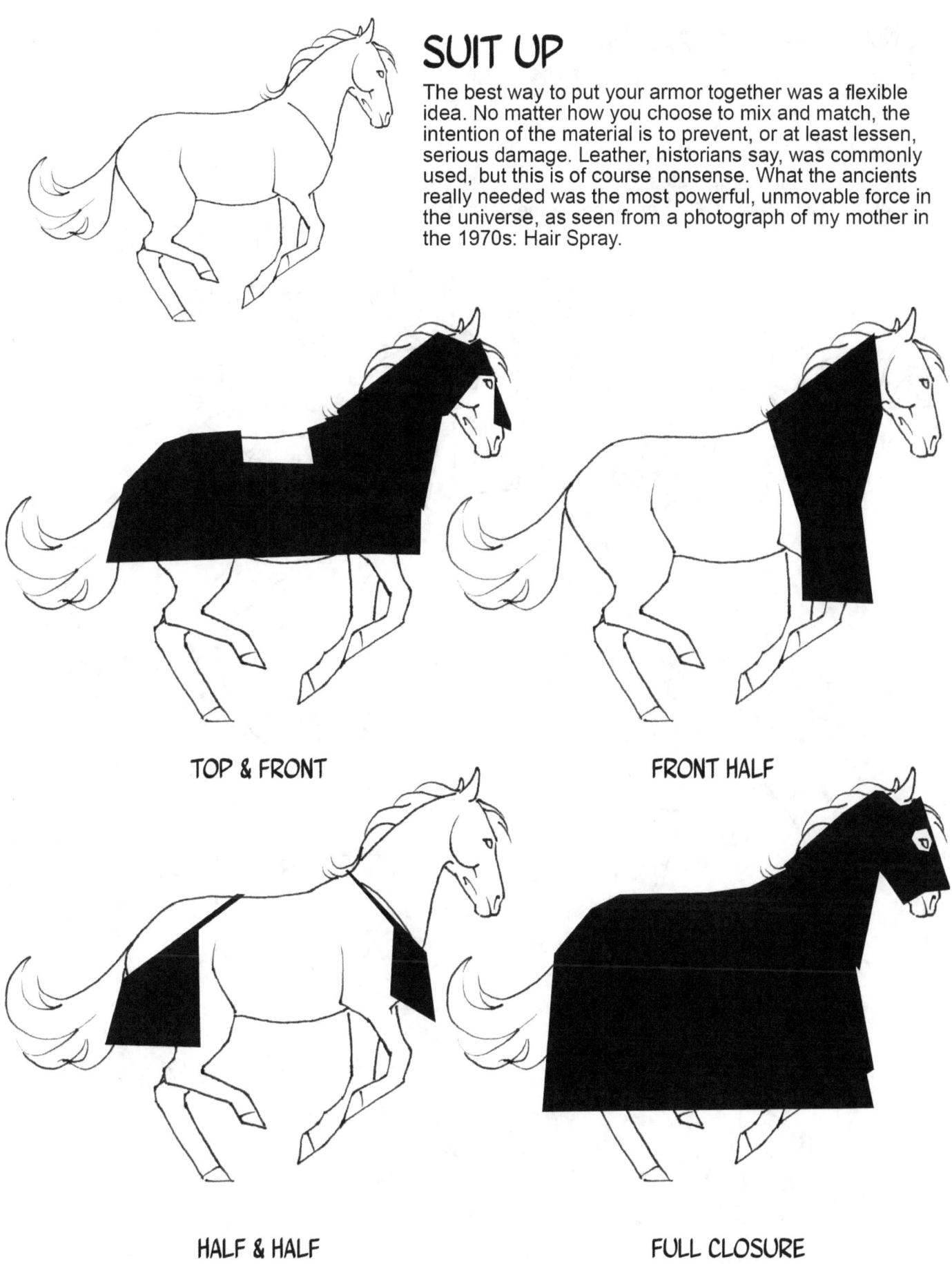

TOP & FRONT

FRONT HALF

HALF & HALF

FULL CLOSURE

UNDERSTANDING ARMOR

There are three, basic designs you need be familiar
with when it comes to equine armors and recall,
that you can mix and match:

LAMELLAR ~ Think little plates.
LAMINAR ~ Think large plates.
SCALE ~ Think Global. Everybody has some version.

LAMELLAR
This has horizontal plates,
laced together for protection.

JAPANESE BARDING

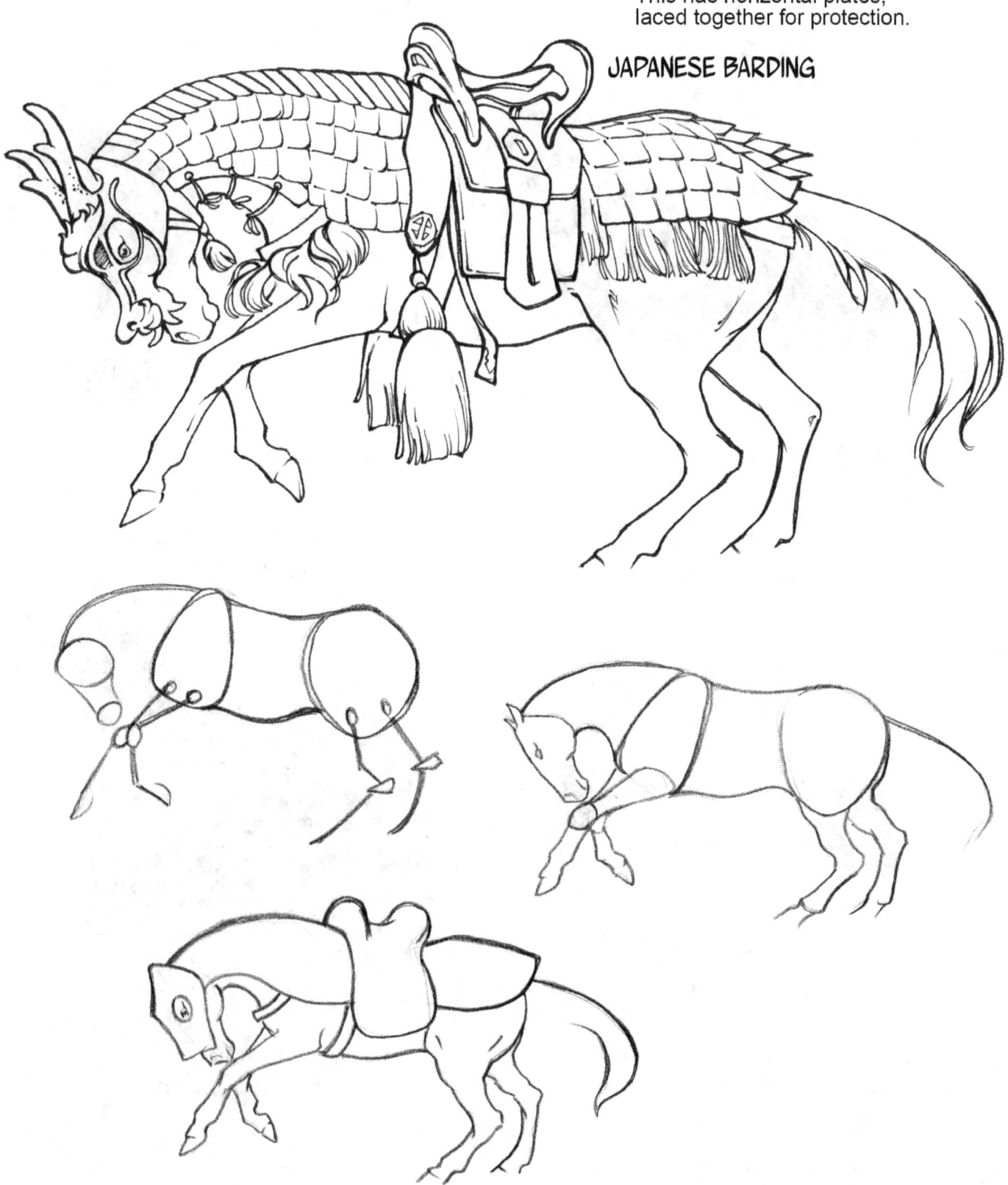

LAMINAR

These are horizontal rows of pates, which overlap. Romans were not early adopters of horse armor, but many of the people that they conquered, such as the Celts, who are credited with creating mail, were a tish more inclined towards protection.

CRINET

While Roman emperors were busy being killed to death by their own troops around the 2nd-3rd centuries AD, their horses sport this sort of look, mostly minus the crinet.

Crinet won't become more common until we get into the middle ages.

LEATHER REAR GUARD

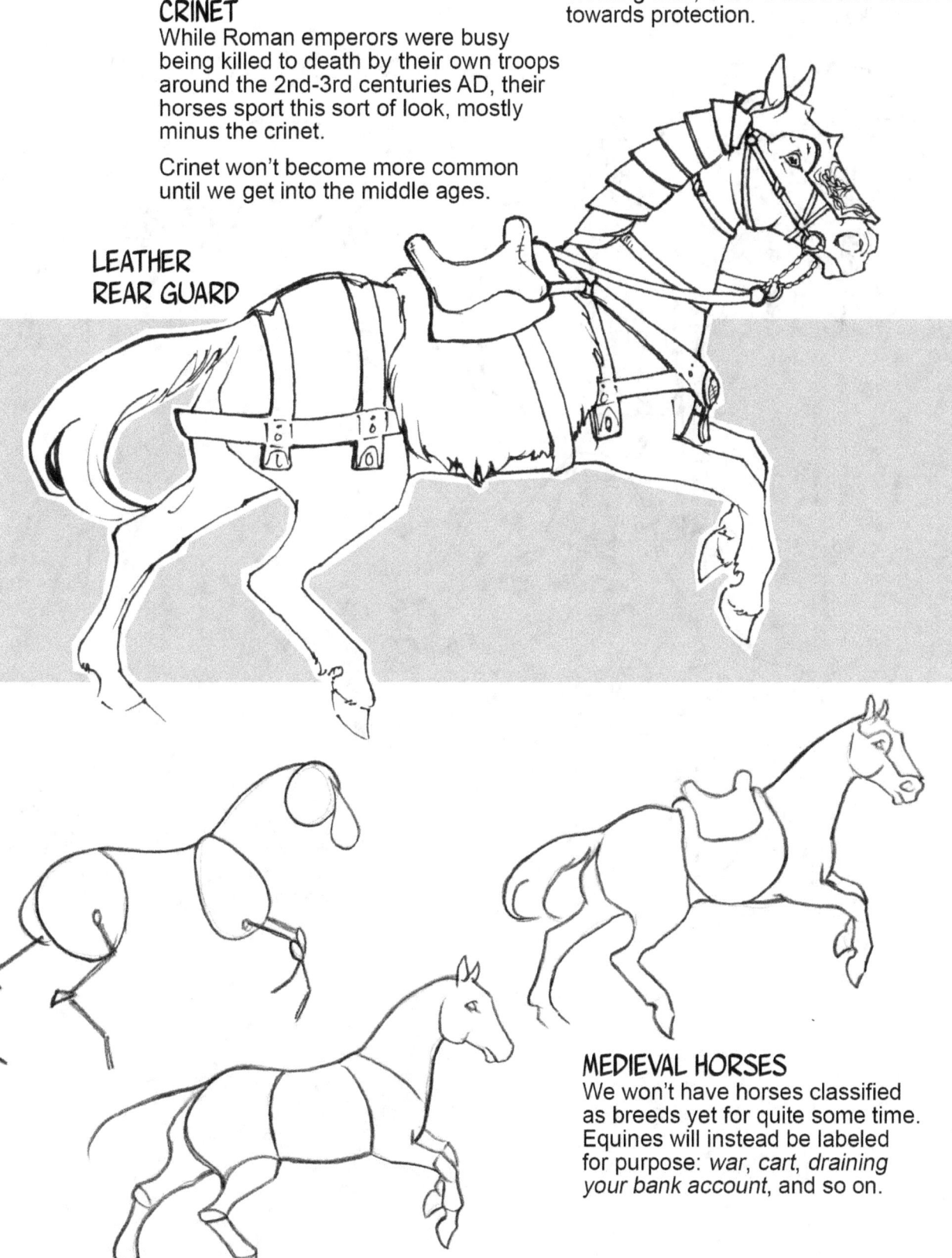

MEDIEVAL HORSES

We won't have horses classified as breeds yet for quite some time. Equines will instead be labeled for purpose: *war*, *cart*, *draining your bank account*, and so on.

SCALE

These are universally diverse plates/scales which are sewn onto a backing and overlap. As light cavalry, it's a good investment. Unless you're in full gear, somewhere quite warm. In which case, I assume you would cook like a bun on a stove.

PERSIAN CATAPHRACT – LIGHT CAVALRY

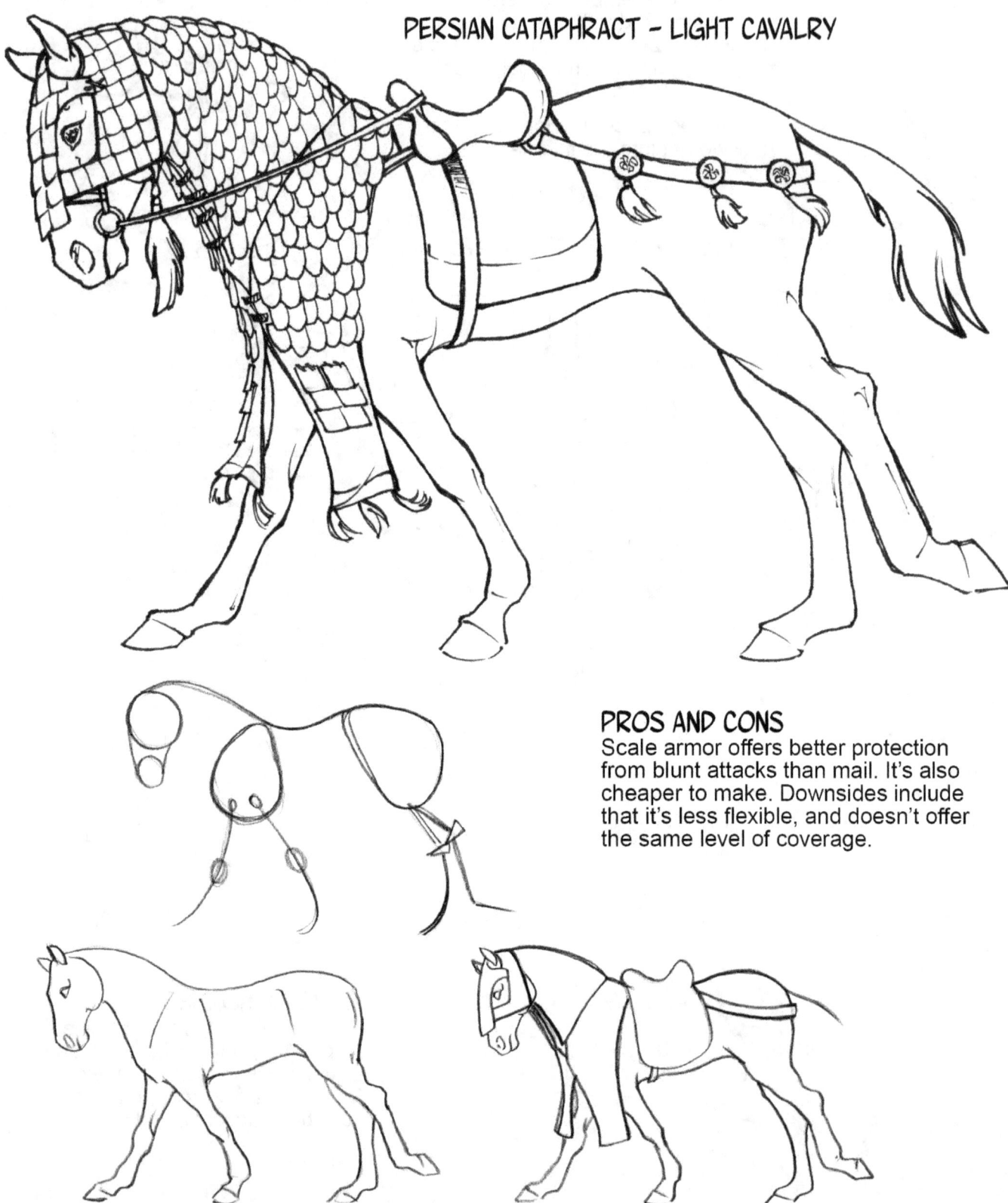

PROS AND CONS

Scale armor offers better protection from blunt attacks than mail. It's also cheaper to make. Downsides include that it's less flexible, and doesn't offer the same level of coverage.

BIT + REINS

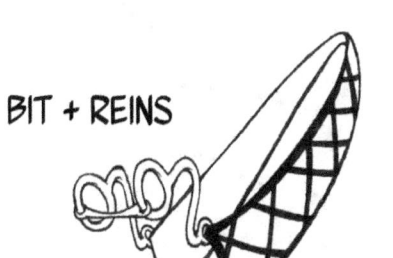

MEDIEVAL BARDING
Everyone is in love with the gear that comes out of the late middle ages. The trouble is, there's not a lot of surviving examples of it about. This combination of mail, leather, and plate is designed to keep you alive, not to be light or comfortable.

The truth is, most of this gear is in response to that other brilliant, medieval invention, the longbow.

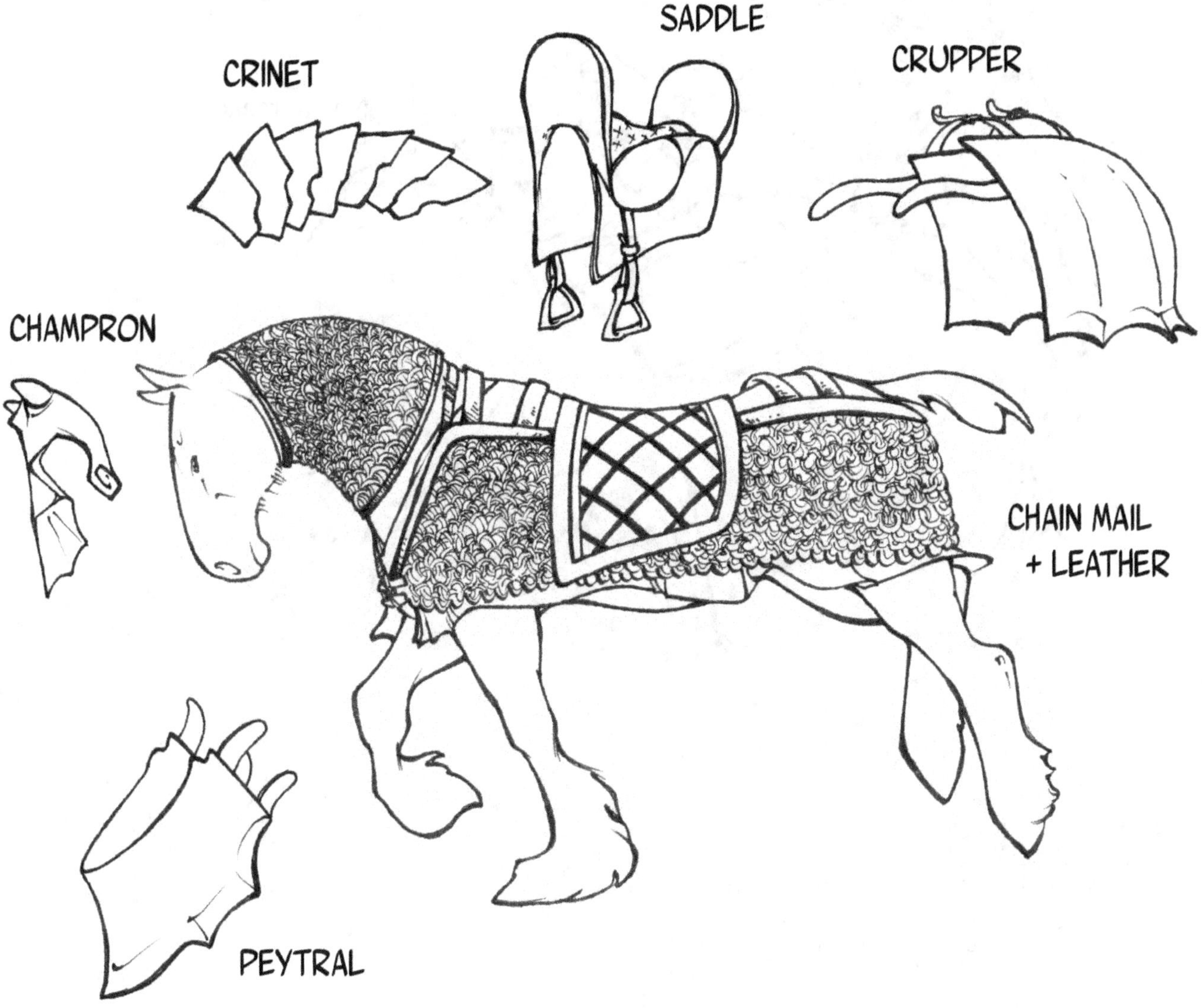

SADDLE

CRINET

CRUPPER

CHAMPRON

CHAIN MAIL + LEATHER

PEYTRAL

MEDIEVAL HORSES
Most people who read this will know that the Belgians, Percherons and other really large draft breeds were bred for agriculture, not to be knight's horses, but I'll repeat that fact anyway.

I agree, they look great playing the part in the movies, and I know I'm going to get another email about it, but for the record: not really medieval horses.

WHY FEATHERS?
Things aren't always as they are now.

Many stocky, medieval-times horses had some feathering. Over time, the desires changed from the need for destriers, palfreys, coursers, and rouncies. Just about any modern breed can fit into the broad characterizations of the middle ages, and nearly all horses will grow longer hair on the lower legs and back of the fetlocks at times. We just don't call it feathers.

So. In that overly wordy way, that's "why feathers."

MYTHOLOGY

There is not an academically agreed upon definition of what expounds a religion vs. mythology.

So however you might personally define it, please remember that it would be really ridiculous to blow up the Internet because of a joke in a how-to-draw-horses book.

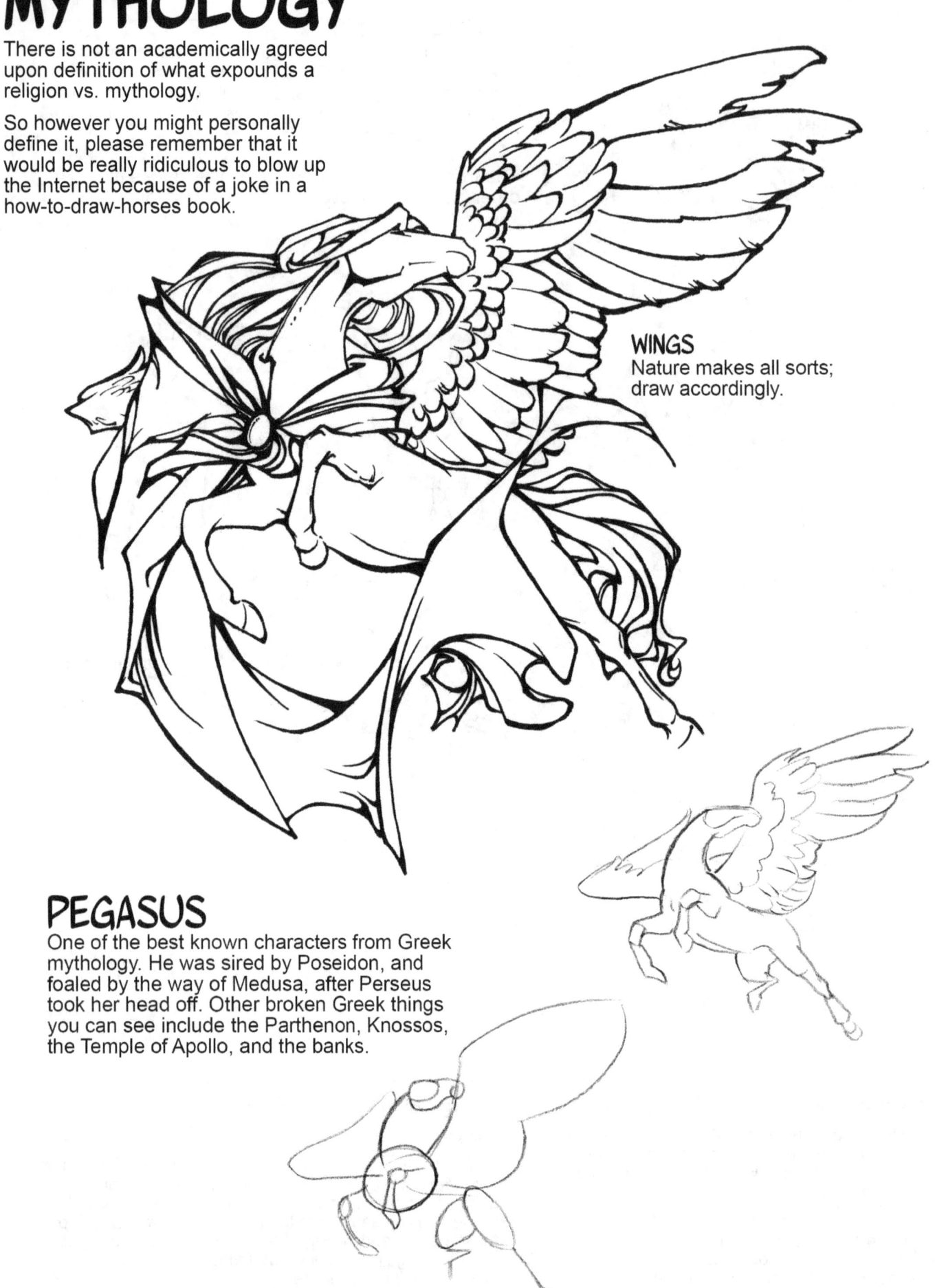

WINGS
Nature makes all sorts; draw accordingly.

PEGASUS
One of the best known characters from Greek mythology. He was sired by Poseidon, and foaled by the way of Medusa, after Perseus took her head off. Other broken Greek things you can see include the Parthenon, Knossos, the Temple of Apollo, and the banks.

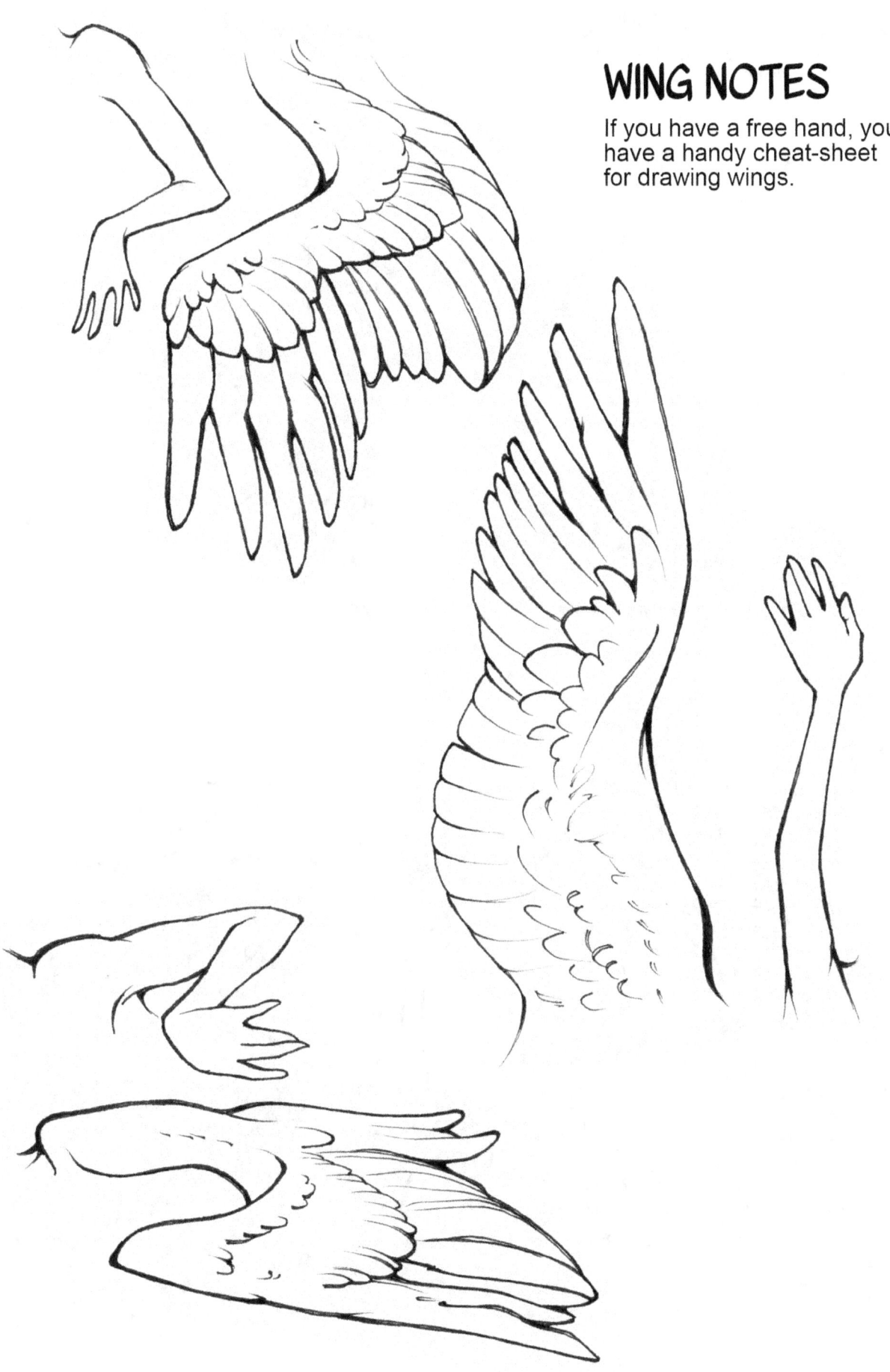

WING NOTES

If you have a free hand, you have a handy cheat-sheet for drawing wings.

BALIUS + XANTHUS

These horses were a gift that Achilles took to draw his chariot during the Trojan War.
Like you do.

HORSES OF HELIOS

These horses pulled the sun chariot, but it's a matter
of who you ask as to what they were called.*

HOMER: Abraxas, Therbeeo

OVID: Pyrois, Eous, Aethon, and Phlegon

EUMELUS OF CORINTH: Eous, Aethiops - males and trace horses;
Bronte, Sterope - female, and yoked

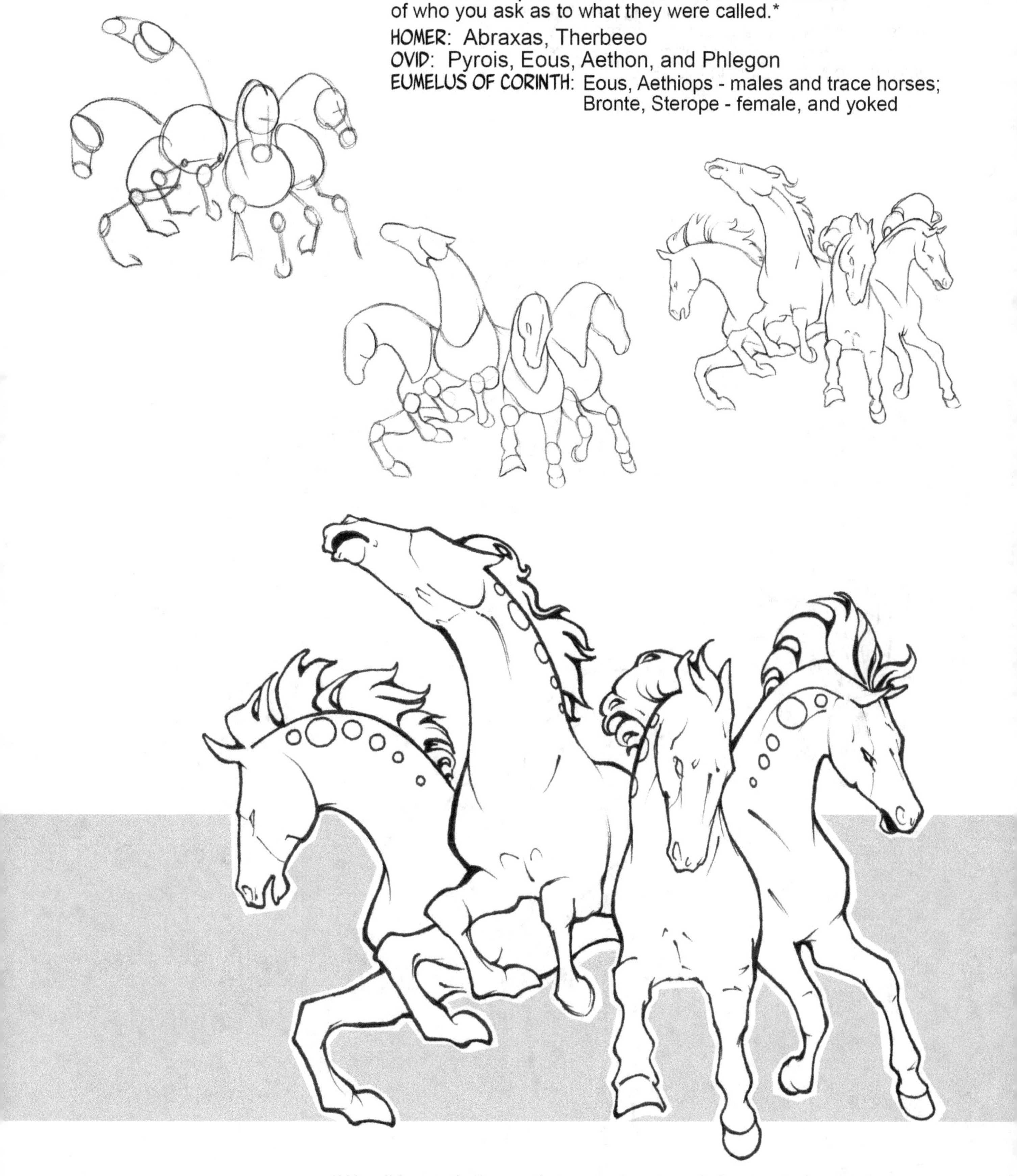

*We all know that over the centuries, translations get changed.

ARION

Sired by Poseidon* and foaled by Demeter in some versions, or Gaia in others. The big points about Arion were that he was extremely fast, immortal, which comes in handy, and went on to have a career advertising Mitsubishis in the 1980s.

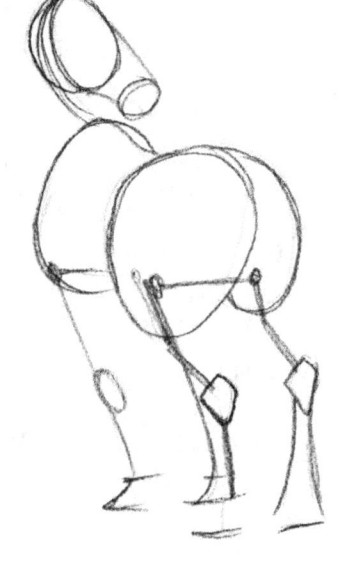

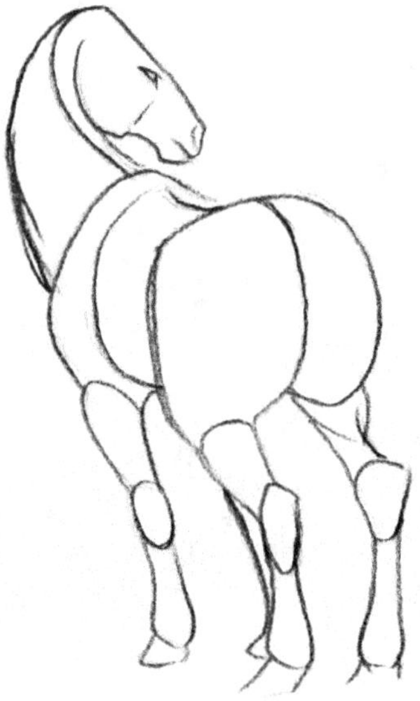

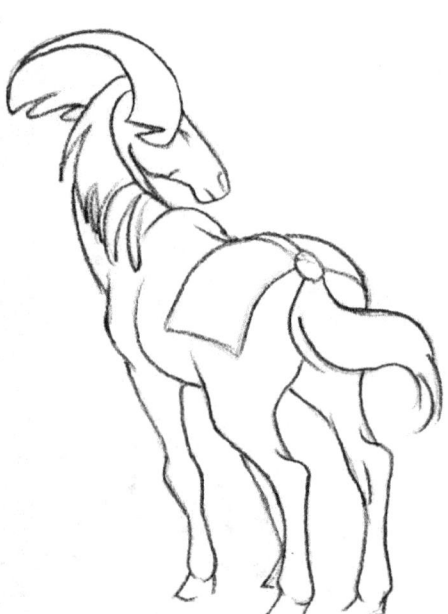

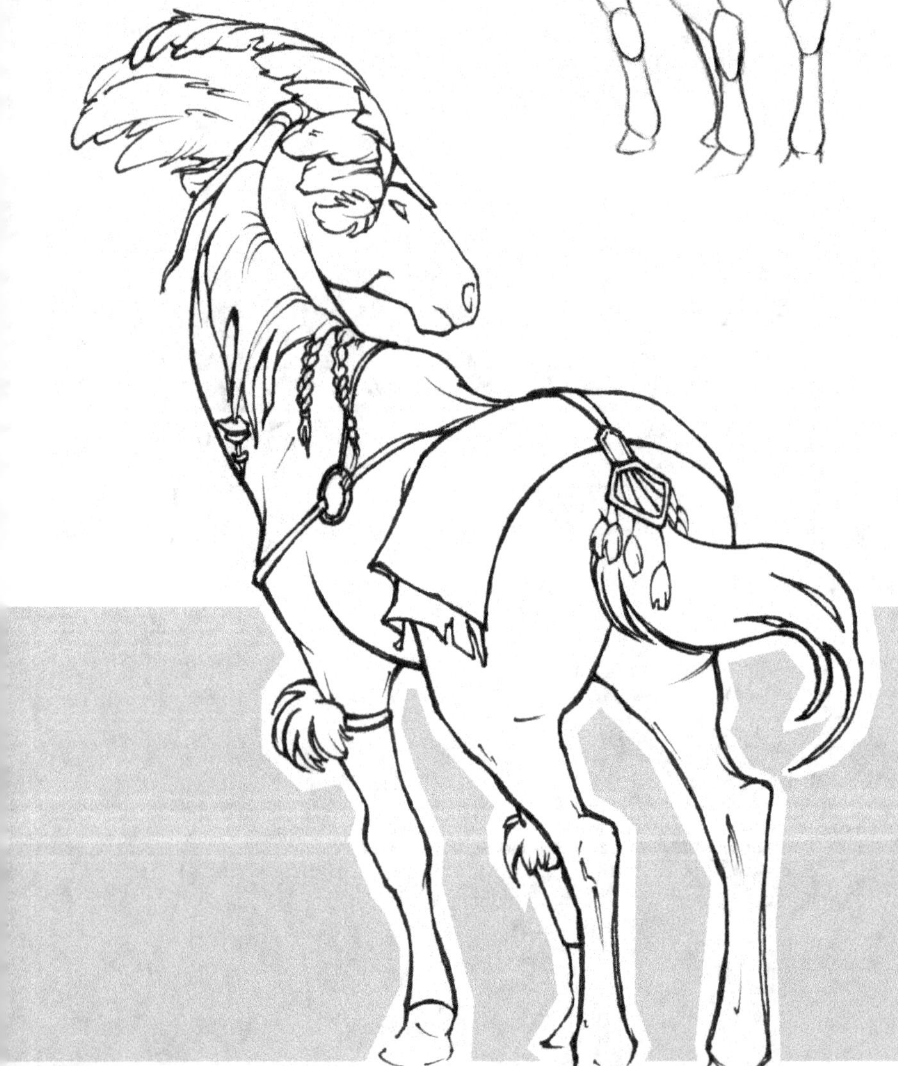

*The gods did a lot of "siring."

MARES OF DIOMEDES

These mares were a bit exciteable and had the unusual habit of eating people. Which probably means their advert read "Fun to Ride!" (Assuming you're a thrill-seeker.)

All versions of the story involve Hercules showing up, Diomedes, the giant-king of Thrace going down, and nobody really mentioning the mares much after that.

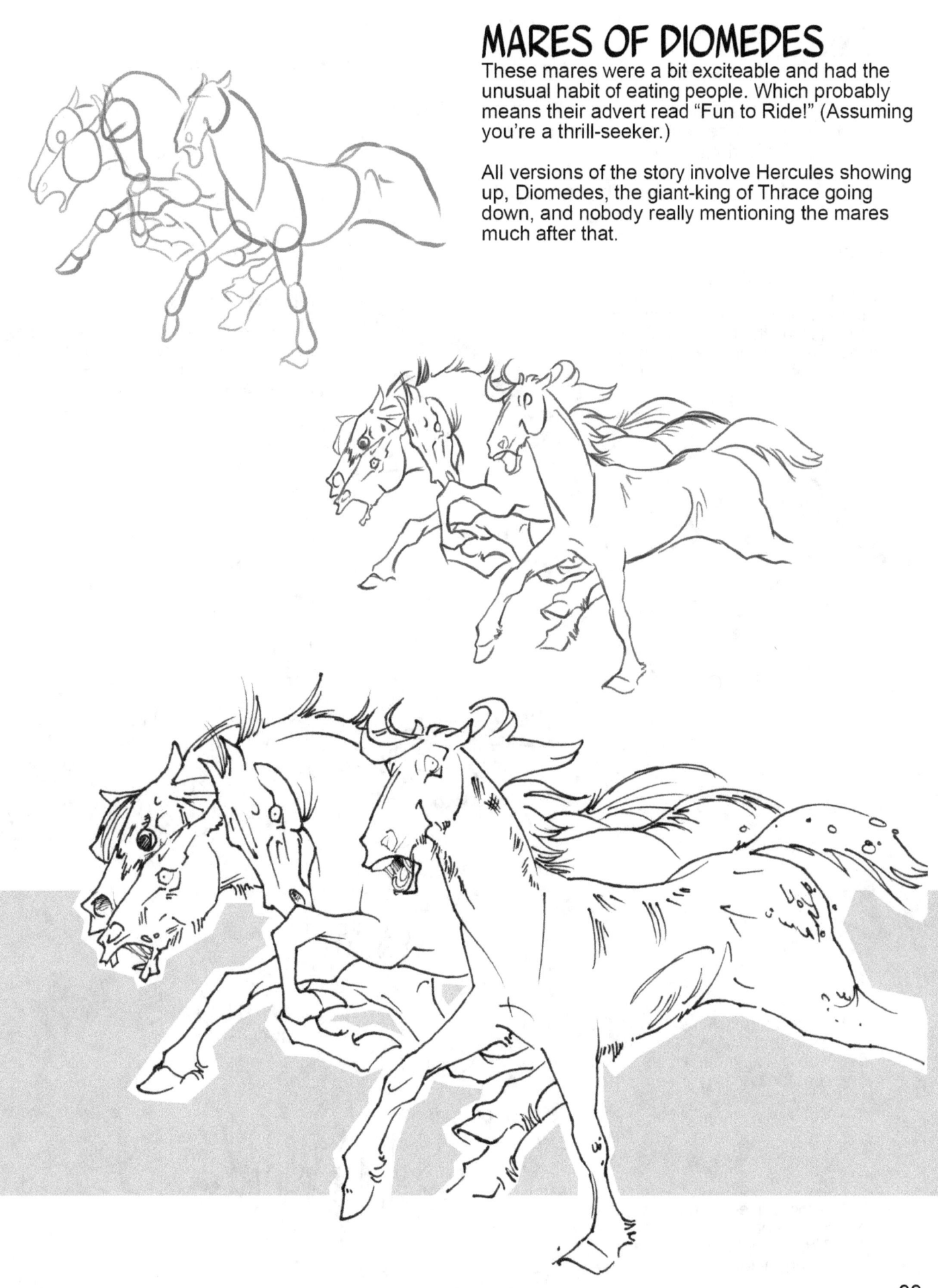

UNICORN

Every culture has some version of this beauty. It has had so many makeovers and comes in so many versions that much like pizza toppings, no two people in the same room are going to agree on what's right.

Let your imagination run free. The ancients did.

GREEKS

Greek writers had them in India, being red, black, and white, although Strabo, centuries later, says that in the Caucasus there were one-horned horses with stag-like heads. Then again, Strabo says a lot of stuff.*

MEDIEVAL EUROPE

People kept the horsey-goatish-wild ass idea, but added lore and romance to the tale. The pure-white characteristics get added to later versions.

CHINESE

Qilins looks more chimeras with the body of a deer, the head of a lion, scales and a long-curved horn. They often have fishy whiskers too.

*If this looks like a wild ass with a horn on the front of it's face, that's because it is. The ancients were also fond of describing rhinos.

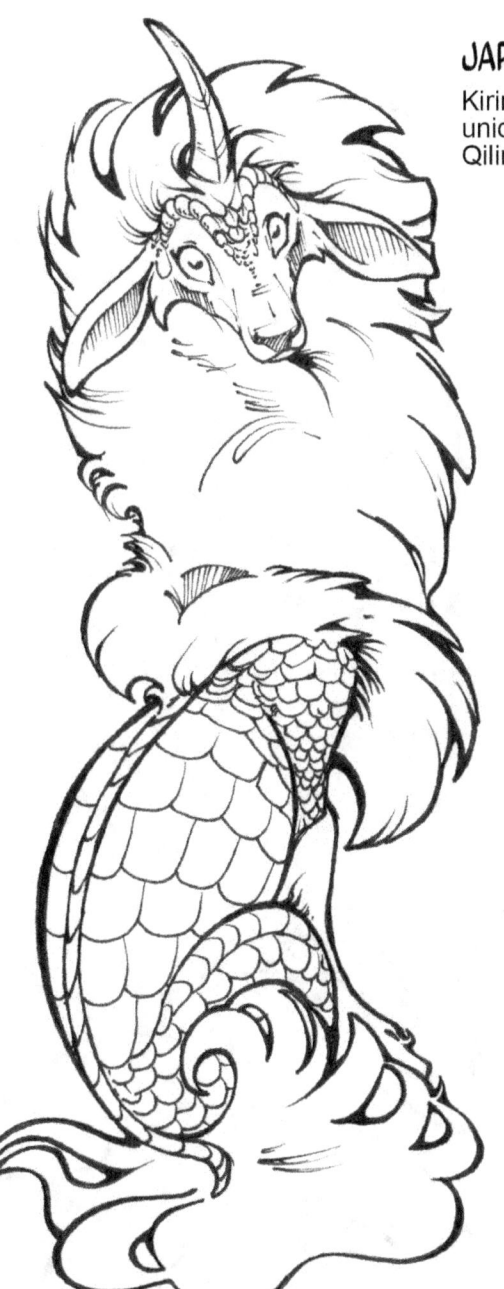

JAPANESE

Kirins look more like a western-styled unicorn, even though it is based on the Qilin version.

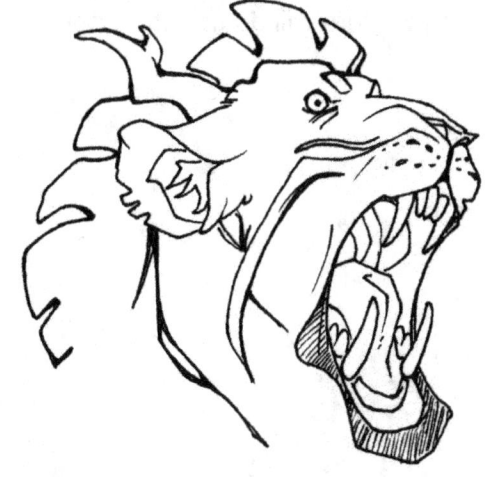

KOREAN

Of course there's a Korean version, but with the body of a deer, the tail of a cow, hooves, a mane, and a single horn on it's head, it makes you think it'd need a lot of airbrushing in Photoshop.

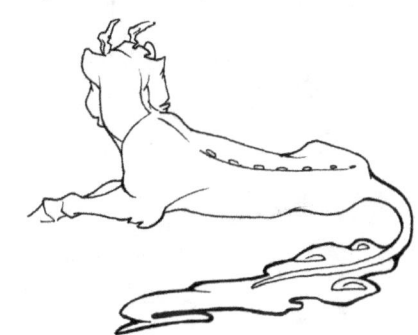

BIBLICAL

Tachash? Re'em?
Wild Ox? Unicorn?*
Depends on who you ask.

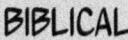

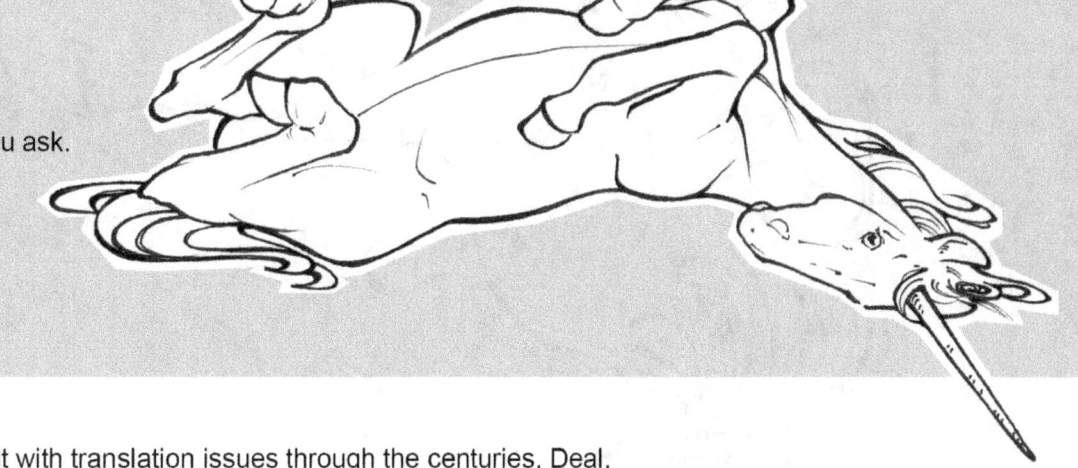

*We've already dealt with translation issues through the centuries. Deal.

HIPPOCAMP

These are great sea horses that get their start with Poseidon, but also turn up in Etruscan art, and even Pictish culture, although, whether they're hippocamps scribbled on stones in Scotland, or Kelpies, or something else, is also plausable.

Long winters will do that to people.

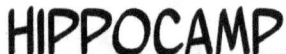

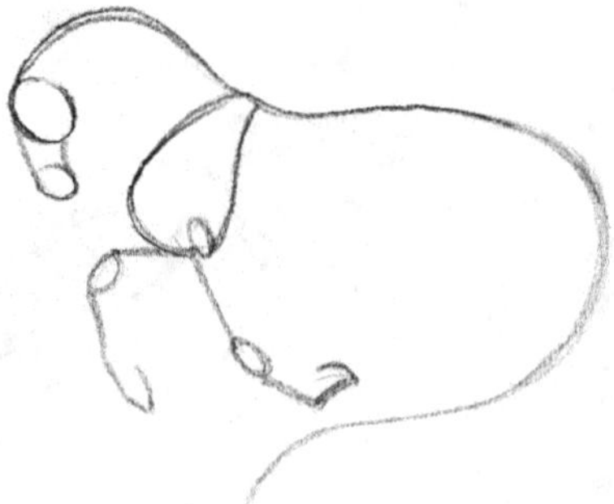

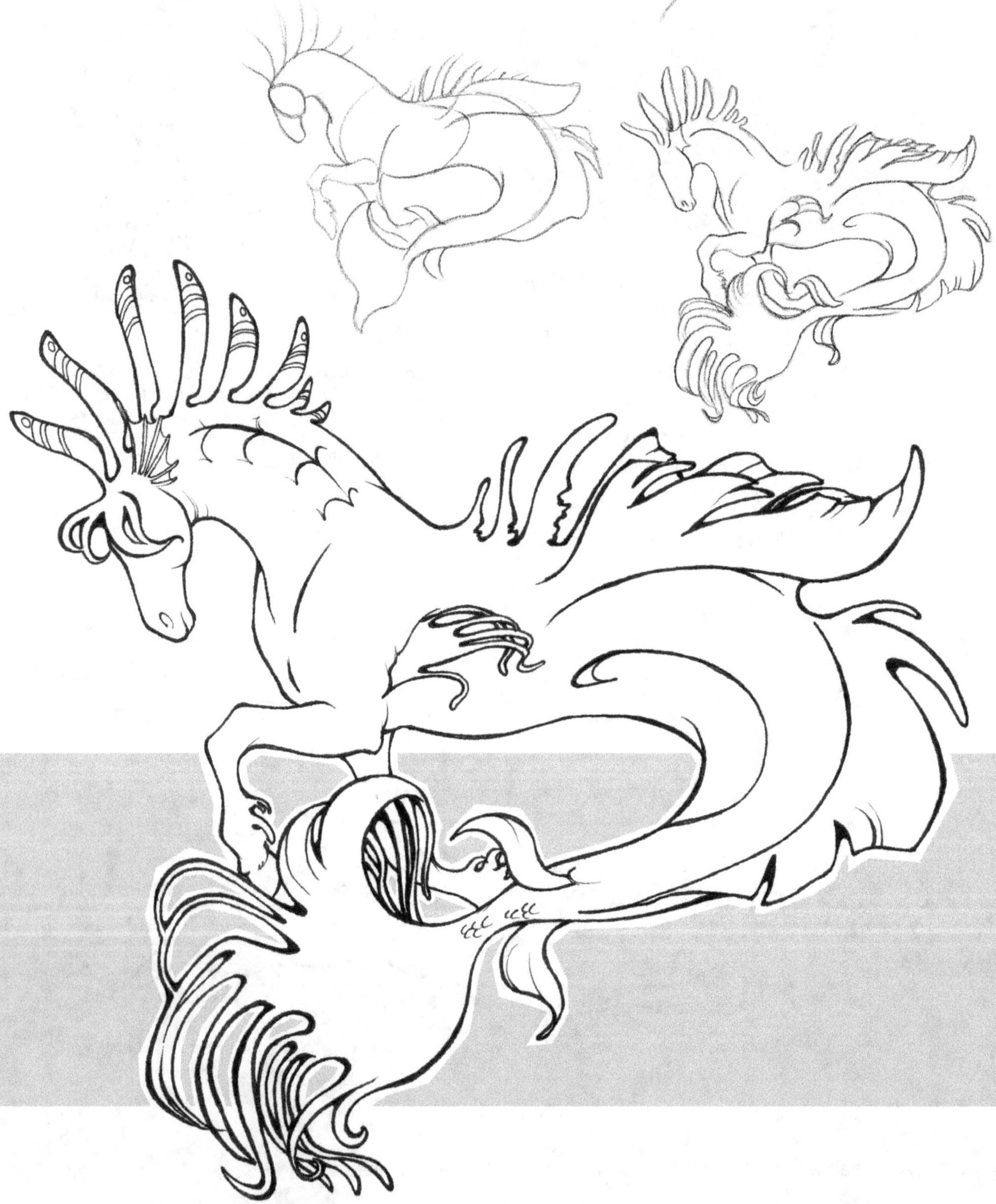

HIPPALECTRYON

I can only guess that this is a horribly mangled Greek attempt at a griffin knock-off.
There are different hybrids, chicken, vulture, etc., all of them having a horse front, while the rear, makes for a massively tempting opportunity to make seriously juvenile, inappropriate, double entendre jokes regarding *giant roosters*.

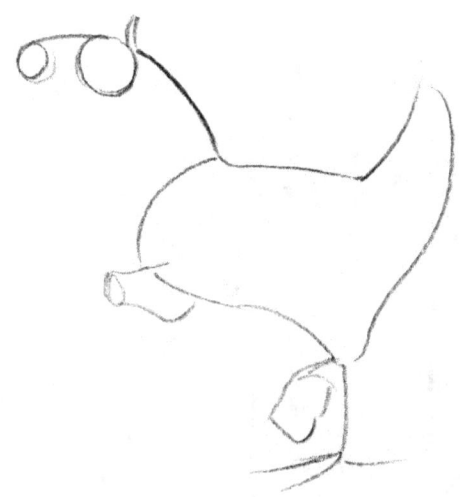

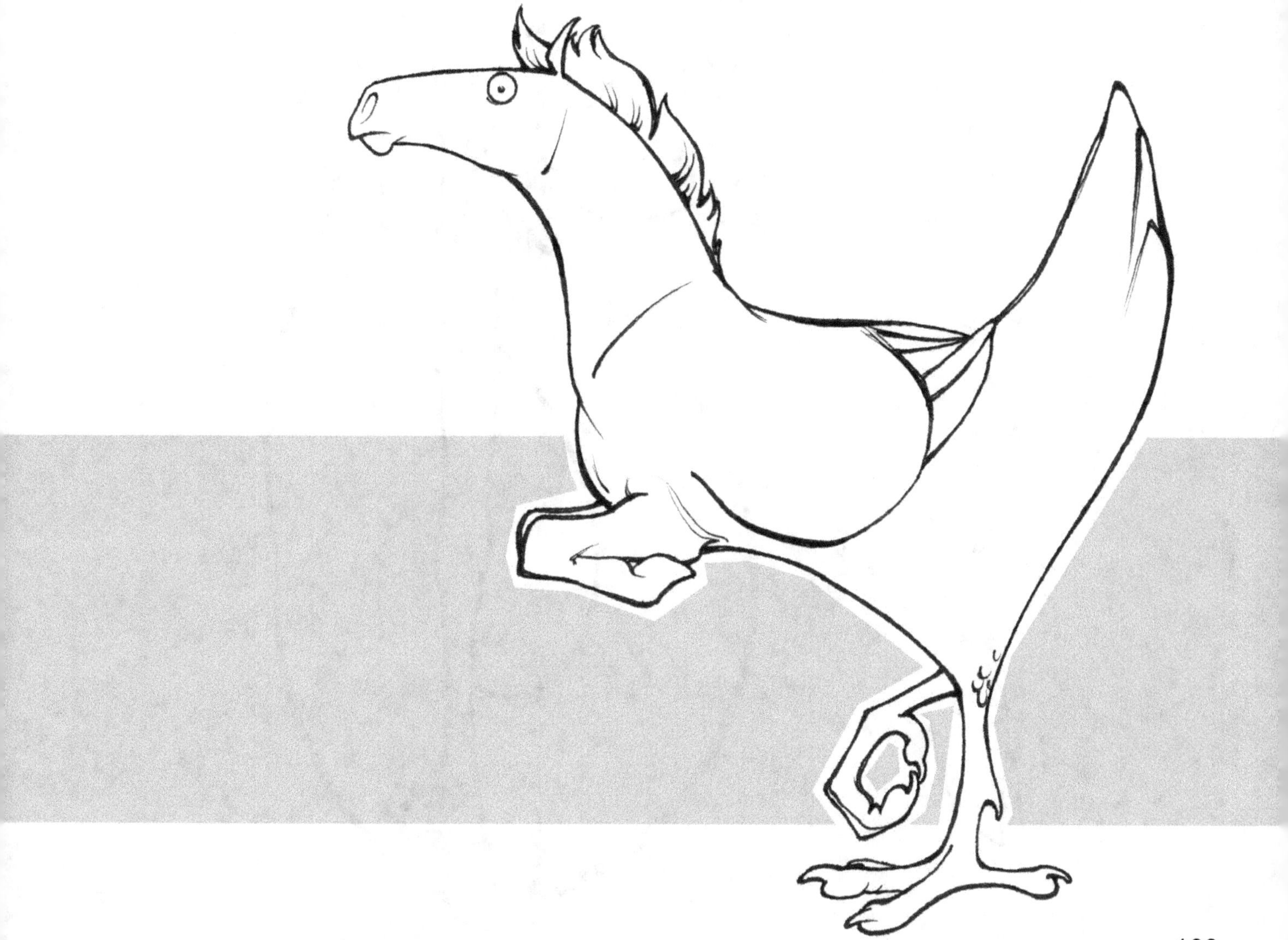

KELPIES

The kelpie is from Celtic folklore, and the story varies by region. They are said to inhabit the waters of Scotland and Ireland, and like any good ghost story, lure the living to their graves.

Known by many names/versions:
Scandanivia: Bäckahästen
Norway: Nøkken
Iceland: Nykur
Wales: Ceffyl Dŵr

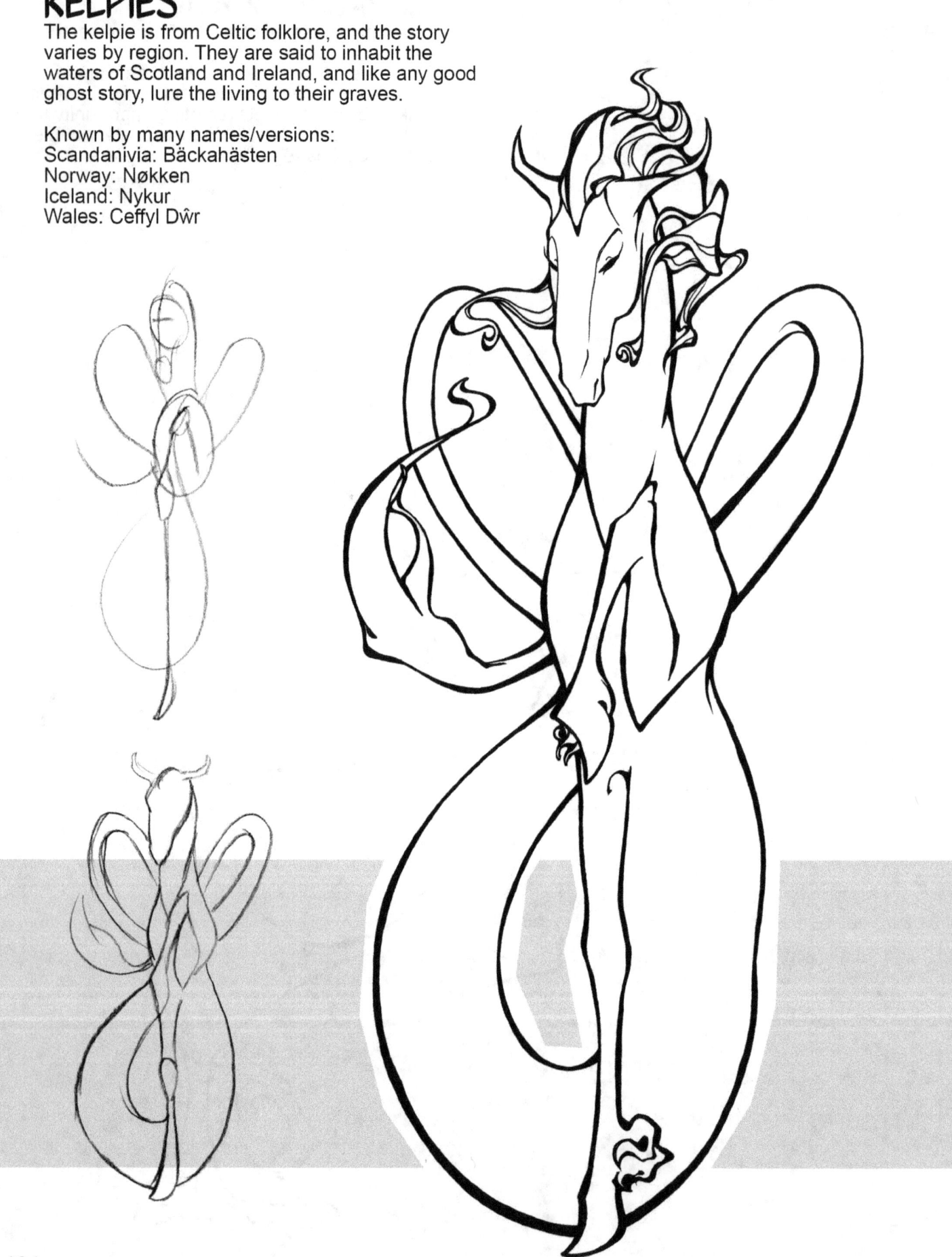

EACH-UISGE

A lot like the kelpie, but more known for bouts of unecessary roughness and anger issues.

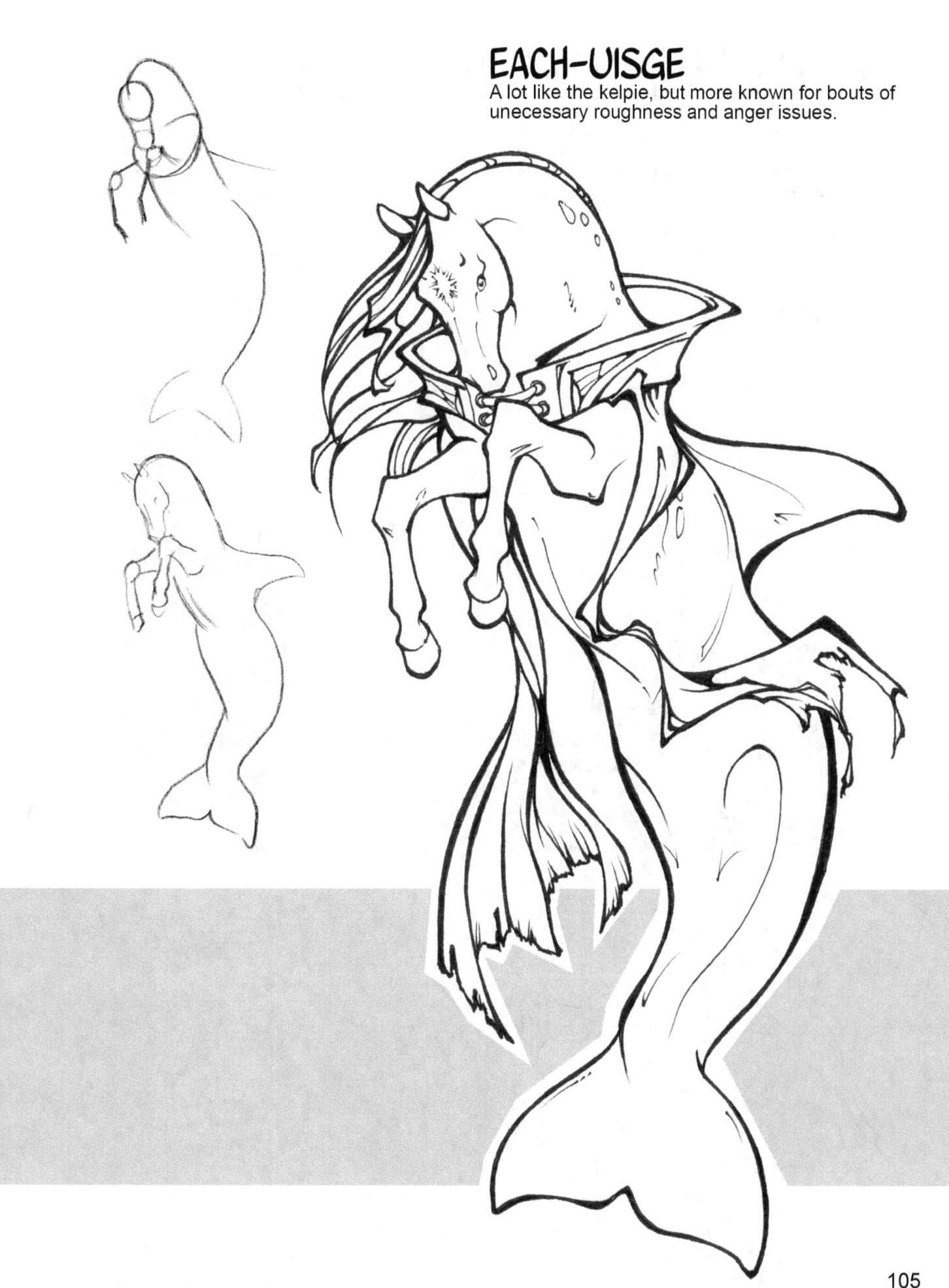

105

CABALLO MARINO CHILOTE

These hippocamp-like creatures come from the Chilote mythology of Chile. An invisible creature, which can only be seen by those with magical powers, sorcerers use them for transportation to the Caleuche ghost ship, which is crewed by the drowned.

Beat that, Johnny Depp.

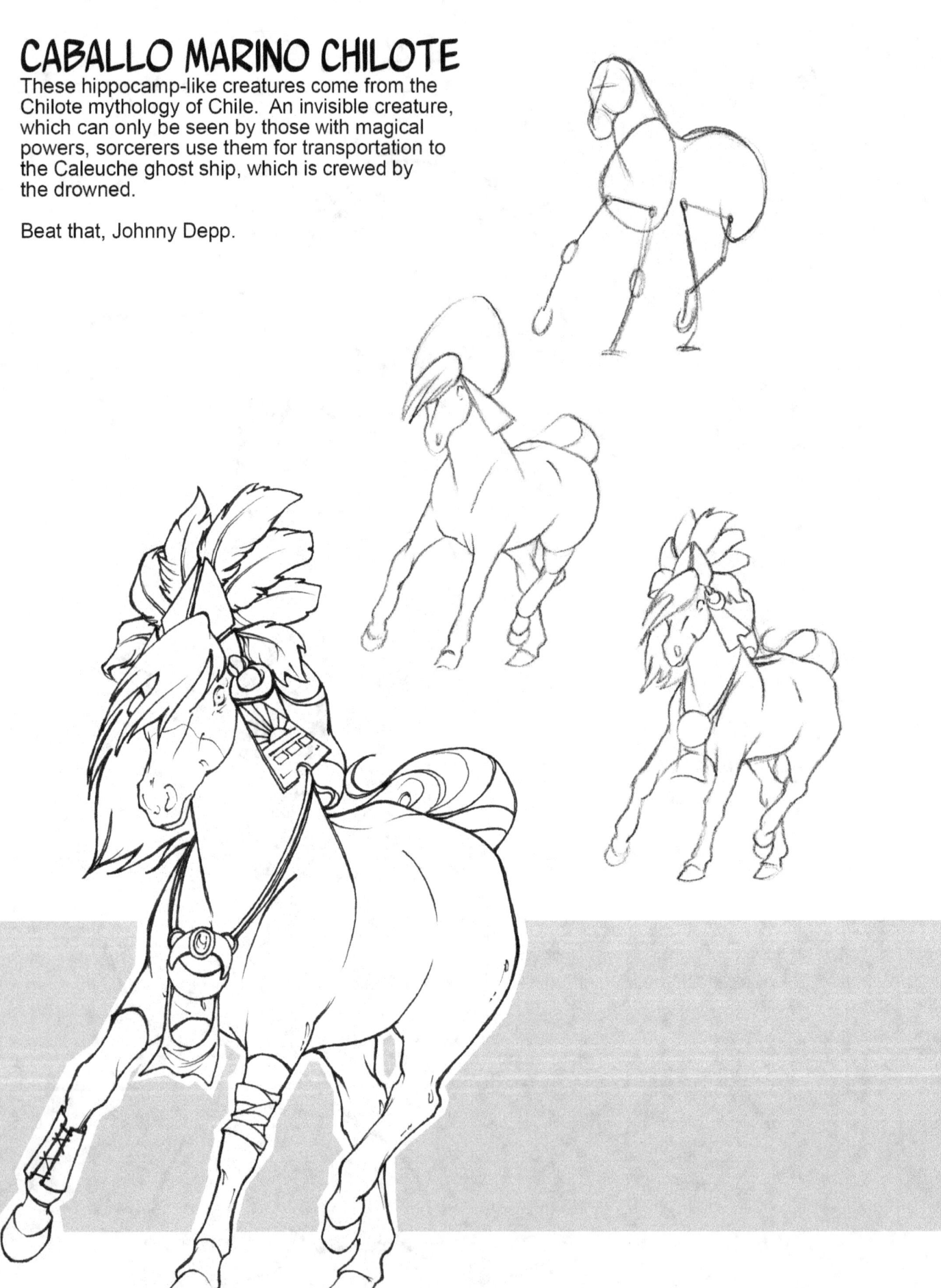

GRANI

This is the son of Odin's own, Selipnir. He comes from Norse mythology, but he doesn't do anything super-amazing.

He is just famous for being famous. Kind of like a Kardashian, but more Scandinavian.

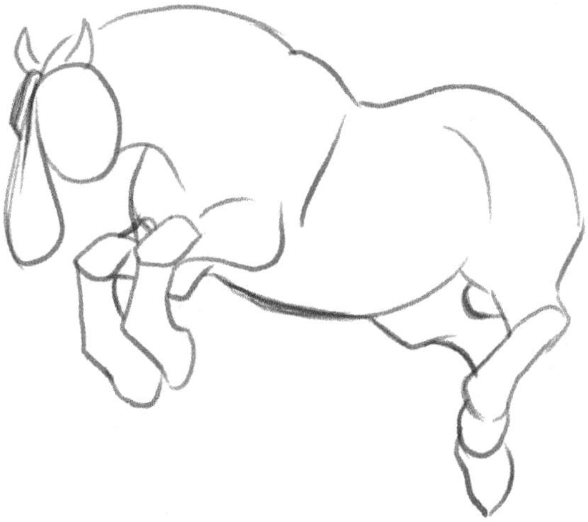

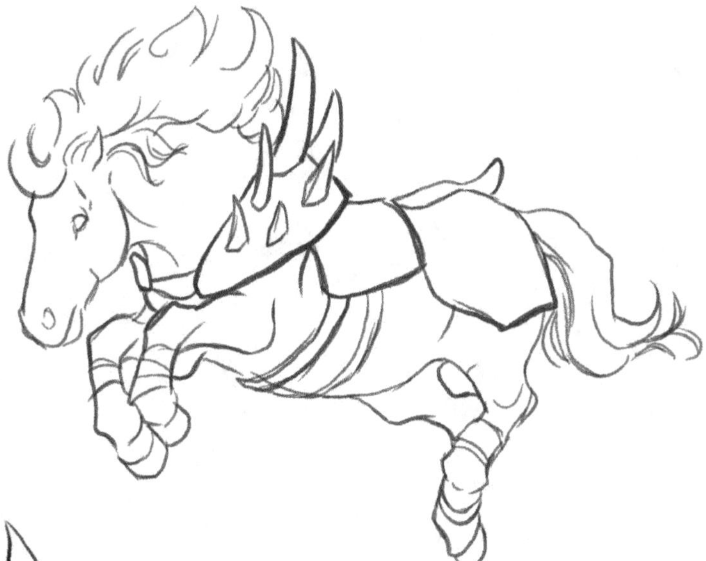

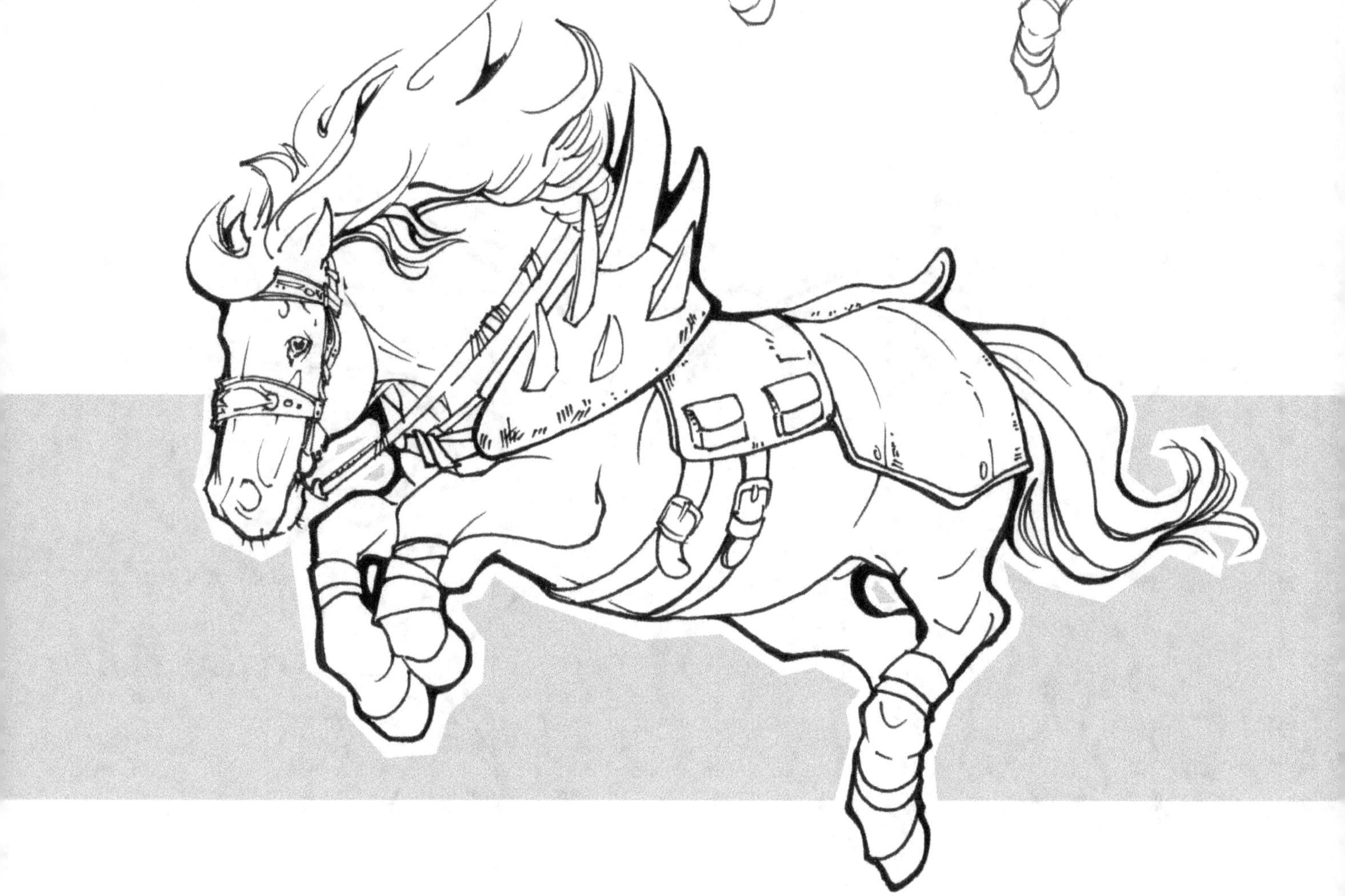

SLEIPNIR

This eight legged freak is the horse of Odin, who is found in lots of intense-bad-day stuff: Like, if you found yourself near something radioactive that was explo_ding_, you would need _iod_ine, and probably some Vic_odin_.

Historians will always tell you that the Vikings were sailing off, looking about for silver, songs, and various parts of Europe to set on fire, which is of course, silly.

There's plenty of Scandanvia that's quite flammable, and everybody knows, there's no such thing as Norway.

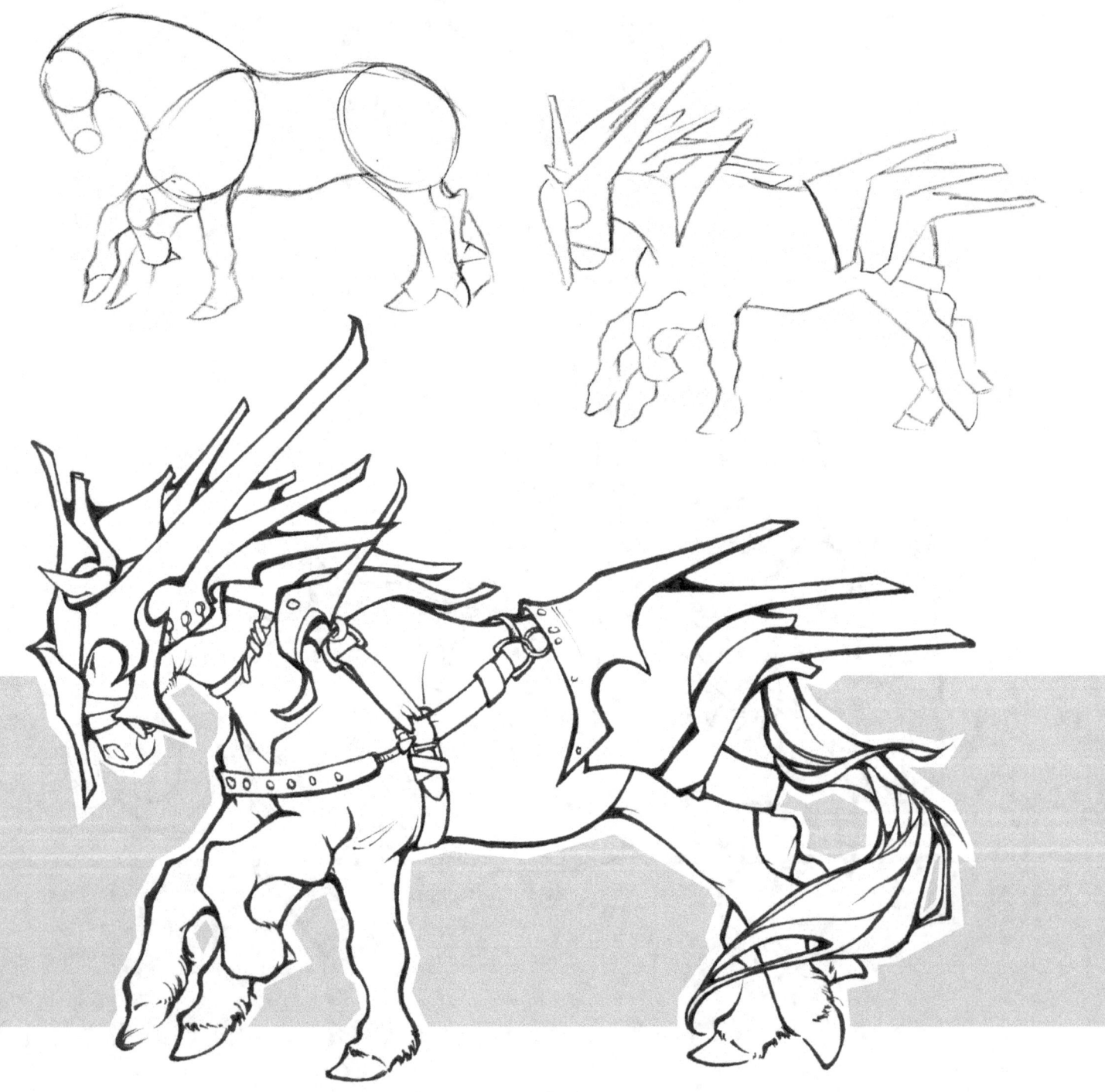

ENBARR

Enbarr of Manannán, Irish, could travel over land and water. The name of this horse is spelled many, many different ways, as you would expect in a world before editors and spell checks. Enbarr belongs to Lugh more or less, and conveniently shows up as the story requires, and then goes away to join the stash of other super-powered gifts mythical heroes always have to stack the odds in their favor.

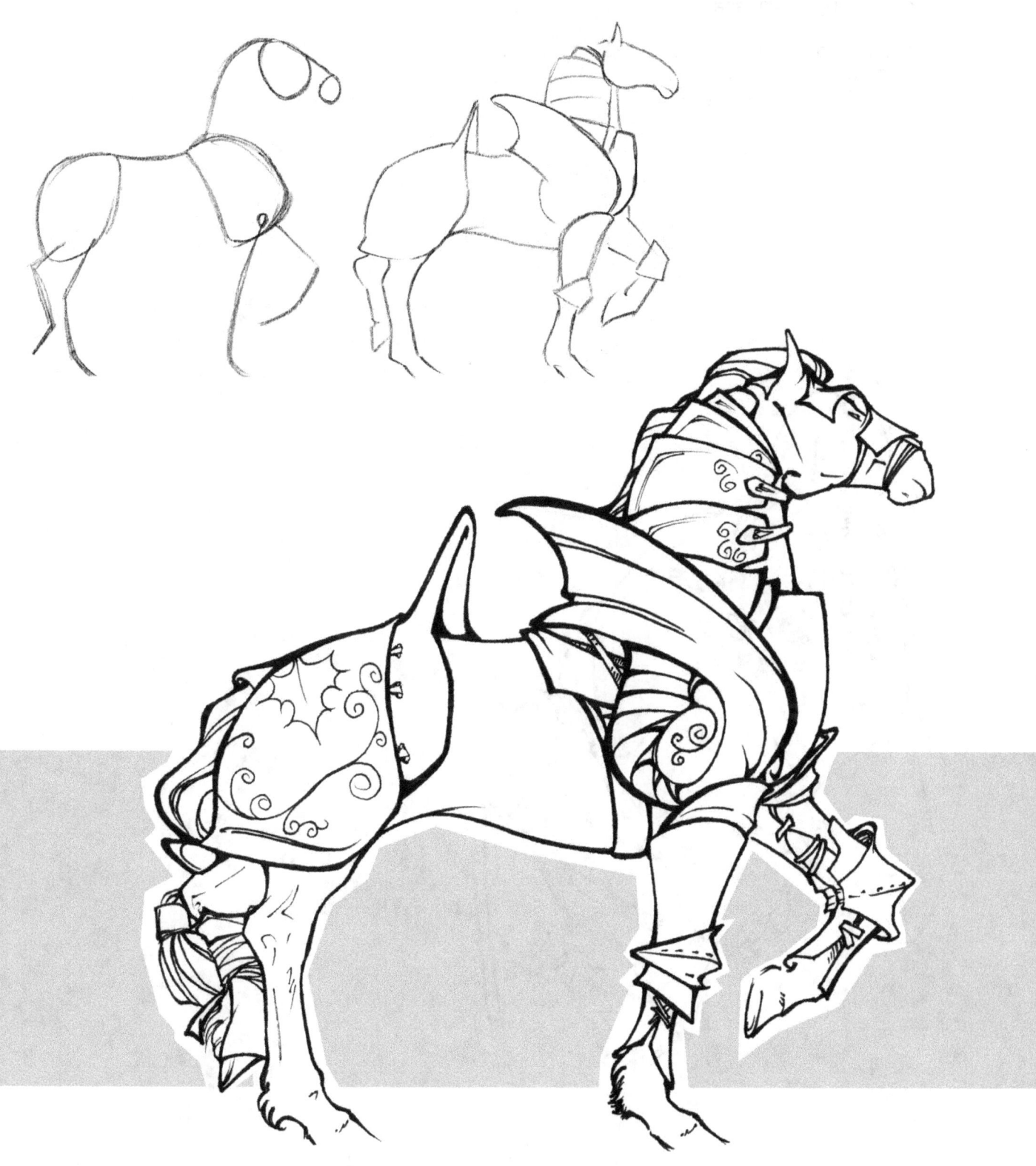

UCHCHAIHSHRAVAS

Bless you! Wait. No. This is a sort of king of horses in Hindu mythology. There's a lot of being created, and being destroyed, and being reborn, and so on, so in some versions, Uchi is the horse of the king of heaven, and in others, he's the horse of the king of demons. But most versions agree that he's a white stallion, and he's one of the great treasures to come out of the churning, milky sea.

You might also notice him because technically, he's a flying horse with seven heads.

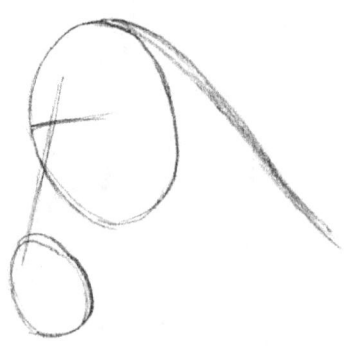

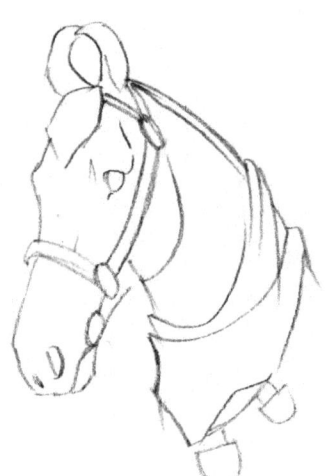

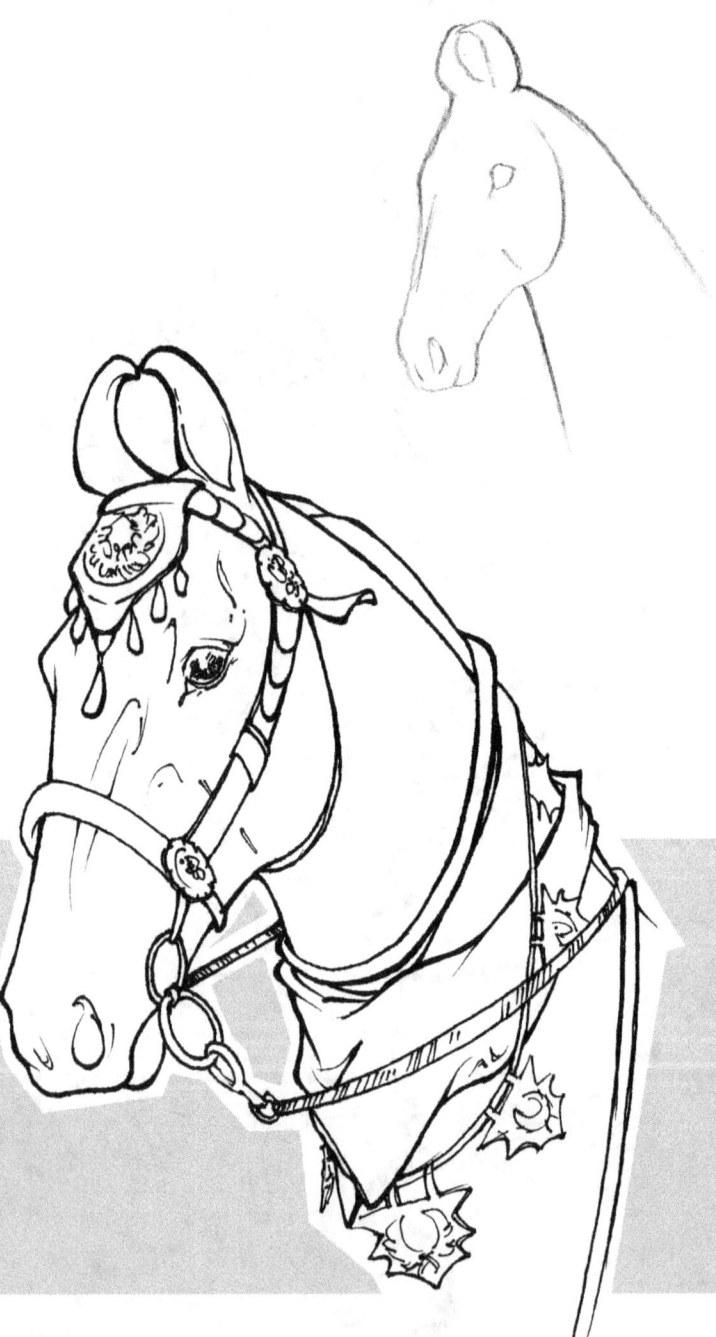

DRAW THIS
Now draw it
6 more times.

KANTHAKA

The white horse of of Prince Siddhartha, who later became Gautama Buddha. The prince uses Kanthaka to display his prowess with horsemanship and thus win the hand of the princess, Yashodara. While out on a chariot drive, he is shocked to learn that there is suffering in the world, which for a guy who is supposed to have powerful methods of observation, doesn't stand out as particularly Sherlock-level of deductive reasoning, if you catch our drift, but, he's moved to take up the ascetic life*, and Kanthaka carries him away from the palace.

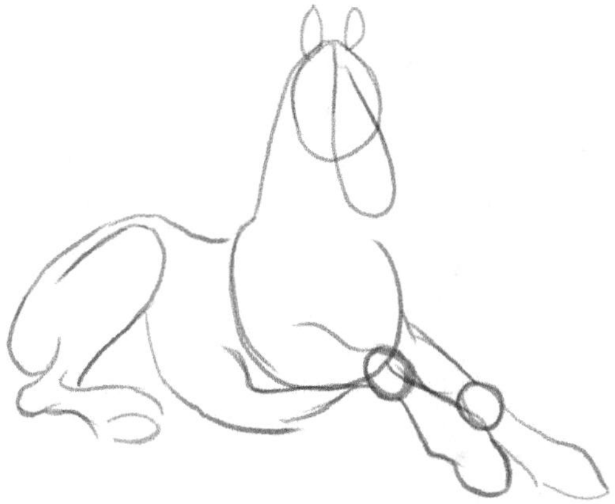

Kanthaka is said to have died of a broken heart after the prince left. But he's reborn as a brahmin and attains enlightenment, so, I guess it all works out.

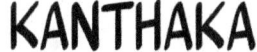

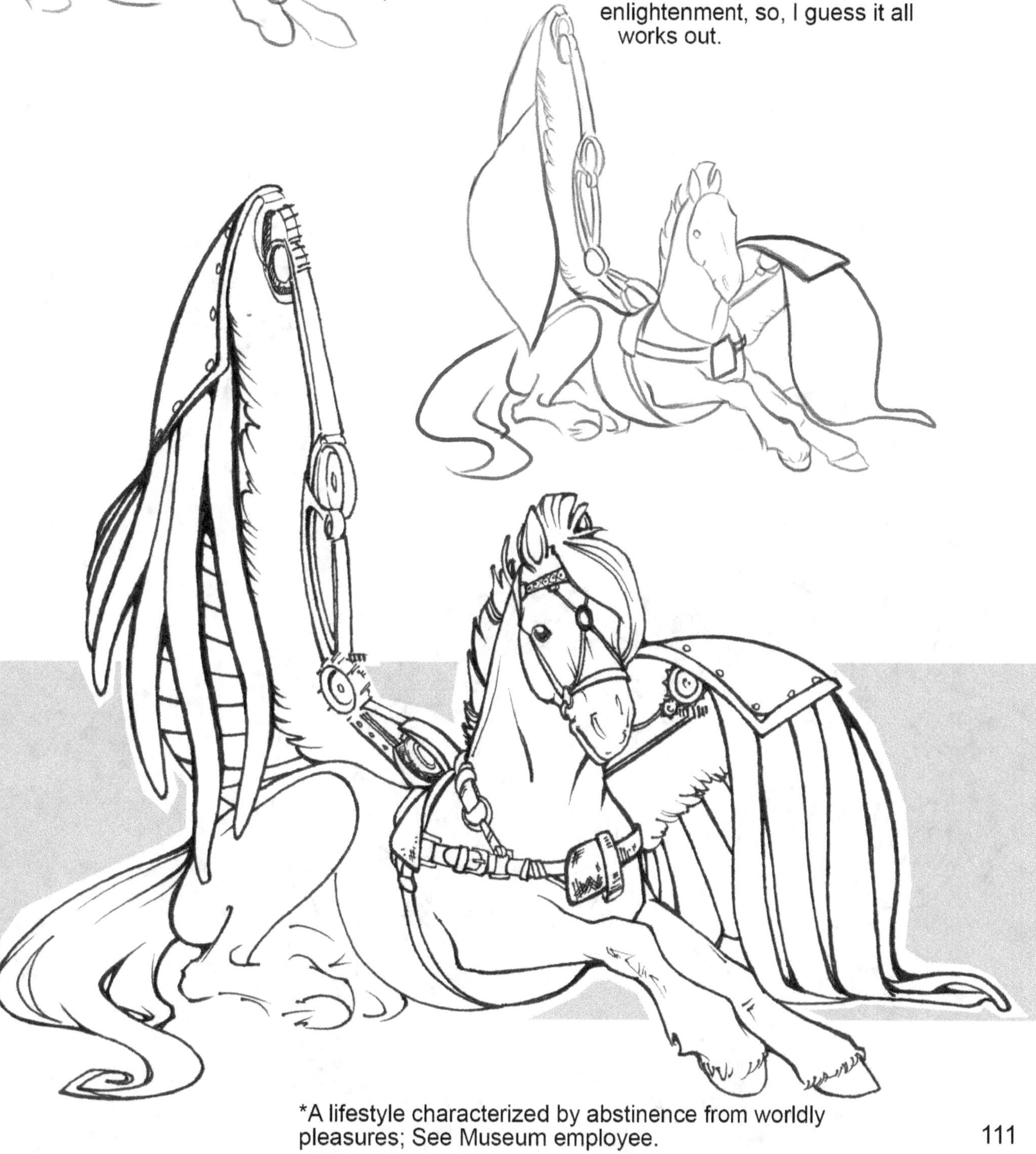

*A lifestyle characterized by abstinence from worldly pleasures; See Museum employee.

EPONA

While most pagan deities were rather a local thing, the Gaul-Celtic goddess Epona went like wildfire across the Roman empire. She was the blessed protector of equines, she performed some leading around in the after-life, and was the goddess of several other things you should go ask your mom about.

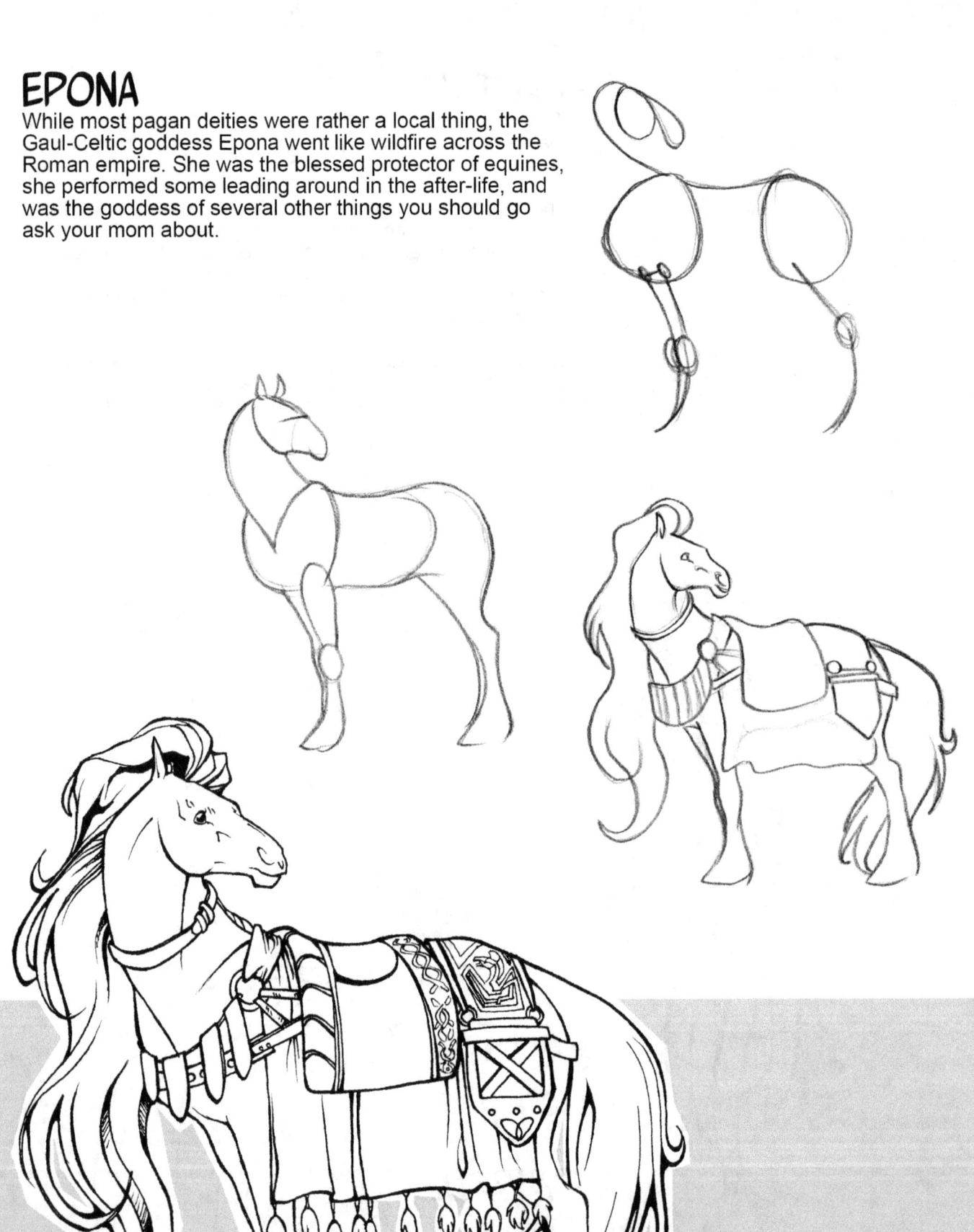

RAKHSH

This stallion is from the Persian national epic, Shahnameh. He is of course strong, beautiful, and brave, and dies with the hero, Rostam, because the poet Ferdowsi is the George R. R. Martin of Persian literature.

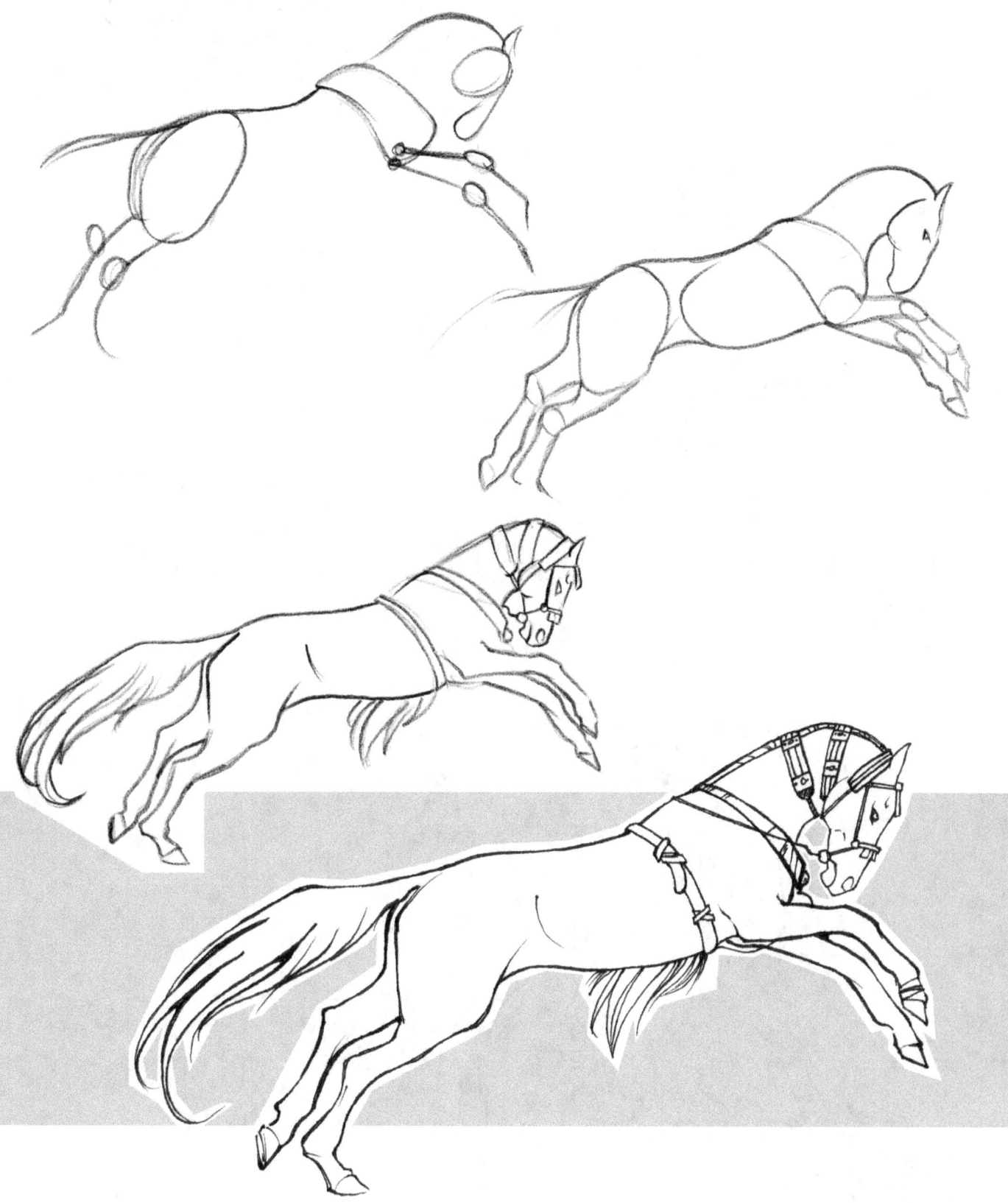

AL-BURAQ

This heavenly horse is most known for transporting the prophet Muhammad from Mecca to Jerusalem and back during the "Night Journey." Al is often depicted with a human face, along with wings from his back or his rump, and the tail of a peacock.

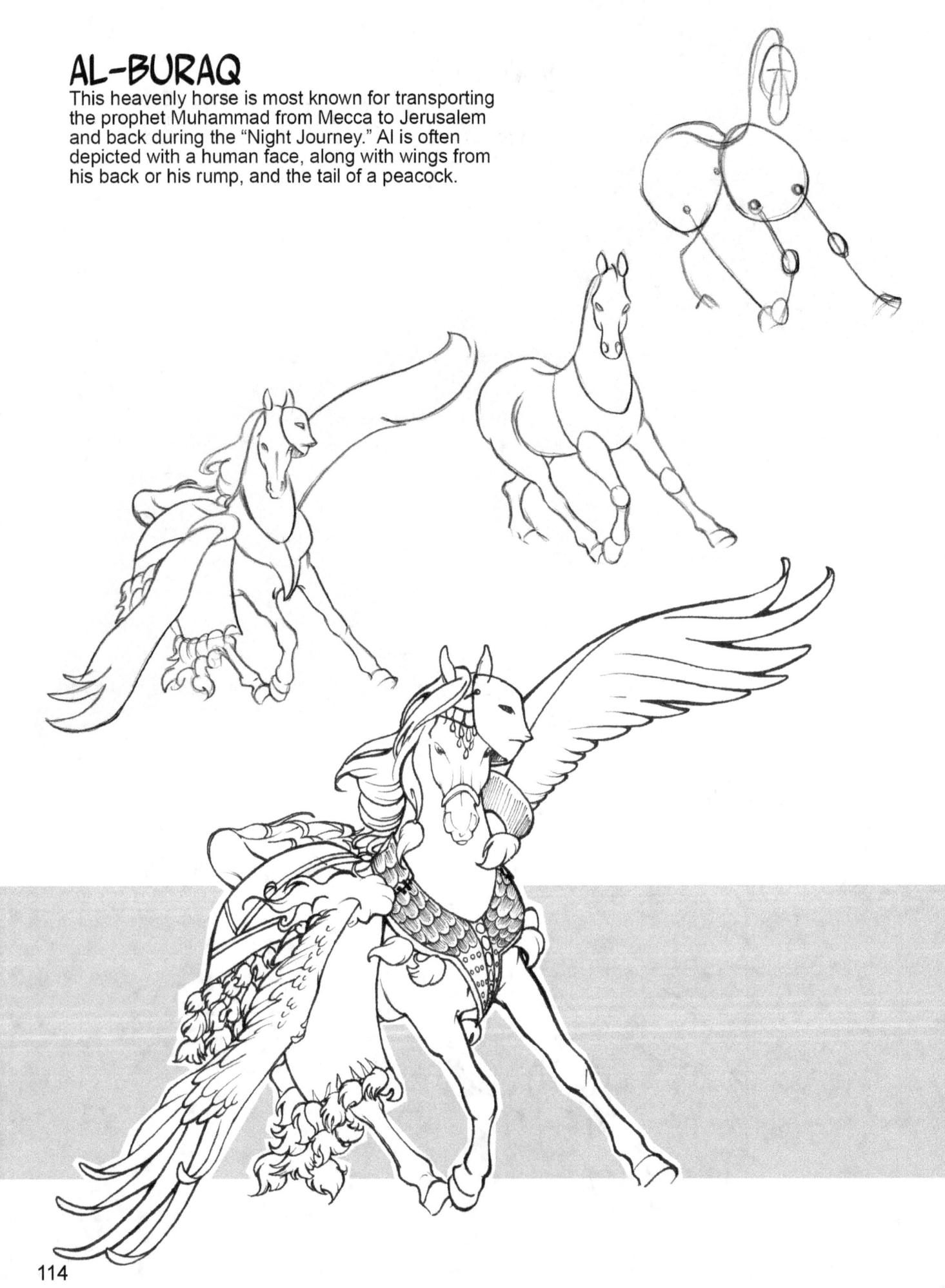

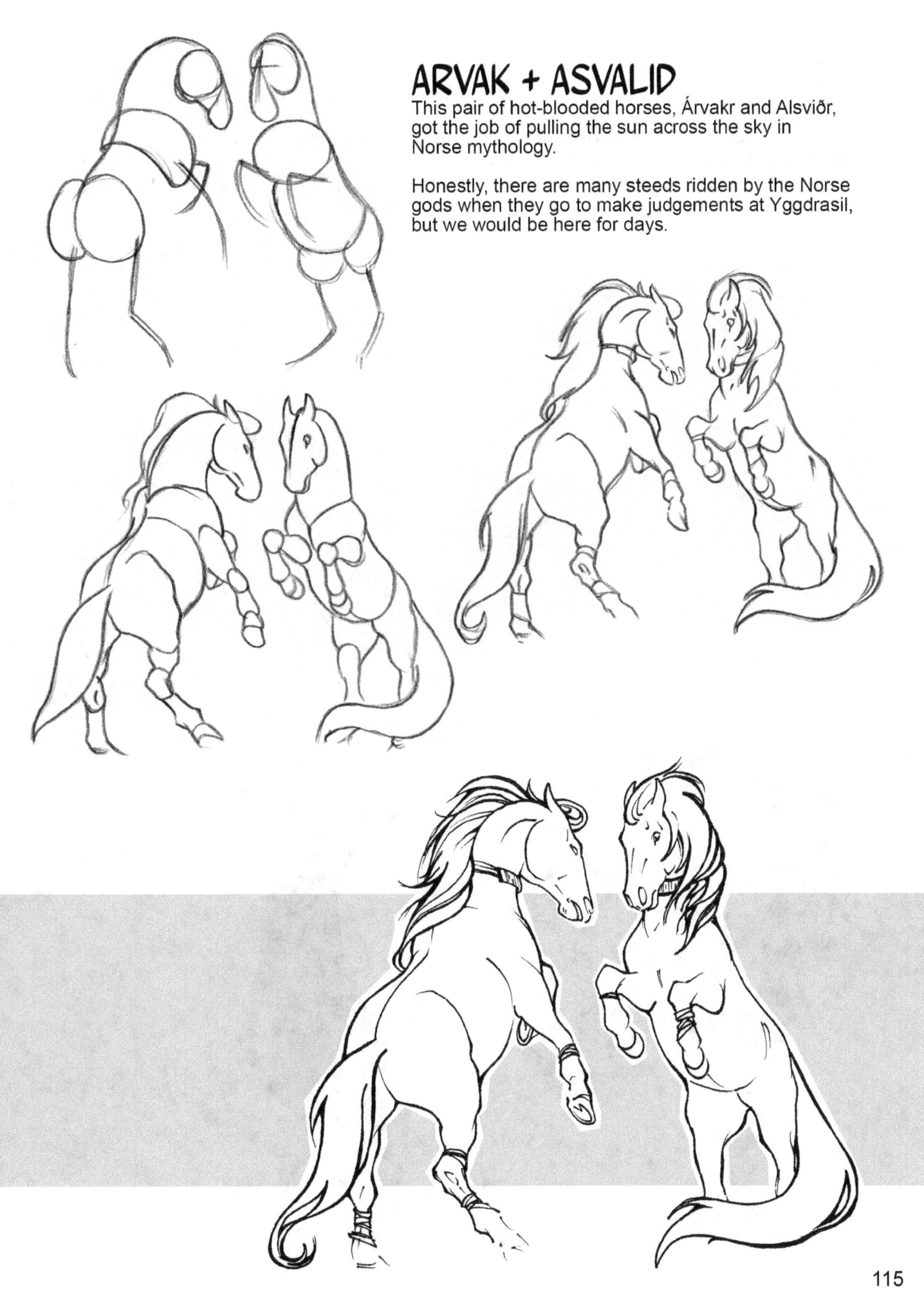

ARVAK + ASVALID

This pair of hot-blooded horses, Árvakr and Alsviðr, got the job of pulling the sun across the sky in Norse mythology.

Honestly, there are many steeds ridden by the Norse gods when they go to make judgements at Yggdrasil, but we would be here for days.

HELHEST

Helhest is a Danish horse of death. What does Hel do,
you ask? It does death. That really is about it.
In that upbeat-rainbow-and-sunshine sort of tale that
the Scandinavian countries are known for. And he only
has three legs.

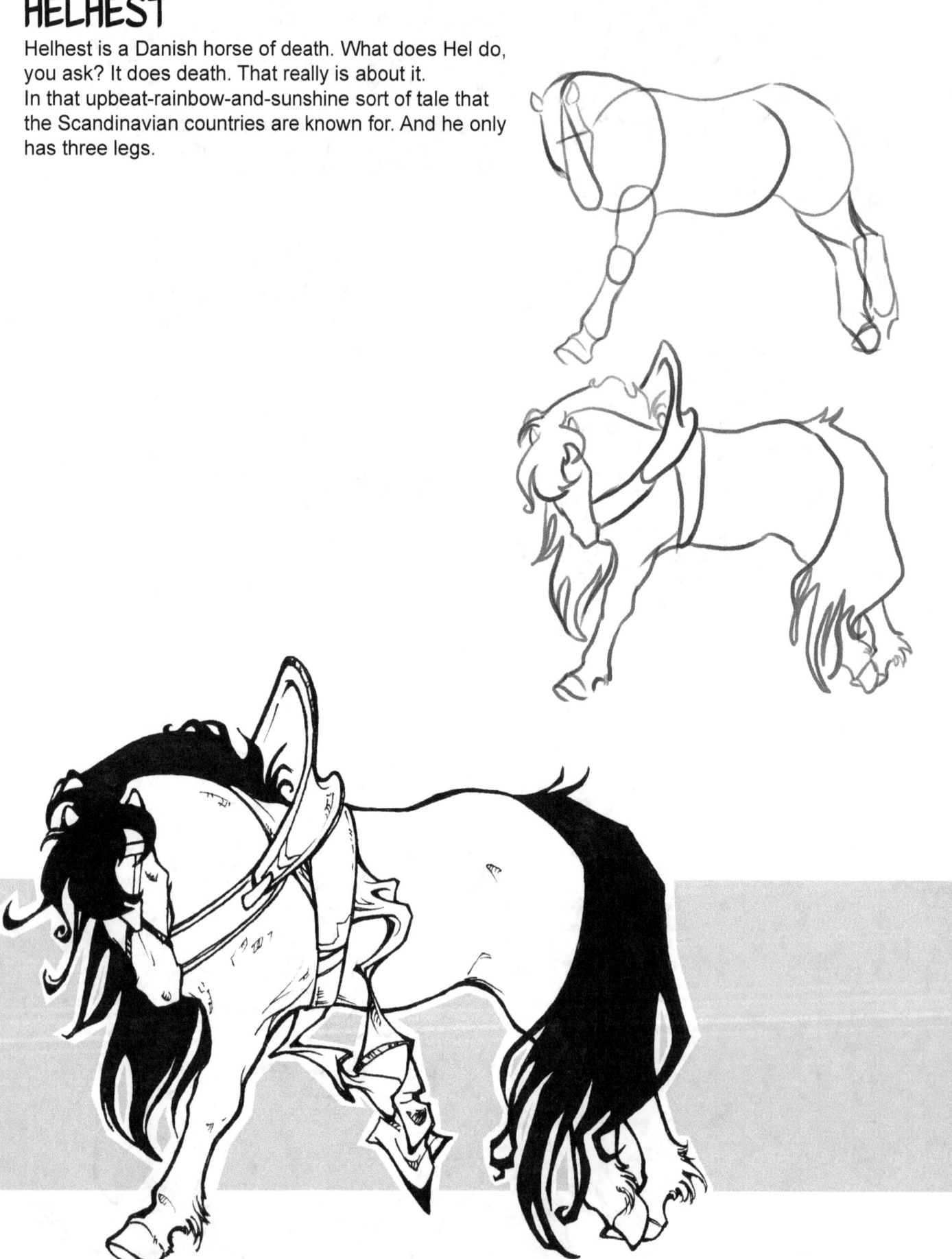

RIDING SCHOOL

If you can handle shapes, you can draw a rider just
as easily as you did their horse. No, really!

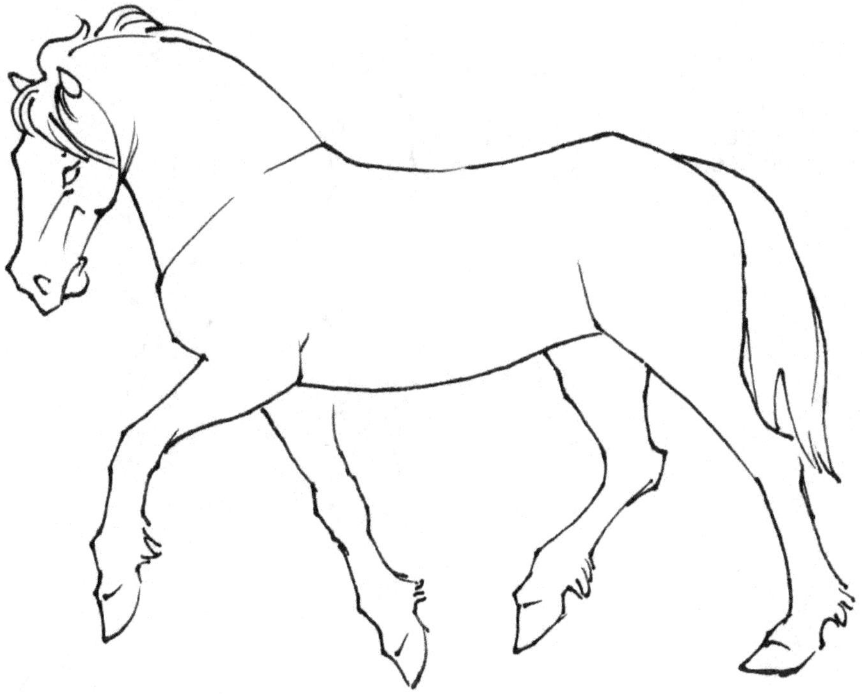

Let's start with
this lady.

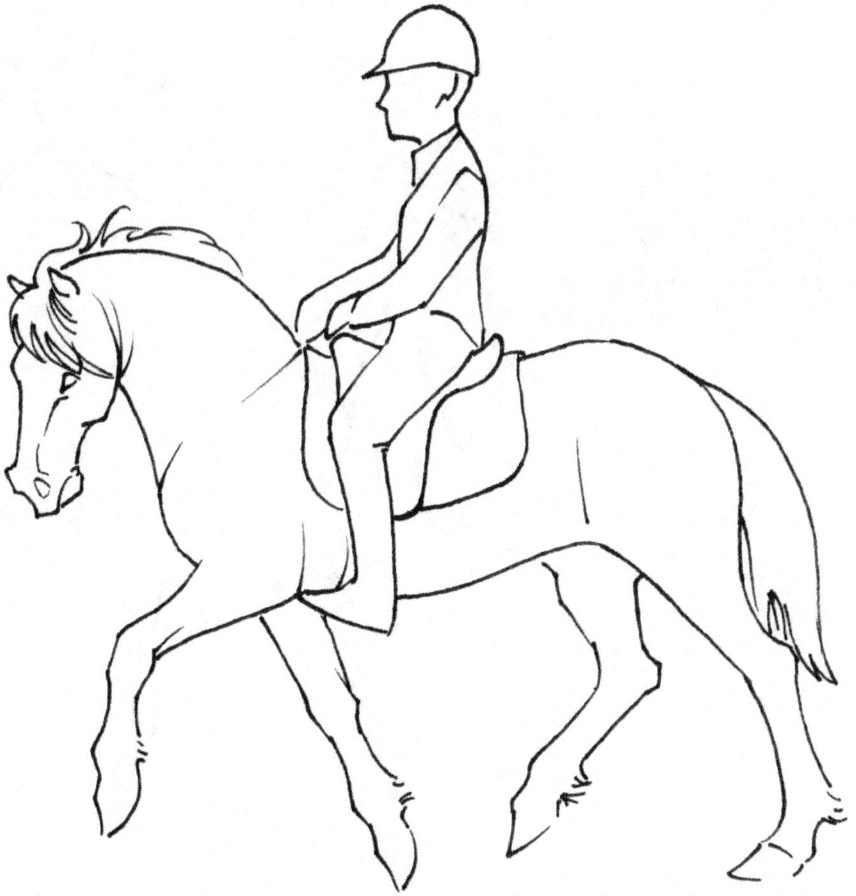

MODERN EXAMPLE
Has the luxuries of
solid saddle trees,
stirrups, and will
be drawn correctly:
shoulders back, heels
down.

ANCIENT EXAMPLE
A rider in the ancient
world is going bareback,
which is much less
forgiving of error.

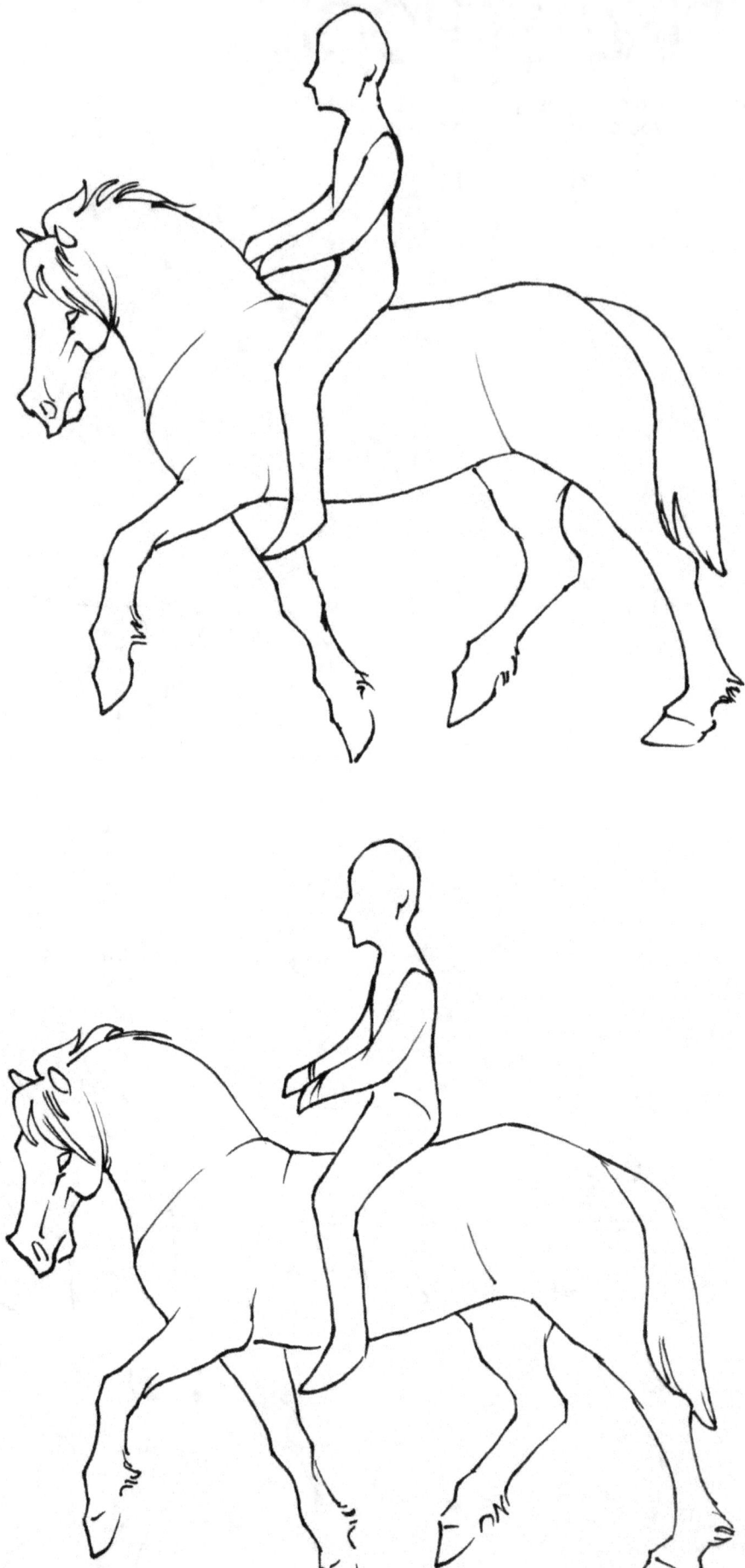

And the rider has the
ability to slide backwards.

A rider in the 'ye olden time of yore' must
jump,canter, and perform every other task
bareback as well, which in a world with hardly
any roads sounds beyond terrifying.

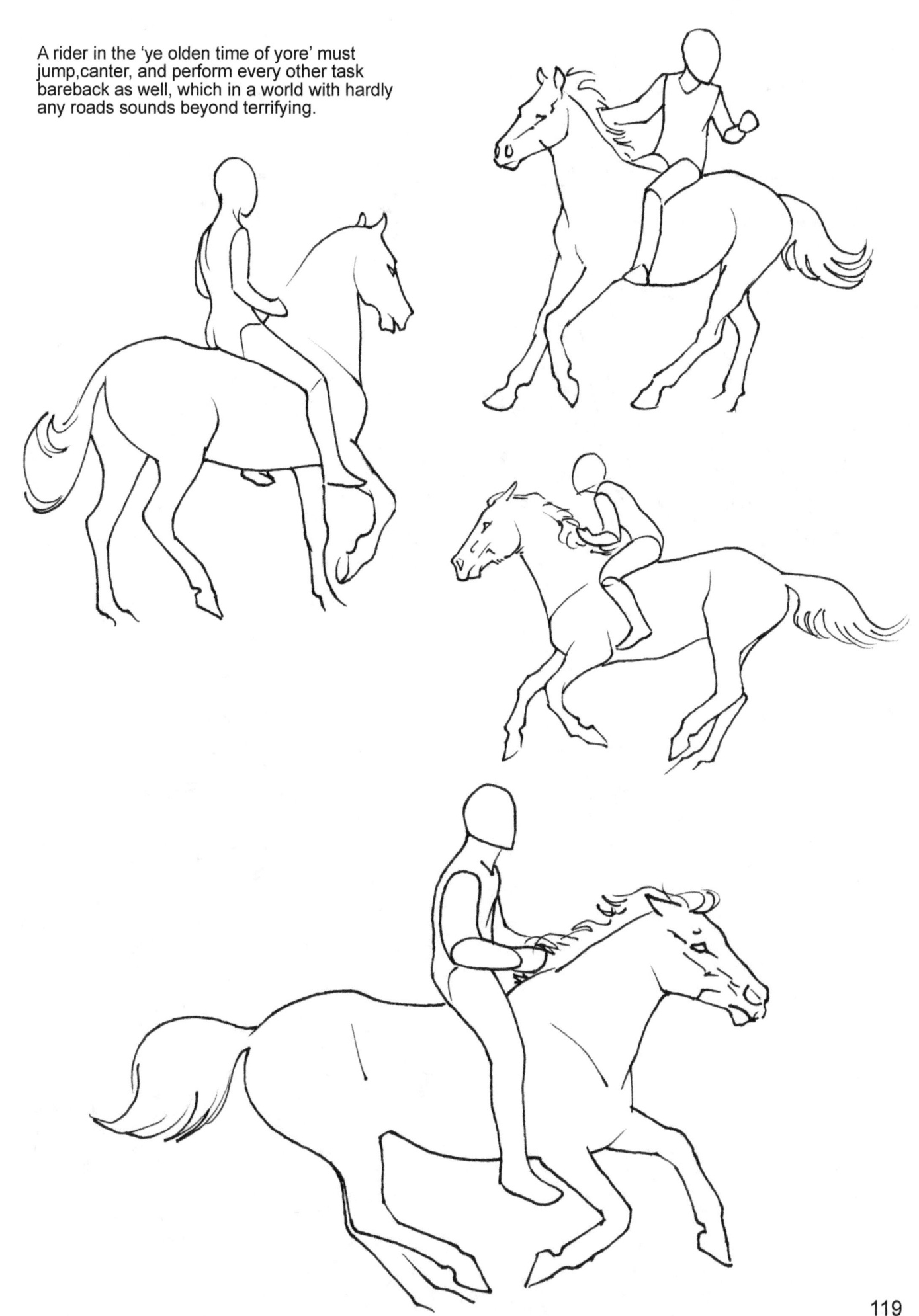

REARING

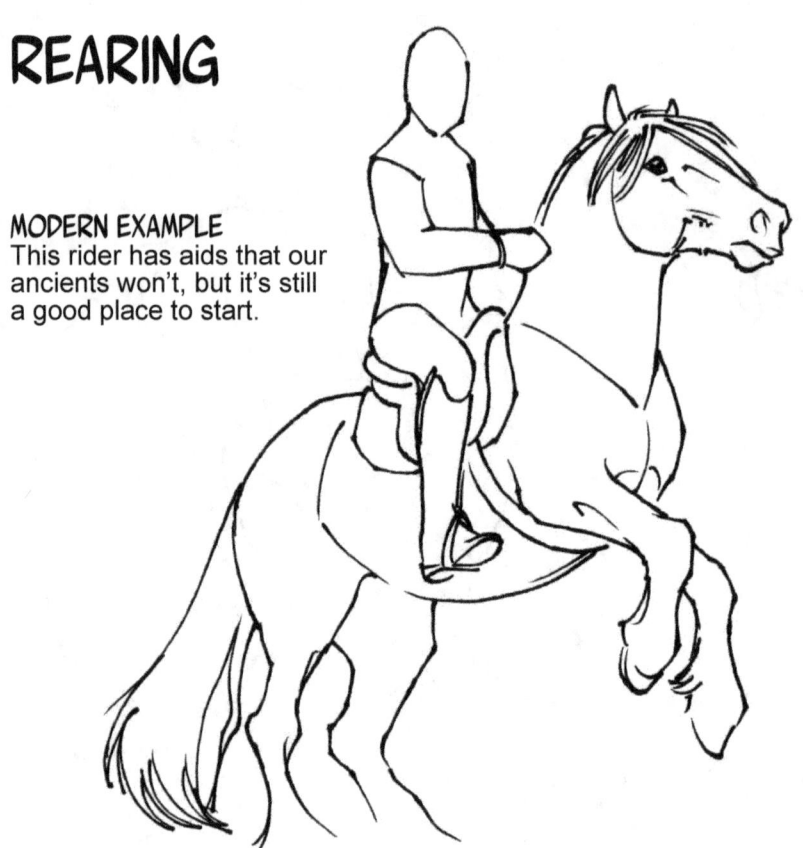

MODERN EXAMPLE
This rider has aids that our ancients won't, but it's still a good place to start.

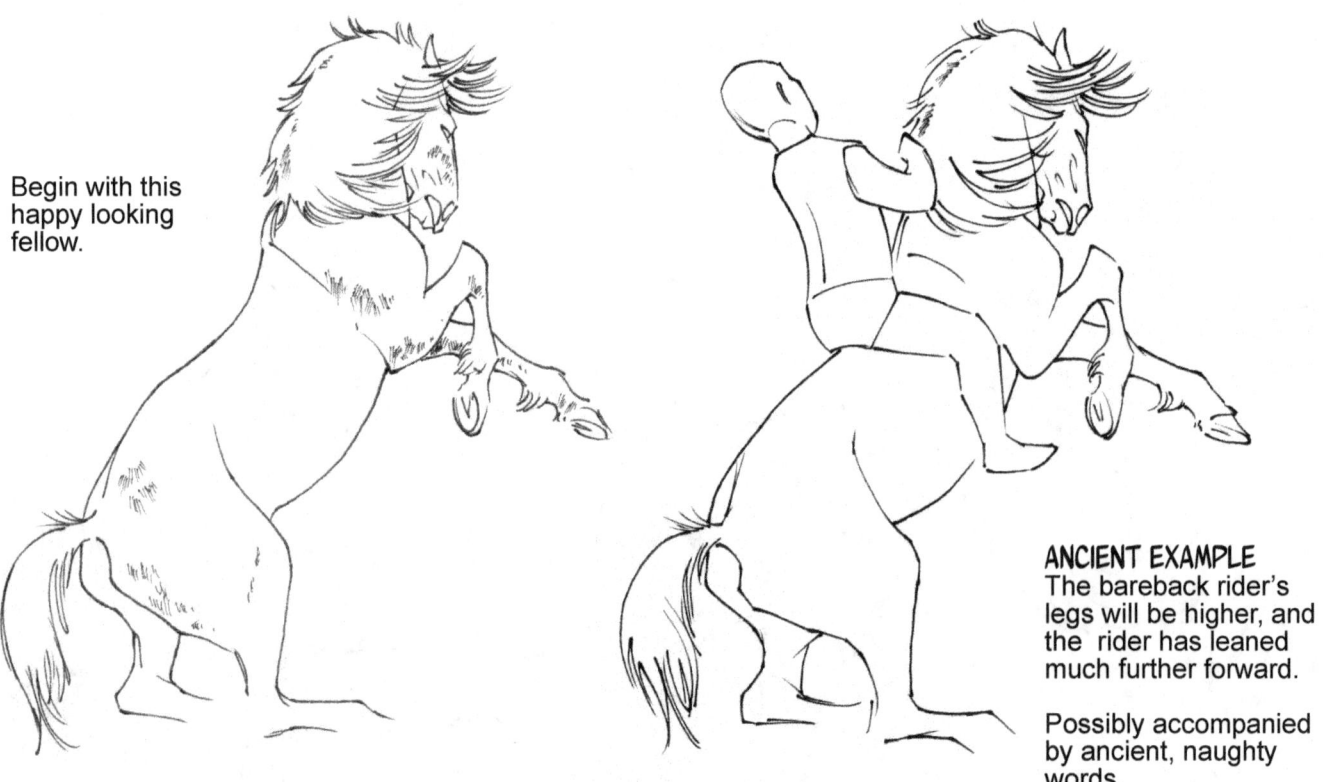

Begin with this happy looking fellow.

ANCIENT EXAMPLE
The bareback rider's legs will be higher, and the rider has leaned much further forward.

Possibly accompanied by ancient, naughty words.

RIDING POSES

There's no way to get good at drawing a horse and rider besides practice. A lot.

CENTER LINE
If it helps, you can usually draw a line of balance between your horse and rider.

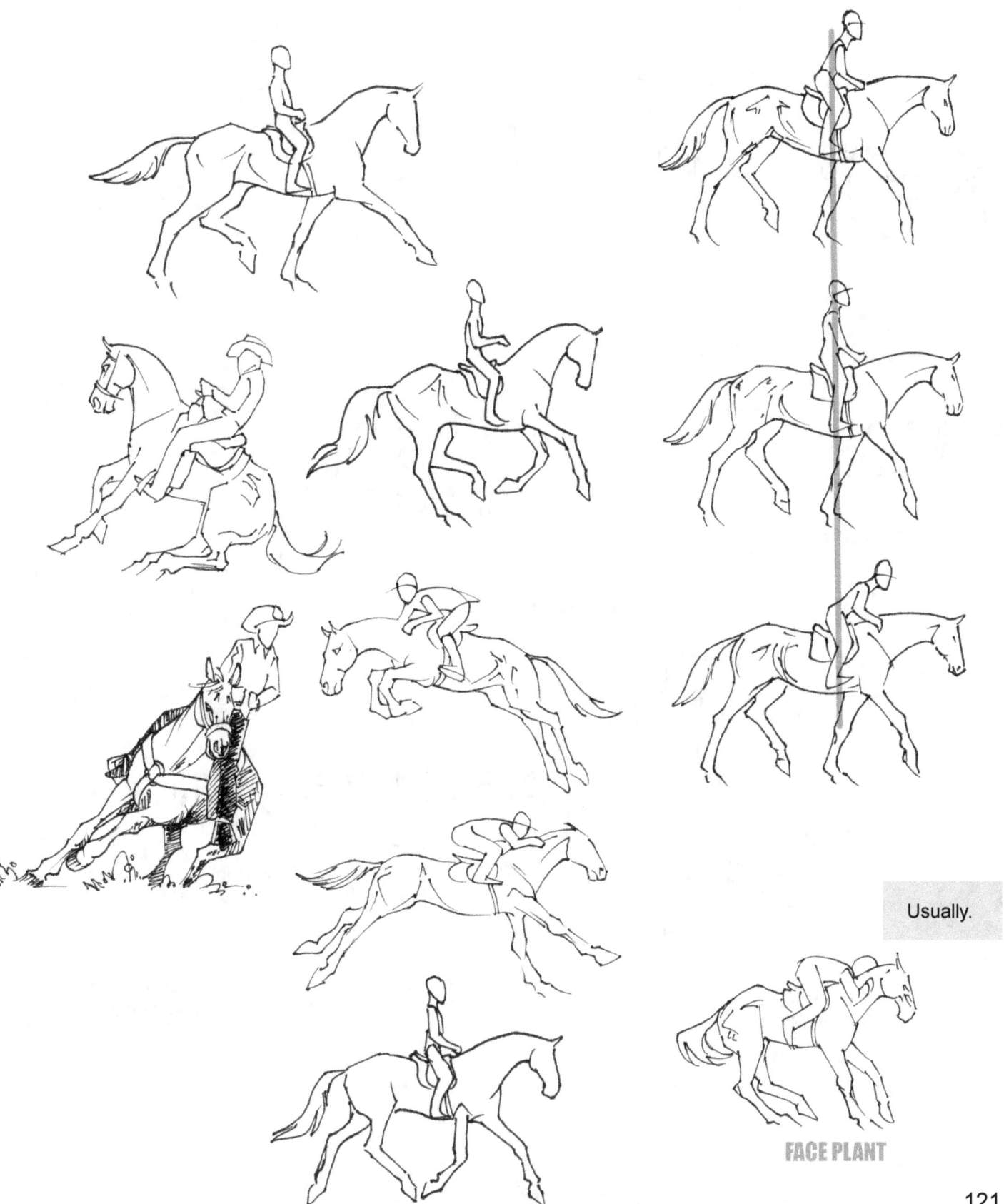

Usually.

FACE PLANT

LINEAR PERSPECTIVE

We are able to see out to a distance of about 42 billion light-years - our cosmic visual horizon. And it just might be that there is not one universe - but an infinite series of multiverses.

Either way, we should probably learn how to handle some space.

LEVEL FEATURES
You only need to work out one subject from a distance if they are level.

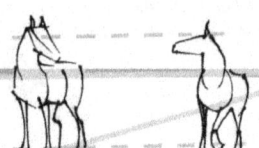

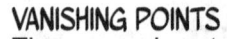

VANISHING POINTS
These are almost always off the page. Use your good judgement.

2-POINT PERSPECTIVE
Very often used for horse scenes in paintings.

3-POINT PERSPECTIVE
Mostly used for extreme views from above or below. Or a very close viewpoint.

OTHER TRICKS FOR DEPTH

TONE
Tonal intensity increases the closer you get to the viewer.

DETAIL
Closer subjects will be in sharper focus.

OVERLAPPING
You can block a subject to make it look further away.

SIZE
Closer subjects will appear larger. Our brains love to trick us like that.

CARTOONS

Now that we've learned lots of rules, lets have fun breaking them.

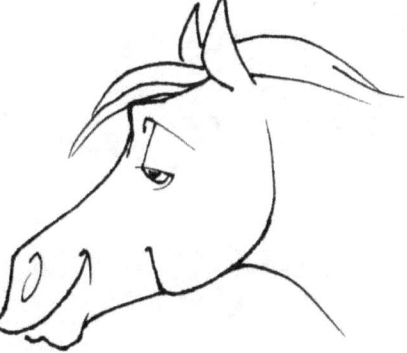

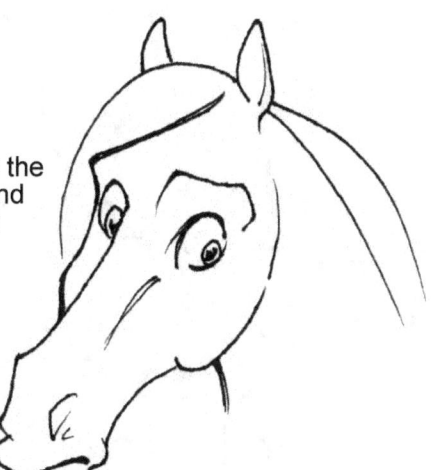

EYES
These will work to the front of the face and become large and expressive.

MOUTH
Will be able to enchance the expression.

MANE
Becomes stylized, and gender specific.

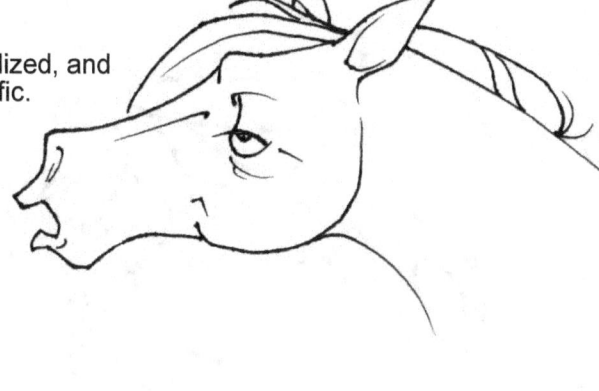

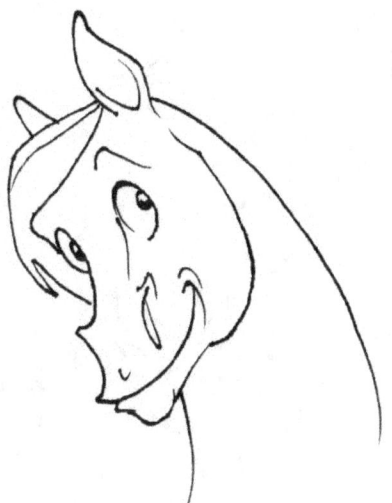

EARS
Stretch and squeeze for any gesture.

EYEBROWS
Don't forget the expressive power of the eyebrows!

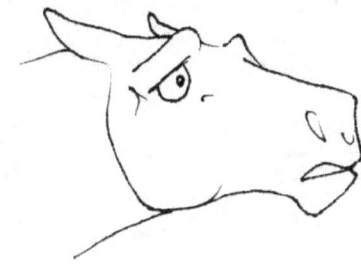

EXPRESSIONS

Happy, Anger, Scared, Sad - these
are the four primary emotions
humans use... ... the
world of ...
the hu...
beyon...

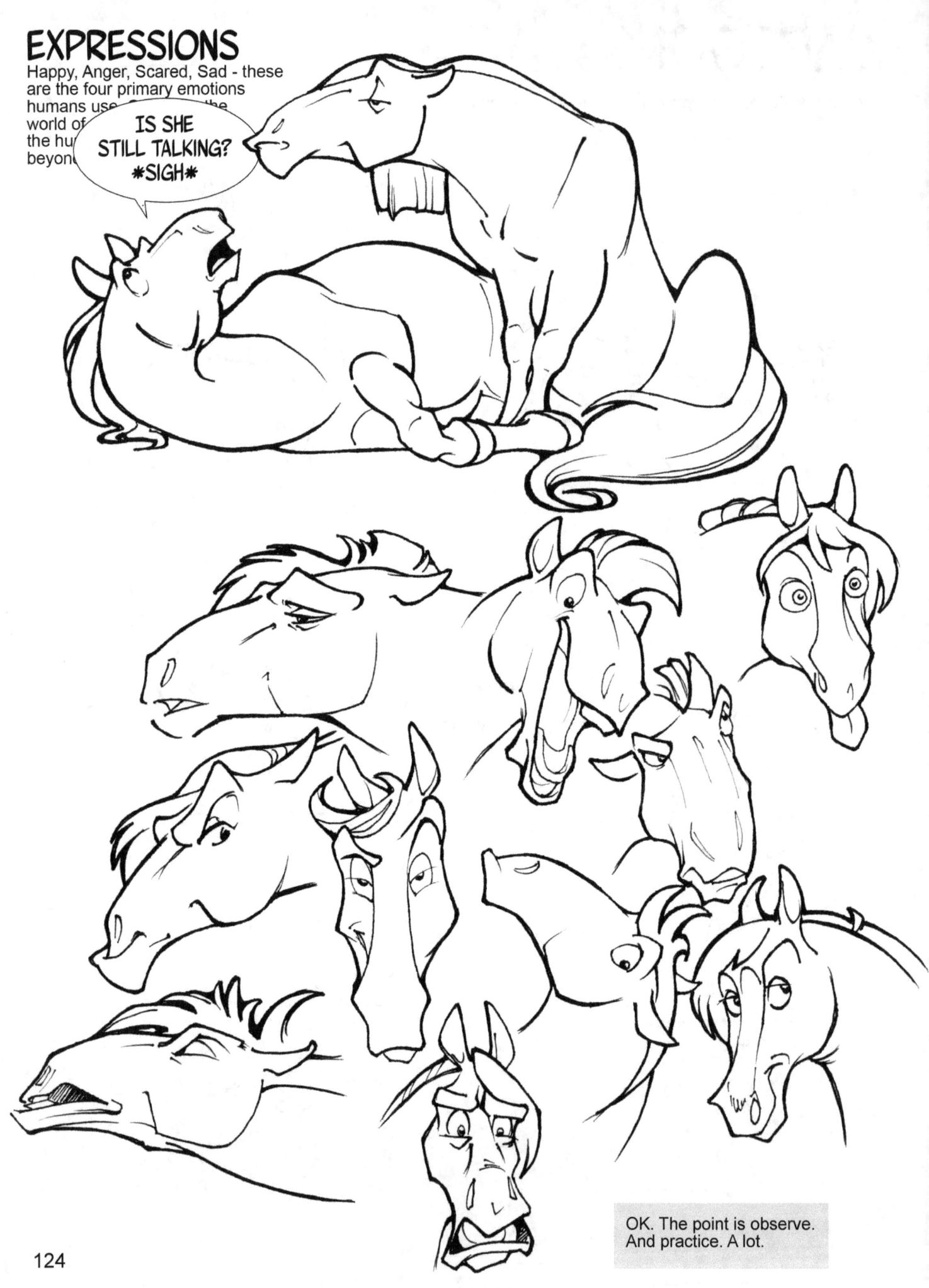

OK. The point is observe.
And practice. A lot.

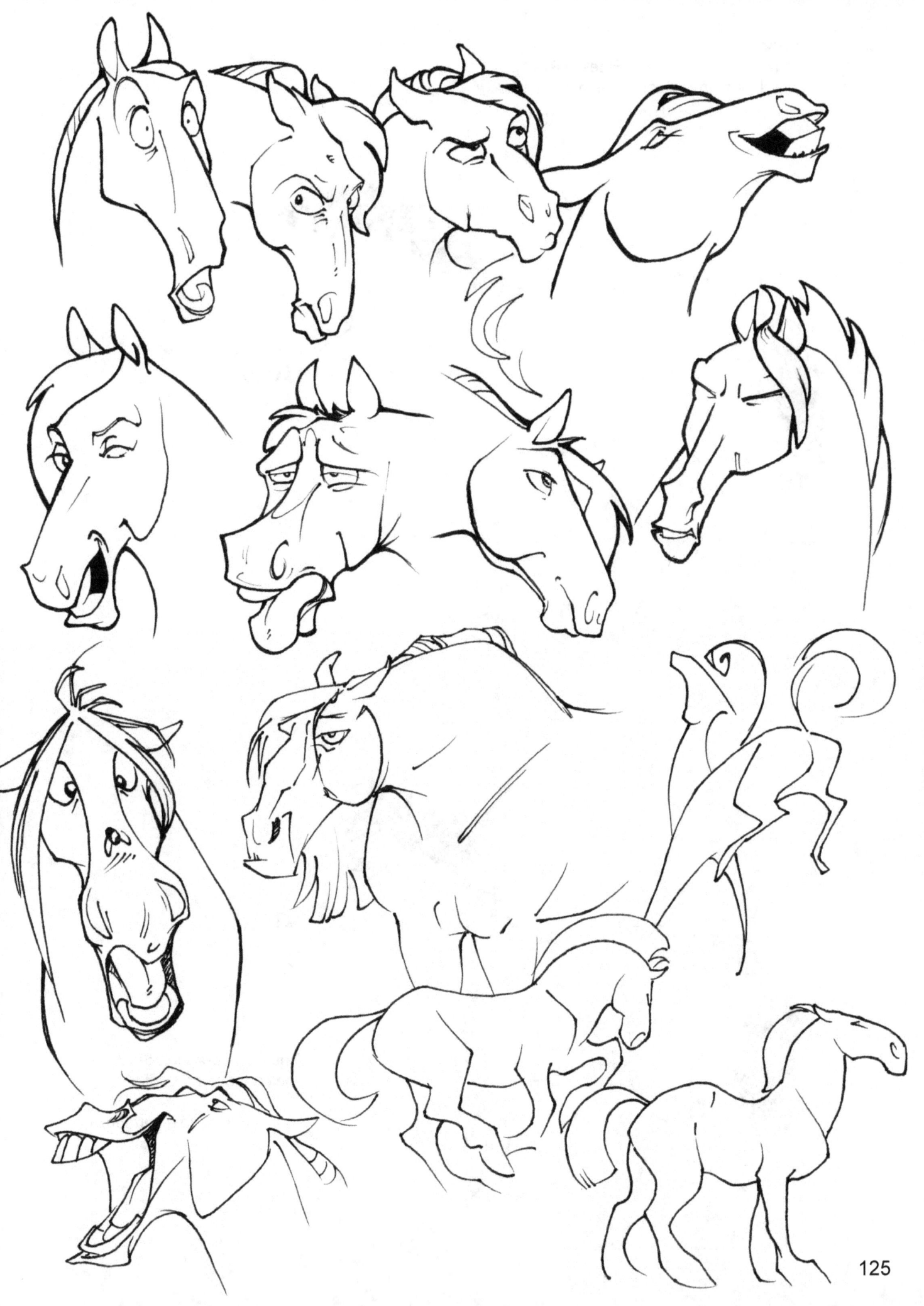

PRACTICE HARD

You can take any subject, such as a Przewalski's horse, and throw the real, anatomical boundries out the window.

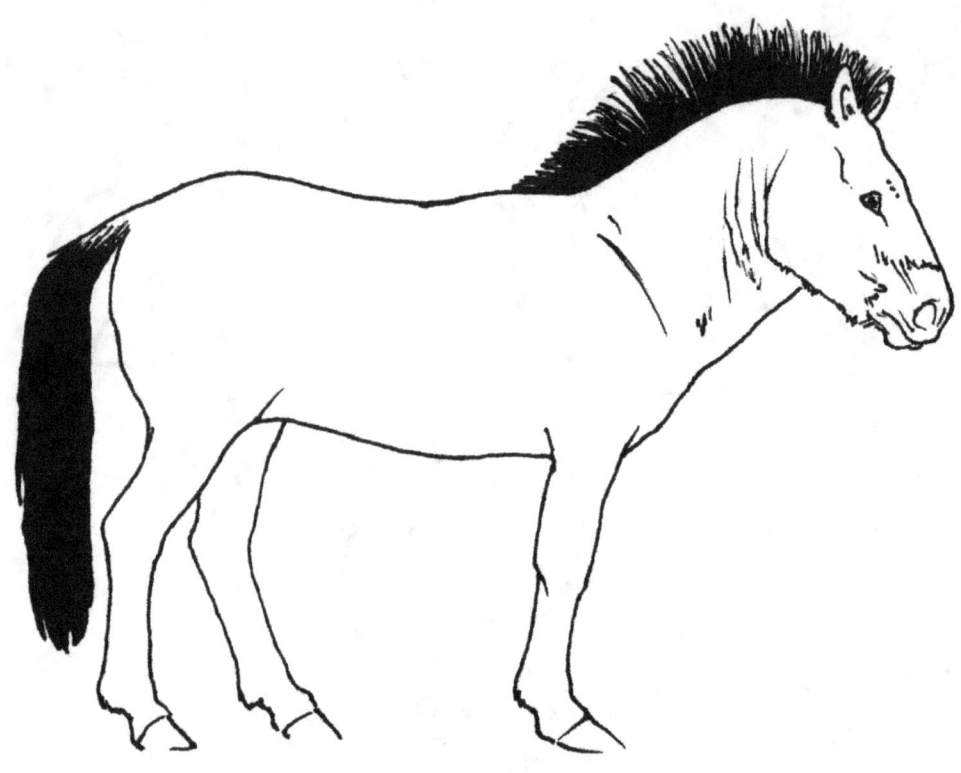

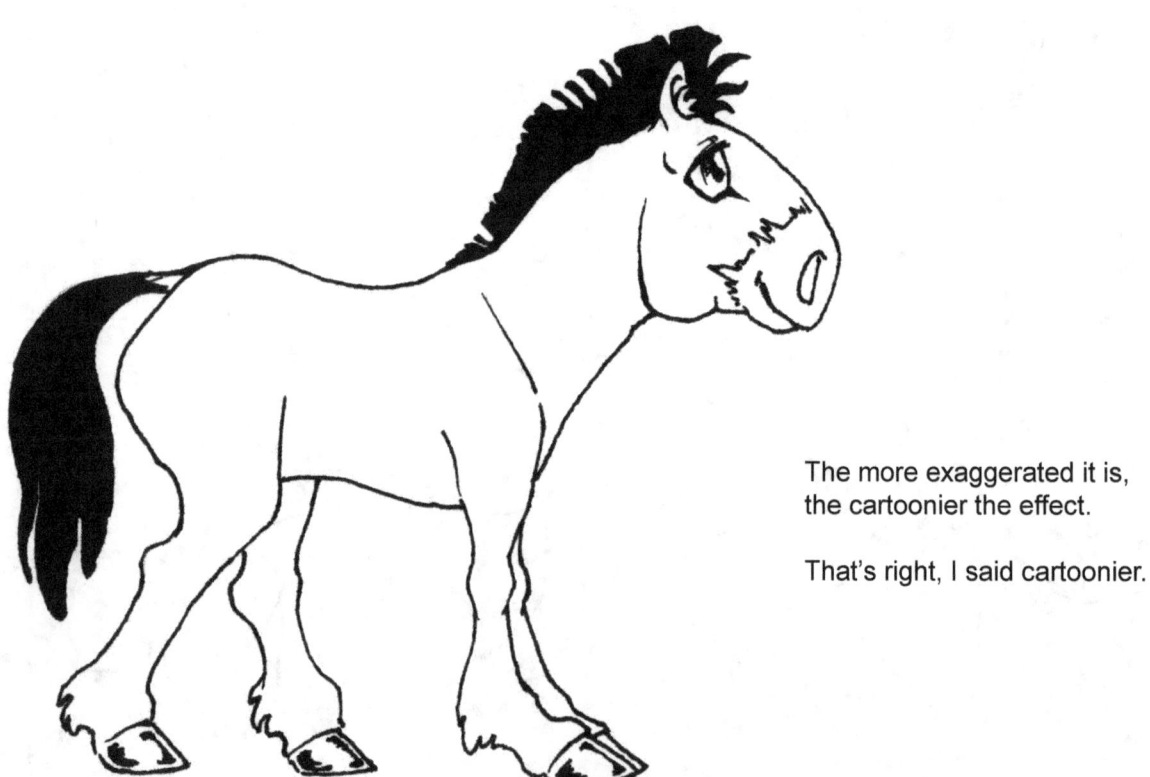

The more exaggerated it is, the cartoonier the effect.

That's right, I said cartoonier.

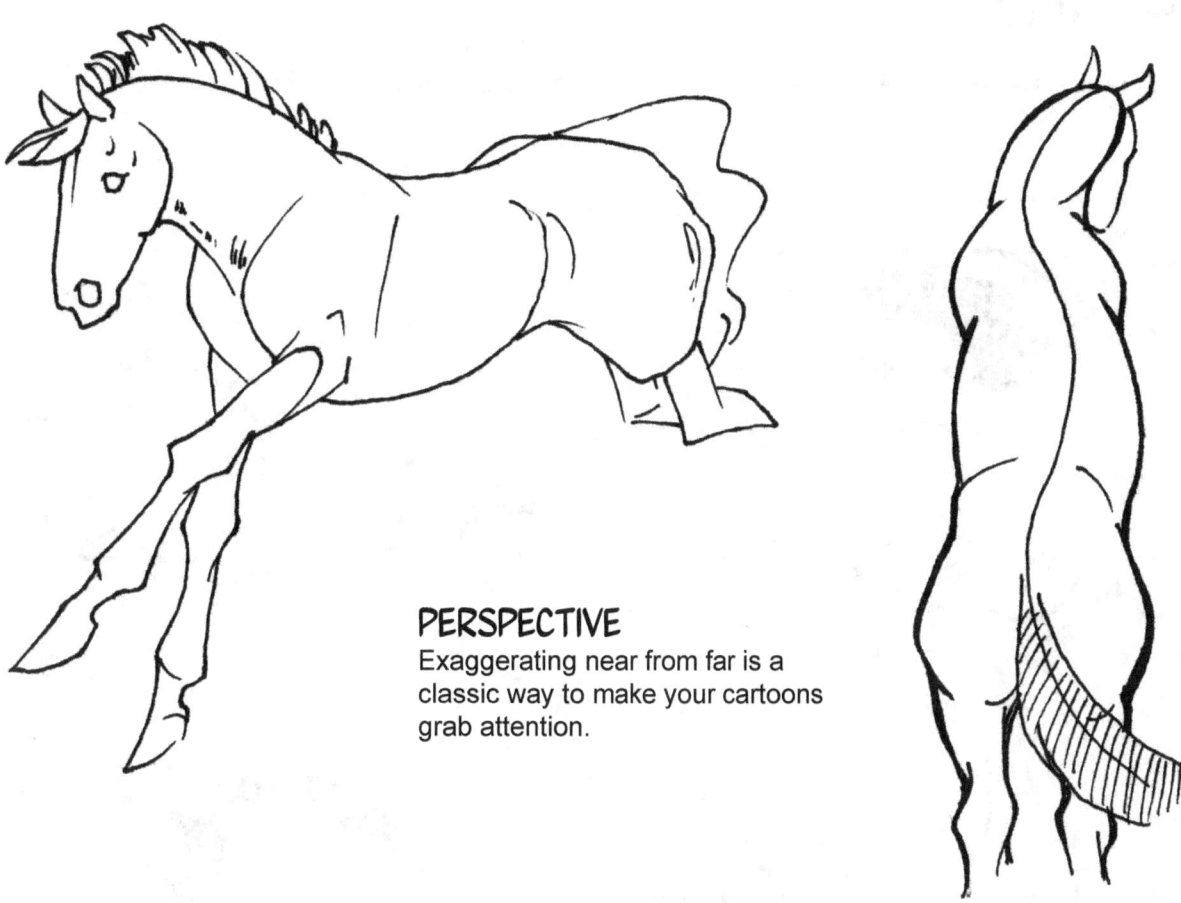

PERSPECTIVE
Exaggerating near from far is a classic way to make your cartoons grab attention.

PROPS
Distorting the size of the gear can sell the effect as well.

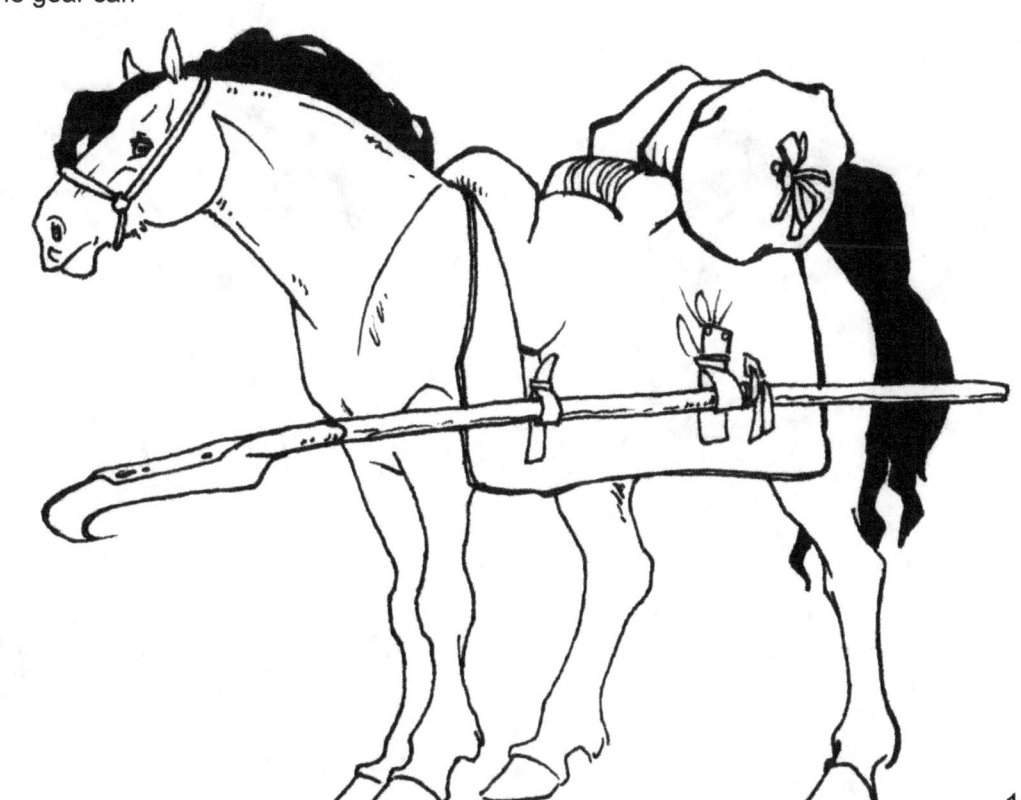

EYE CONTACT

The likes of big animation empires have this sugar-loaded look down to a science.
The magic ratio usually being eyes = 2/3 of the head, and the mouth being close to the eyes.

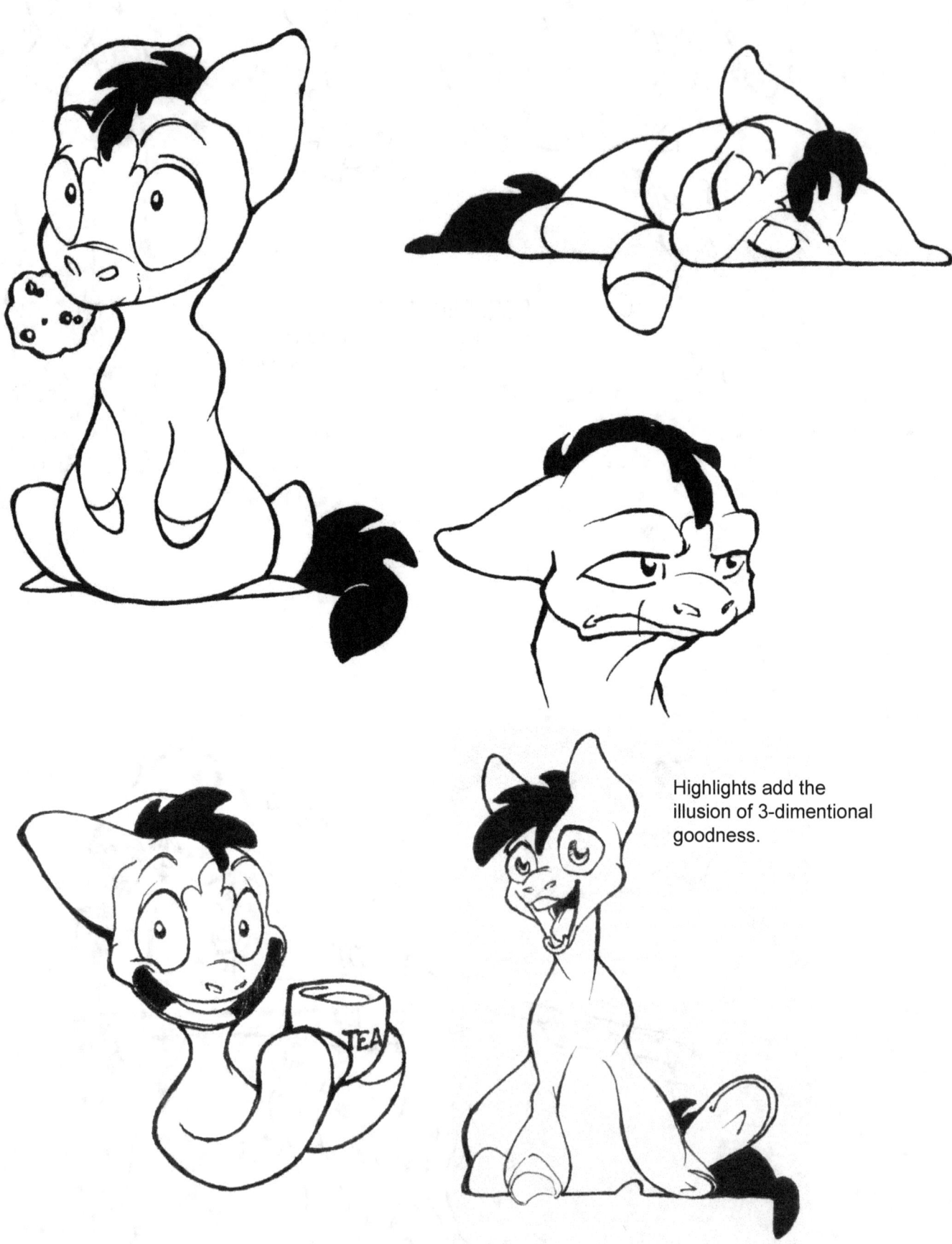

Highlights add the
illusion of 3-dimentional
goodness.

Other ideas for influence:

GREEK/ASIAN

FANTASY

EMO-HORSE

WHEREVER THE MUSIC
TAKES YOU

REFERENCES

I would like to thank every reference, person, and resource that helped to make this book what it is. Because honestly, it isn't their fault.

Azzaroli, Augusto. *An Early History of Horsemanship*. Leiden: E.J. Brill/W. Backhuys, 1985.

Clutton-Brock, Juliet. *Horse Power: A History of the Horse and the Donkey in Human Societies*. Cambridge, MA: Harvard UP, 1992.

Davidson, H. R. Ellis. *"Gods and Myths of Northern Europe." Google Books*. 2014.

Dent, Anthony Austen. *The Horse, through Fifty Centuries of Civilization*. New York: Holt, Rinehart and Winston, 1974.

Ewart, J. C. "XX.—On Skulls of Horses from the Roman Fort at Newstead, near Melrose, with Observations on the Origin of Domestic Horses." Transactions of the Royal Society of Edinburgh 45.03 (1907): British Veterinary Journal Vol 63. *Google Books*. Web.

Goldsworthy, Adrian Keith. *Caesar: Life of a Colossus*. New Haven: Yale UP, 2006. Print.

H. R. E. Davidsen. *Myths and Symbols in Pagan Europe: Early Scandinavian and Celtic Religions. Google Books*. N.p., n.d. Web.

Hyland, Ann. *The Horse in the Ancient World*. Westport, CT: Praeger, 2003.

Hyland, Ann. *The Medieval Warhorse from Byzantium to the Crusades*. Far Thrupp, Stroud, Gloucestershire: Alan Sutton, 1994.

Karl F. Friday. *Samaurai, Warfare and the State in Early Medieval Japan.*

Lee, Sherman E. *A History of Far Eastern Art*. New York: Harry N. Abrams, 1982.

Livy. *History of Rome*. Whitefish, MT: Kessinger Pub., 2004.

Michael Pfrommer. *Metalwork from the Hellenized East* - J. Paul Getty Museum.

Nakamura, Shunsuke, and Akihiko Magoori. "7th-century Horse Tack Unearthed in Kyushu." *The Asahi Shimbun* 19 Apr. 2013

Nicolay, Johan. *Armed Batavians: Use and Significance of Weaponry and Horse Gear from Non-military Contexts in the Rhine Delta (50 BC to AD 450)*. Amsterdam: Amsterdam UP, 2007.

Philip Sidnell. *Warhorse, Cavalry in Ancient Warfare*. London: Hambledon Continuum, 2006.

Polybius. *Histories. Google Books*. N.p., n.d. Web.

Rufus, Quintus Curtius, John Yardley, and Waldemar Heckel. *History of Alexander*. Harmondsworth, Middlesex, England: Penguin, 1984.

Telegin, Yakolevich Dmitriy. *Dereivka: a Settlement and Cemetery of Copper Age Horse Keepers on the Middle Dnieper. Google Books*. Web.

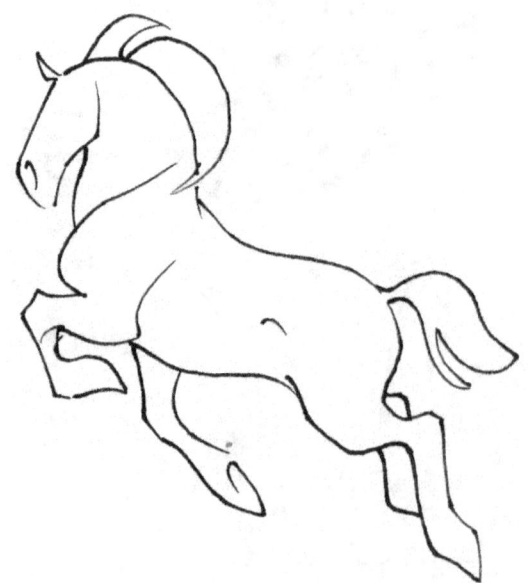

Thompson, F. M. L. *Horses in European Economic History: A Preliminary Canter*. Reading: British Agricultural History Society, 1983.

Thucydides. *History of the Peloponnesian War. Google Books*.

WWW.HTDHORSES.COM

Xenophon. *The Art of Horsemanship.* London: J.A. Allen, 1962.

Xenophon, Rex Warner, and George Cawkwell. *The Persian Expedition.* Harmondsworth, Eng.: Penguin, 1972.

Other sites:

A Song for Horse Nation - Smithsonian, National Museum of the American Indian - http://nmai.si.edu/exhibitions/horsenation/index.html

Horse. AMNH. http://www.amnh.org/exhibitions/past-exhibitions/horse

North Dakota Heritage Center and State Museum - history.nd.gov

The British Museum - britishmuseum.org

The Hermitage Museum - hermitagemuseum.org

The Harvard Art Museums - harvardartmuseums.org

Christies - http://www.christies.com